POLITICIANS
AND
DEFENCE

POLITICIANS AND DEFENCE

STUDIES IN THE FORMULATION OF BRITISH DEFENCE POLICY 1845-1970

edited by **IAN BECKETT** and **JOHN GOOCH**

MANCHESTER UNIVERSITY PRESS

Published by
Manchester University Press
Oxford Road, Manchester M13 9PL

British Library cataloguing in publication data

Politicians and defence.
  1. Great Britain – Military policy
  2. Great Britain – History
  I. Beckett, Ian
  II. Gooch, John
  355.03'35'41   VA647

  ISBN 0–7190–0818–2

Material from the Royal Archives appears by gracious permission of H.M. the Queen

Computerised Phototypesetting
by G.C. Typeset Ltd., Bolton, Greater Manchester
Printed in Great Britain
by the Alden Press, Oxford

CONTENTS

ILLUSTRATIONS

INTRODUCTION

Today's Minister of Defence, master of missiles and submarines which operate on a world stage dominated by two super-powers, seems far removed from his Victorian predecessor at the War Office, concerned largely with redcoat garrisons and with conducting the expeditions and small wars which were the chief concerns of the world's largest imperial power. Yet both are linked by the avenues within which the minister responsible for defence must try to formulate policy and convert it into reality. The purposes for which the armed forces exist, and their capacity to carry out Britain's diplomatic and treaty commitments; the effectiveness with which professional advice can be marshalled to guide and inform ministerial decisions; the place of the ministry in Cabinet, and the relationship of its civil head with the Prime Minister of the day—these considerations form the basis of a minister's approach to his task now, and have done so for over a century and a half. Though the substantive issues have changed during that time, the overall parameters within which defence policy must be formulated have not. Today's minister is, in these matters, very much the heir of his forerunners.

The War Office was traditionally the grave of many a promising career in politics. When, in 1903, St John Brodrick left office, to be replaced by Arnold Forster, he was comforted by Lord Curzon on having quit 'a place where the most strenuous endeavours meet with the smallest return, and from which little is to be got save vituperation'.[1] Many came to the War Office unwillingly, among them Sir George Cornewall-Lewis, Hugh Childers, the Marquess of Hartington, Henry Campbell-Bannerman and W. H. Smith; and Sidney Herbert, Edward Stanhope and Hugh Arnold-Forster were among those whose health was fatally affected by their exertions there. One of the chief causes of a minister's difficulties when grappling with the Office before 1904 was the chaotic state of the administrative machine with which he was entrusted. Before the outbreak of the Crimean war in 1854 thirteen separate authorities competed with one another for executive control over the various branches of the administration, and when they were brought under a single roof during that war the situation became intolerable. Florence Nightingale, a shrewd observer of the defects of the War Office as well as an effective reformer, had no illusions about a minister's problems on this score: he had in his charge 'a very slow office, an enormously expensive office, a not very efficient office, and one in which the minister's intentions can be entirely negatived by all his sub-departments, and those of each of the sub-departments by every other'.[2] One way to overide this obstructionism might have been to fall back on the example of most European powers and install a serving soldier as Secretary of State; however, although Cardwell did suggest in 1871 that a general be given the post, this course never seems to have been seriously considered.

Administrative reform was the path which eased the minister's burden in this regard, and which also gave him a single consolidated body of advice. In 1870, by means of the War Office Act, Cardwell split executive responsibility into three: the Commander-in-Chief had sole responsibility for tendering military advice, a Surveyor General of Ordnance oversaw questions of *matériel*, and a civilian Financial Secretary was responsible for the Estimates and Accounts. This division of responsibility partially masked the confrontation over policy between soldiers and civilians which was at the root of the Secretary's administrative difficulties, but not for long. As a result of equipment failures during the campaign in Egypt of 1884–85, some of them quite spectacular, the then minister, Edward Stanhope, suppressed the special office for equipment and in 1888 formalised the division of the War Office into two halves, civilian and military. Rivalries which had previously been diffuse at once became clarified.

The question of how effectively a civilian could oversee the business of a complex military department had by that time been closely examined by the Stephen Commission (1887). Its conclusions, which were directed at by-passing the minister and giving more power and authority to the Commander-in-Chief, were that the Secretary of State was overburdened with responsibility, that the system provided no clear guide as to what kind of army was required, and that an annual report to Parliament on the army's state of readiness was the best way to safeguard military efficiency. This last was a suggestion of Lord Wolseley, who was looking ahead to the time when he would succeed the Duke of Cambridge as C-in-C, and was one to which he clung throughout his career.[3] The Stephen Commission had also criticised the system by which financial requirements were determined: one in which the soldiers had deliberately pitched their demands high in the expectation that the civilians would cut them back. 'Extravagance controlled by stinginess is not likely to result either in economy or efficiency,' they reported.[4] Civilian management also found itself under attack before the Select Committee on Army and Navy Estimates in 1887, though it survived an examination into the army's manufacturing departments in the same year. For this and other reasons a general inquiry into the administration of the military department was pressing, and one was shortly afterwards undertaken by a commission under the chairmanship of the Marquess of Hartington.

The second report of the Hartington Commission (1890) found overcentralisation on the person of the Commander-in-Chief and remarked on the lack of a satisfactory system to enable the Secretary of State to get independent advice. To improve the co-ordination of military advice by way of the C-in-C, a War Office Council was founded, or rather re-founded, in May 1890; a precursor had existed since 1870 but had met only sporadically in the C-in-C's office and had dealt mostly with matters such as the effects of flogging on recruiting, individual cases of half-pay or retirement and terms of service. The new body soon foundered on a lack of any clear definition of its duties. The Hartington Commission had suggested it as part of a package which included creating a Chief of the General Staff and a Defence Committee of the Cabinet, and abolishing the post of C-in-C. None of its other recommendations got as far as did the Council: Queen Victoria and Wolseley combined to resist interfering with the powers of the Commander-in-Chief—the one in order to avoid diminishing the powers of the Crown, the other to preserve the office to which he was to succeed in 1895. The Cabinet was not disposed to allow the intervention of a chief of staff 'in any form', and the Prime Minister, Lord Salisbury, did not approve.

The system had reached a most unhappy compromise on the eve of the South African war (1899–1902), when an Order in Council of 1895 made the Commander-in-Chief responsible to the Secretary of State for all decisions on military matters, whilst allowing the heads of the military departments separate access to the civilian head and increased responsibility. With a board on Hartingtonian lines and a strong C-in-C, the hapless Secretary of State now enjoyed the worst of all possible worlds, both in terms of running his department effectively and in receiving, and in turn tendering, considered and approved military advice. It was perhaps small wonder that Salisbury chose to ignore official channels and seek counsel from soldiers such as Sir Evelyn Wood and Sir Redvers Buller, and civilians such as Spenser Wilkinson and Sir Charles Dilke. In this he was following a precedent set by Disraeli in 1878, when the Prime Minister had been advised on military policy not by the C-in-C but by Lintorn Simmons, Inspector General of Fortifications, and Robert Home of the Topographical and Statistical Branch. Indeed, the Duke of Cambridge pressed unsuccessfully to be allowed to attend Cabinet meetings at which military matters were to be discussed.

The fluidity of a Cabinet system which permitted, or even encouraged, a Prime Minister to seek military advice where he would represented a second factor which made the job of Secretary of State for War arduous and at the same time diminished its standing. Not until 1895, as part of the scheme put forward by Campbell-Bannerman which had split the War Office into two parts, did any arrangement appear which formalised Cabinet consideration of expert military advice within a specialist forum. Then the Standing Defence Committee of the Cabinet was established to focus ministerial attention on defence issues. Unfortunately this development did not improve the situation in which the Secretary of State found himself, for the committee met irregularly and tended, when it did come together, to deal in administrative details. Queen Victoria, who seems to have supported this important development in Cabinet responsibility, was inclined to blame the chairman of the new body for its dilatoriness, remarking to St John Brodrick that she thought 'it might be more actively worked than by the Duke of Devonshire'.[5] In fairness the Cabinet itself was as much to blame for under-using the new instrument, for it was largely preoccupied during the decade before the Boer war with domestic legislation. Lord Lansdowne, explaining to the Director of Military

Intelligence the Cabinet's failure to conduct a strategic review of the situation in the eastern Mediterranean during the summer of 1896, remarked that 'as the summer wore on, and we all became busier and busier with Land Bills and suchlike rubbish, this really big question slid into the background'.[6] This was a phenomenon not unfamiliar to Lansdowne's twentieth-century successors.

Another factor with which nineteenth-century incumbents of the War Office had to come to terms was the Treasury, and this too became increasingly important during the following century. The need to make economies was as much a part of Earl Grey's stewardship as it was of Denis Healey's; where the centuries differed was in the attitude struck by the Treasury towards military expenditure in general. Up till 1914 that attitude was one of barely disguised hostility. In 1887 the Treasury was watching the growth of the Intelligence Division at the War Office like a hawk, and objected strongly to a request for a 20 per cent increase in its budget. This drew from Goschen, newly installed as Chancellor of the Exchequer, the comment 'I have been rather struck by the uniform and almost constant attitude of positive hostility in language taken up by various Officers of the Treasury towards Naval and Military Officers generally'. [7]Some twenty years later the Treasury was defending its position of parsimony on the grounds that, under section 27 of the Exchequer and Audits Act of 1886, it had the power to forbid the sanction of any expenditure included in a parliamentary Appropriations account which, in the opinion of the Comptroller and Auditor General, was not supported by the Treasury. The issue was one of principle, and financial control never seems to have taken the more aggressive path before 1914; but a strong impression remains that the turn-of-the-century Treasury official would have been equally at home with the defence 'rationing' of the 1930s and the defence budgeting of the 1960s.

No single event had greater influence on the post of Secretary of State for War than did the Boer war. It awoke the realisation that much more efficiency was needed in generating authoritative military advice, that articulated control of the military administration was vital, and that the structure and functioning of the Cabinet must be changed to fix the importance of defence issues in the political mind. Each of these developments reinforced the post of civilian head of the ministry, so that it emerged from half a decade of reform more powerful than it had ever been.

In 1900 St John Brodrick, the Secretary of State, allowed the War Office Council to absorb the Army Board, set up the previous year in order to get a more efficient vehicle for tendering military policy, and followed a deliberate tactic of bringing the soldiers and the civilians in the War Office together rather than allowing them to maintain separate existences as antagonistic bodies preoccupied with keeping checks on one another. The following year a Director General of Mobilisation and Military Intelligence was created, with Brodrick's support, and entrusted with the preparation and maintenance of detailed plans for the military defence of the empire and with devising schemes of offensive and defensive operations; by this means the Secretary of State was at last provided with support and guidance on strategic questions, something he had never enjoyed during the reign of the 'strong' C-in-C. Then, in 1902, Brodrick joined with Selborne, his opposite number at the Admiralty, to propose a new defence committee of the Cabinet: it was to comprise only a president, the Prime Minister (if he were not the president), and the two defence ministers, and was to have the power to call strategic experts from both services to assist its deliberations.[8] This initiative had profound results, for on 11 February 1903, as a direct consequence, the Committee of Imperial Defence came into being as the special Cabinet forum for the discussion of defence questions. From it were to spring the many sub-committees of the Cabinet and of the defence staffs which grew up in the 1930s and 1940s. As yet, however, the CID lacked vital ingredients, not the least of which was experience: writing to his uncle, Edward VII, to acquaint him with progress by the new committee on the question of Russia and the defence of India, Prince Louis of Battenburg remarked that 'the fact is that the deeper we get into some of these subjects, the more difficult we find the solution'.[9]

The defects in War Office administration were so deeply displayed by the war in South Africa that the government could not avoid conducting a full inquiry into them; nor did it wish to do so. Accordingly a Royal Commission under the chairmanship of Lord Elgin set to work in 1902. It sat for fifty-five days, asked 22,200 questions of 114 witnesses, and concluded that a 'strong' C-in-C had failed. Wolseley was severely criticised for failing to exercise his responsibilities for the preparation of schemes of offence and defence in any systematic manner, and it was pointed out that his hapless master had had to learn of intelligence reports from the Secretary of State for the Colonies. As a direct consequence of the findings of this commission a small executive committee was set up under the chairmanship of Lord Esher, an able and influential courtier who enjoyed the trust of the King and the friendship and confidence of almost everyone who mattered in politics, with instructions to make proposals for the reorganisation of the War Office. Its main recommendations were the abolition of the post of C-in-C, the creation of a Chief of the General Staff, the establishment of an Army Council containing military and civilian members with defined administrative responsibilities sitting as a body under the chairmanship of the Secretary of State, and the provision of a secretariat to give the CID an efficient bureaucratic mechanism with which to service the Cabinet. All these suggestions were adopted, and with their implementation the age of 'defence by committee' began. Despite defects inherent in Esher's blueprint, especially with regard to the exact role of the secretary to the CID, the new system greatly improved the position of the Secretary of State. He was now firmly set at the apex of an efficient bureaucratic structure, and established as an authoritative voice in the counsels of the Cabinet, themselves formalised and improved beyond recognition.

With the onset of war in 1914, power was everywhere in Europe handed to the soldiers, and for once Britain was no exception to Continental practice. The War Office was in an unstable position owing to the Curragh 'mutiny' some five months earlier, as a consequence of which the Secretary of State for War had resigned and the Prime Minister had taken over the seals of office. Under a cruel misapprehension, Asquith eagerly handed over the position to the best known soldier in the empire, Lord Kitchener. He failed to realise that Kitchener's very background disqualified him from the post, for he was almost totally ignorant of European matters and knew nothing of the workings of the War Office, though it should be said that Kitchener was aware of his unfitness for the post and tried to resist it. Once in office, Kitchener's tortuous secretiveness towards the War Cabinet, combined with the failure at the Dardanelles (1915) and the obvious lack of firm and clear military advice at the centre, produced an important change in the balance between the civil head of the War Office and his chief strategic adviser. Sir William Robertson was brought back from the western front in December 1915 to take the post of Chief of the Imperial General Staff to provide professional stategic advice to the Cabinet, and the powers of the post were expanded to include those of countersigning all executive orders; the Secretary of State's position declined to that of raiser of forces to the Cabinet, and little more.[10]

This was the situation which faced Kitchener's successor, Lord Derby, and Asquith's successor, David Lloyd George. While Derby seems to have accepted it, Lloyd George chose to exert his control over the running of the war not by reviving the independent powers of the Secretary of State, which would have diminished his own uncontested dominance in defence matters, but by trying to replace Robertson with military advisers more ready to view the war in wider confines than those of the Flanders deadlock to which the CIGS seemed so stubbornly attached. Thus, leaving Derby to manage conscription, Lloyd George at first put British armies temporarily under the command of a French general, Nivelle, who promised better results, and then created the new post of military representative on the Allied Supreme War Council, with powers which cut into those enjoyed by Robertson, who was then offered a choice: CIGS with reduced powers, or

Allied representative. Disliking both, Robertson resigned over the issue, leaving Lloyd George to put his own nominees into both positions and to savour the victory of prime ministerial authority over what had been a temporarily over-mighty military subject.

The end of the first world war found Britain quickly faced with the need for drastic economic retrenchment whilst at the same time responsible for an empire which had reached its largest physical extent, and which now required protecting from internal dissidents rather than defending from external enemies. As the Geddes axe began to bite into the service ministries and the Ten Year Rule (1919) signalled the expectation that Britain would not have to fight a major war for at least the next decade, the economics of defence began to play an increasingly dominant role in decision-making, depriving the minister and the War Office alike of much force in the government's counsels. The Royal Air Force won the tender to police the empire on grounds of cost, thereby at the same time establishing itself and cutting away one of the army's traditional roles. It was not until the middle of the following decade, when Britain faced hostile powers in Europe, the Mediterranean and the Far East, that the influence of the War Office began to revive as its role in defence slowly increased; but even then it had to face both the strategic dominance of the RAF and the power of the Treasury. Until then the office reverted to being one of the posts of state offering least opportunity to make or even to influence policy.

Cabinet development helped deprive a Secretary of State for War of any real chance to exert influence. In June 1920 the CID had met for the first time since 1915 and had established a standing Defence Sub-committee. Lloyd George, then Prime Minister, was not much interested in it and generally delegated the chair to a senior minister, so that by the following October Sir Maurice Hankey, secretary of the CID and of the Cabinet, was complaining of the stagnation of the new body and of the difficulties of finding a chairman.[11] In 1922 it was recommended that the CID be in constant session, and the same year, during the Chanak incident, the three chiefs of staff began to meet informally; the following year this arrangement was put on a formal basis with the creation of the Chiefs of Staff sub-committee of the CID. What might have proved a beneficial development became little more than an arena for inter-service wrangling over roles and resources; and after the departure of Lord Trenchard, Chief of Air Staff, in 1929 and Lord Milne, CIGS, in 1933 the service officials on the sub-committee were, in the opinion of Sir Warren Fisher of the Treasury, a poor lot.

The years 1914–18 had demonstrated the complexities of modern war and the need for co-ordination and integration in defence planning and organisation, and soon after the end of the war pressure to create a

Minister of Defence began to grow. Such a post might have created the kind of political leverage from which an able man could have imposed more unity on the chiefs of staff, and increased the military voice in defence counsels against the increasing power of the Treasury. However, such a development was consistently opposed throughout the 1920s by Hankey, and when it came up once more in 1931 under the attractive head of a saving in administrative budgets, Hankey sank it once again. There can be little doubt that he saw it as a threat to the weight of influence he could exert on defence planning—and Hankey stood as one of the reasons why the Secretaries of State for War had small influence in these years. However, it was also the case that Hankey, by now clerk to the Privy Council in addition to his other two heavy responsibilities, was increasingly preoccupied with non-defence matters.[12] This meant that he could not give such issues the full-time attention they both warranted and deserved, whilst at the same time no individual service minister had the authority or the influence to take on such a role himself.

The announcement of German rearmament in 1935, and the Italian war against Abyssinia that same year, highlighted the mounting conviction—voiced by Churchill among others—that effective defence planning demanded the kind of co-ordination Hankey had for so long resisted, and in February 1936, in direct response to public pressure, the post of Minister for the Co-ordination of Defence was created, with Sir Thomas Inskip as its first incumbent. By this time, as a consequence of the first report of the Defence Requirements Sub-committee (1934), it had been established that Germany was to be regarded as Britain's main potential enemy and that she was to be deterred from any overt military action by being confronted with an RAF bomber force at least equal in size to her own. The 'parity deterrent', as this principle was termed, had made the air force the dominant voice in defence matters, and the Secretary of State for Air far outweighed his colleagues at the Admiralty and—especially—at the War Office as a consequence. It was also a manifestation of the rivalry between the services which had developed during the previous decade: Sir Arthur Harris, then Deputy Director of Plans, saw the expansion of the RAF as a deterrent aimed at Germany and at staving off the demands of the Admiralty.[13] The army came a poor third.

Once the twin decisions had been taken that Germany was Britain's primary enemy and that the bomber deterrent was the means by which to contain her, the dominant voice in defence counsels had passed from the service ministers to the Treasury. This body took the view in 1936 that the level of forces should be one that could be permanently maintained, and by autumn of the following year was prepared to allow defence spending to reach £200 million a year—two-thirds of the amount the services wanted.

With Treasury influence so strong, and in a situation where most politicians showed a distinct apathy towards the idea of an expeditionary force and a 'Continental commitment' on the part of the army, the position of the Secretary of State for War was weak indeed. The addition of a new minister to the system weakened it still further. In December 1936 Inskip was called upon to arbitrate between Duff Cooper, then at the War Office, who recognised the diplomatic value of the army in any possible future alliance with a European power, and Neville Chamberlain, Chancellor of the Exchequer, who—together with his adviser, Weir—strongly opposed such a concept. The Treasury resisted Cooper's proposals to re-equip the Territorial Army at levels suitable for supporting an expeditionary force on the Continent, and Inskip reached a 'compromise' allowing enough new equipment for two divisions, to be spread over ten in peacetime, which was barely a compromise at all.

Treasury influence mounted still further with the introduction of 'defence rationing'. Limits for defence spending over the five years 1937–41 were set at £1,570 million, and in order to ensure that the three services stayed within their limits Inskip was put in charge of a three-man committee, including Hankey, to vet the annual Estimates for 1937. This meant that priorities had to be determined to guide expenditure, and Hankey had a large hand in drawing them up. First on his list came maintaining the security of the United Kingdom, and last came co-operation with overseas allies. This order of priorities was enshrined in the Inskip Report of December 1937, which altered Britain's long-term defence policy from parity deterrence to holding out to Germany the prospect of a long war in which Britain's superior economic weight could be brought to bear on her opponent. In the immediate future, the report reversed RAF policy by concentrating on the various means of defence against the bomber, instead of operating on Baldwin's much-quoted dictum that 'the bomber will always get through'.

These important decisions had been reached with little influence from the War Office, whose unfortunate occupant had small leverage in decision-making as long as the agreed role for his service remained no more than a peripheral imperial operation, probably in Egypt. It is even possible that Chamberlain chose Hore-Belisha to succeed Duff Cooper at the War Office in 1937 in the hope that he would produce internal disorder among the military in the course of a bold shake-up, and thus leave the War Office poorly placed to resist the Inskip policy.[14]

Hore-Belisha certainly did produce an upheaval in his new office, and his unofficial adviser, Liddell Hart, ensured by his advocacy of defensive ideas and his opposition to a Continental expeditionary force that the Secretary of State lacked the backing to renew a contest Duff Cooper had lost. But by the summer of 1938 Liddell Hart was moving towards acceptance of such a force, the need for which the War Office had already recognised.[15] After Munich the army's star began to rise once again as Britain became drawn into a *de facto* alliance with France against Germany, and the French pressed for land forces to replace the thirty-five lost Czech divisions. However, Chamberlain was still resistant enough to the idea of fully fledged preparation for war to dismiss Inskip in January 1939 for urging the creation of a Ministry of Supply and replace him with a former First Sea Lord, Lord Chatfield.

The nature of Cabinet control over military matters did not undergo noticeable change in the first eight months of the war under Chamberlain's continued rule. However, Churchill's advent to the office of Prime Minister in May 1940 was to produce striking changes. The Prime Minister took to himself the newly minted title Minister of Defence—a signal of his determination to have complete charge of defence matters—and slimmed down the War Cabinet by dismissing the service ministers from it, shunting them off into a Special Defence Committee. Thereafter Churchill's fertile mind, strategic inventiveness and readiness to concern himself with minutiae continued a process whereby the War Office became what it had been from 1916 to 1919—an administrative adjunct to the Prime Minister's office, and not much more. There was, however, to be no repetition of the rivalry between Robertson and Sir Henry Wilson to mar the course of civil–military relations in this war. Churchill was fortunate to have as his CIGS first Sir John Dill and then the incomparable Sir Alan Brooke; through them, and with the aid of Ismay at the Cabinet Office, the Prime Minister's impulsiveness was tempered and strategic policy was drawn up.

During the second world war Britain was one member of an alliance which enfolded first Russia and then the United States. Alliance diplomacy and alliance strategy required co-ordination, between all three allies but especially between the Western pair, which further removed the Secretary of State for War from a position of influence. Policy was made at the series of international conferences beginning in August 1941 at Argentia Bay and ending at Potsdam in July 1945, and at those conferences the political leaders surrounded themselves with batteries of professional advisers but generally took care to keep their civilian colleagues well away. The system perfectly suited a politician who liked the spotlight to be on him, and who was prepared to be prompted from the wings but not to share the stage with any minor star.

The end of the war thus produced a system which had been serviced by strong professional advisers, and in which most defence matters had been centralised under the Prime Minister's hand. Post-war politicians were to be faced with a generation of experienced professionals who were accustomed to having their views heard and, frequently, acted upon without prior reference to competing civil authorities. The task facing the first Labour government, containing as it did politicians who lacked experience of high government office, and with whom many of the military were temperamentally out of sympathy, was not to be an easy one. The problem was accentuated by a number of additional factors which combined to weaken not only Labour ministers but their Conservative successors.

At the institutional level the Chiefs of Staff gained when, in 1946, the CID was replaced by the Cabinet Defence Committee. To a large extent the Ministry of Defence still existed in name only: Shinwell, for example, did not have even a Parliamentary Secretary when he became minister in 1950. In such circumstances most plans submitted to the Defence Committee tended to originate within the service ministries. The minister was only deputy chairman of the committee and dealt largely with administrative questions. Since both chiefs of staff and ministers sat on the Defence Committee, Churchill tended to address them direct, leaving the minister in a highly ambiguous position. The service ministers, though no longer in the Cabinet, retained their previous constitutional responsibilities and powers intact; their function was to translate the decisions of the committee into executive action. The minister was thus reduced to what Macmillan termed 'a co-ordinator, not a master'.[16] The Defence Committee itself proved an imperfect instrument, unable to resolve issues involving long-term aims or to integrate foreign and defence policy in a way that seriously affected Britain's world role.[17]

Immediate post-war ministers were rarely able to impose their personality over either political or professional colleagues as a way of offsetting their institutional weakness. Though not quite in the position of Crewe, of whom it was said in 1931 'he is dead and has been appointed as a measure of economy',[18] ministers such as A. V. Alexander and Shinwell lacked political weight. The Chiefs of Staff clearly regarded Alexander as a 'passenger', so much so that Montgomery as CIGS attempted to persuade his colleagues collectively to demand the minister's dismissal. Shinwell had previously been demoted from the Ministry of Fuel and Power, with a seat in Cabinet, to Secretary of State for War before being brought back into the Cabinet as minister. Labour Secretaries of State for War were equally lacking in influence. Apart from the demoted Shinwell, Lawson was forced to retire through ill health; Bellenger was unpopular with the Cabinet; and Strachey appeared neither happy nor interested.[19]

The situation did not markedly change with the return of Conservative governments. Perhaps understandably, Churchill was reluctant to regard his Minister of Defence as anything more than a deputy. The clearest example of this trait was perhaps the appointment of Earl Alexander in 1952. Alexander never sought to impose control over his subordinates or, in turn, to stand up to Churchill on their behalf; his remark to a Conservative Foreign Affairs Committee meeting in 1954, when asked his opinion on the evacuation of the Canal Zone, that such decisions rested with his colleagues, was symptomatic of his posture.[20]

Churchill introduced the defence Estimates in the Commons, since Alexander was a peer, and did so again when Macmillan was minister. Eden, too, held that the Prime Minister was 'ultimately responsible for all important decisions on defence'.[21] Monckton's acceptance of the post for a year on condition that he would then become Lord Chief Justice was indicative of a well established tradition: that few ministers expected or wished to remain at the ministry for long. Macmillan believed it unlikely that he would be in the same post for more than a few months.[22] When he duly became Prime Minister he was determined to remedy the situation the minister often found himself in, which led directly to his support for Duncan Sandys.

Eden had already gone some way towards a solution in October 1955 by enlarging the minister's responsibilities to include the composition and balance of the armed forces and the content of service programmes as well as their cost. A new post of Chairman of the Chiefs of Staff was established and a new sub-committee of the Cabinet created to review defence policy. Sandys, however, was given wide powers to make decisions 'on all matters of policy affecting the size, shape, or organisation and disposition of the Armed Forces, their equipment and supply (including defence research and development) and their pay and conditions of service'.[23] Establishing these powers on a more permanent basis proved somewhat difficult, and much was left vague and ill defined in the 1958 White Paper on Defence Organisation. In theory the minister was now to be responsible for the 'formulation and general application of a unified policy relating to the Armed Forces of the Crown as a whole and their requirements', but the means by which this was to be achieved were lacking. A new Defence Board was created, and the Chairman of the Chiefs of Staff became a Chief of Defence Staff. The individual chiefs of staff still retained their right of direct access to the minister and the Prime Minister, however, and the CDS was denied an adequate staff. It has been argued that such important areas as budgeting, procurement, and the construction of a general framework of strategic policy were little affected by these changes, and that what Sandys gained was surrendered, albeit involuntarily, by his successor, Watkinson.[24] Certainly the reorganisation did not lead to the hoped-for co-ordination of high-level planning by means of the Defence Committee and its sub-committees,[25] and even Sandys's authority was challenged by his professional advisers. The dispute with Sir John Cowley is referred to later, and the services also attempted to by-pass the minister through ploys such as the RAF's *Exercise Prospect* in 1958, projecting to civil servants and press correspondents policies contrary to those of their minister, Sandys.[26]

Much of the subsequent redefinition of the relationship between minister and service chiefs, and between them and their service ministers, was due not to a politician but to the endeavours of the second Chief of Defence Staff, Lord Mountbatten. His experience of and belief in inter-service co-operation, together with some frustration at the relative lack of power of his position, led to a series of unified commands in overseas operations, and in 1962 he suggested full integration of the service ministries, with a single Secretary of State assisted by ministers of state and the CDS served by service chiefs. An independent inquiry was instituted by Thorneycroft in January 1963; its findings supported Mountbatten in recommending the subordination of the individual service ministers in an integrated whole, and went so far as to hint at a single integrated service for the future. The White Paper of July 1963 created a single Ministry of Defence, with Thorneycroft now designated Secretary of State for Defence. The former service ministers were reduced to ministers of state, able to attend the new Defence and Overseas Policy Committee of the Cabinet—which replaced the Defence Committee—by invitation only, and required to act through the Secretary of State.

By contrast, the position of the service chiefs did not change as radically as Mountbatten might have wished. The Chiefs of Staff were to be responsible for operations through the CDS, who would issue the necessary authority, and tendered collective advice to the minister through him. When their views differed from those of the CDS he could submit the alternatives to the Prime Minister, but as principal military adviser he could also tender his own advice.[27] With integration came not only an entirely separate procurement arm for the ministry but also a major increase in central staff. A few months after the new organisation had been made effective a new Labour administration came into office.

Further changes were made to the organisation of defence under the new Secretary, Denis Healey. Junior ministers, after briefly enjoying wider spheres of interest than their service portfolios nominally allowed, were further downgraded in 1967 to the rank of Parliamentary Under Secretaries of State, and lost responsibility in key areas to two new junior ministers—a Minister of Defence for Administration and a Minister of Defence for Equipment. In February 1970 the defence White Paper announced the severance of the now virtually powerless junior ministers from the services altogether, and replaced them with Parliamentary

Secretaries with general responsibilities. The two junior ministerial posts created in 1967 were also to be replaced by a single Minister of State for the Armed Forces, all changes becoming effective by the end of the year. In the event the new Conservative ministry introduced the changes on taking office in June 1970. All ministers within the Ministry of Defence, together with the service chiefs, sat on the Defence Council established in 1963, but this met infrequently, and Healey's office became the focus for all policy decisions.[28] Healey exercised more personal authority than any minster since Sandys, but—in theory—the position of the CDS and the professional advisers in general was also enhanced. The lingering suspicion Labour politicians felt about accepting professional advice at face value was illustrated by Healey's creation of the Programme Evaluation Group in 1967; after little more than a year, however, it was replaced by Policy and Operations Staffs, which allowed the professional advisers to 'close ranks' on the minister. In February 1970 the powers of the CDS were also increased, enabling him to initiate staff studies without prior reference to the Chiefs of Staff committee. The situation of 'defence by discussion' under Healey, which had succeeded 'defence by committee' up to 1957 and then 'defence by doctrine' under Sandys, has since remained largely unchanged.[29] The creation of a Procurement Executive reporting direct to a minister of state through its own chief executive has been a notable addition.[30] But, above all, the Secretary of State remains theoretically paramount within the defence structure.

Whatever the complexities of modern defence budgeting and nuclear strategy, and notwithstanding the application of management techniques and operational science to defence, the situation of a Victorian and a modern politician charged with defence responsibilities remain in essence the same. A modern minister such as Healey faced a very similar situation to that confronting Grey or Cardwell in seeking to reconcile competing commitments with limited resources. Sandys had to define priorities in much the same way as Haldane or Hore-Belisha. Financial constraints are at least as pressing now as they were in Arnold-Forster's day, although the claims on state expenditure have increased far beyond the comprehension of a Victorian or an Edwardian. Above all, and by the very nature of the political system, politicians remain transient figures, dependent upon professional advice and, whatever the administrative structure, reliant on winning the respect and confidence of both political and professional colleagues if they are to have much chance of success.   J.G. and I.F.W.B.

Notes

1   Curzon to Brodrick, 5 October 1903, BL Add. MSS 50074.
2   Hampden Gordon, *The War Office*, Putnam, London, 1935, p. 53.
3   Wolseley to Esher, 18 January 1904, Esher papers, 'Army Letters', vol. I.

4   W. S. Hamer, *The British Army: Civil–Military Relations, 1885–1905*, Clarendon Press, Oxford, 1970, p. 66.

5   Note on a conversation with the Queen, 24 November 1900, Public Record Office (hereafter PRO), 30/67/13.

6   Lansdowne to Ardagh, 24 September 1896, PRO 30/40/2.

7   Unheaded memorandum, 21 May 1887, Hamilton papers, PRO T/168/8.

8   Memorandum on the Improvement of the Intellectual Equipment of the Services, 10 November 1902, Royal Archives, RA W32/21.

9   Battenburg to Edward VII, 24 May 1903, Royal Archives, RA W32/28.

10   John Gooch, *The Plans of War: the General Staff and British Military Strategy c. 1900–1916*, Routledge & Kegan Paul, London, 1974, pp. 324–30.

11   S. W. Roskill, *Hankey—Man of Secrets*, II, Collins, London, 1972, p. 156.

12   Brian Bond (ed.), *Chief of Staff:the Diaries of Lieutenant General Sir Henry Pownall*, I, Leo Cooper, London, 1972, p. 40.

13   M. S. Smith, 'The development of British strategic air power doctrine and policy in the period of rearmament preceding the second world war, *c* 1934–1939', unpublished PhD thesis, Lancaster University, 1975, p. 106.

14   Robert Paul Shay jr., *British Rearmament in the Thirties—Politics and Profits*, Princeton University Press, Princeton, N.J., 1977, pp. 169–70.

15   Brian Bond, *Liddell Hart: a Study of his Military Thought*, Cassell, London, 1977, pp. 163–4.

16   Harold Macmillan, *Tides of Fortune*, Macmillan, London, 1969, p. 561.

17   John Baylis, 'Defence decision-making in Britain and determinants of defence policy', *Journal of the Royal United Services Institute for Defence Studies*, CXX, 1975, pp. 42–8.

18   John Ramsden, *A History of the Conservative Party: the Age of Balfour and Baldwin, 1902–1940*, Macmillan, London, 1979, p. 318.

19   Emanuel Shinwell, *Conflict without Malice*, Odhams, London, 1955, pp. 190–200, 209–26; Field Marshal Viscount Montgomery, *Memoirs*, Collins, London, 1958, pp. 430–1, 483–7; Emanuel Shinwell, *I've Lived Through it All*, Gollancz, London, 1973, pp. 211–13.

20   Nigel Nicholson, *Alex*, Weidenfeld & Nicolson, London, 1969, pp. 2–3, 301–13.

21   Anthony Eden, *Full Circle*, Cassell, London, 1960, p. 367.

22   Lord Birkenhead, *Walter Monckton*, Weidenfeld & Nicolson, London, 1969, pp. 303–10; Macmillan, *Tides of Fortune*, p. 560.

23   Eden, *Full Circle*, pp. 374–5; Michael Howard, *The Central Organisation of Defence*, Royal United Services Institute, London, 1970, p. 9.

24   Howard, *Central Organisation*, pp. 9–13.

25   Baylis, 'Defence decision-making', pp. 42–8.

26   John Sabine, 'Civil–military relations', in John Baylis (ed.), *British Defence Policy in a Changing World*, Croom Helm, London, 1977, pp. 243–50; L. W. Martin, 'The market for strategic ideas in Britain: the Sandys era', *American Political Science Review*, LVI, 1962, pp. 23–6.

27   Howard, *Central Organisation*, pp. 14–27.

28   *Ibid.*, pp. 21–3, 39–47.

29   Michael Hobkirk, 'Defence organisation and defence policy-making in the UK and USA', in L. W. Martin (ed.), *The Management of Defence*, Macmillan, London, 1976, pp. 1–13; see David Greenwood, *Budgeting for Defence*, Royal United Services Institute, London, 1972, *passim*.

30   R. M. Hastie-Smith, 'The tin wedding: a study of the evolution of the Ministry of Defence, 1964–1974', in *Seaford House Papers, 1974*, Royal College of Defence Studies, London, 1975, pp. 25–42.

1

LORD GREY AND IMPERIAL DEFENCE

HEW STRACHAN

'Lord Grey is looked upon by the Army as its Greatest enemy', wrote
Lieutenant General the Earl Cathcart to Sidney Herbert on 13 April 1854.[1]
Endowed with strongly held views, a quick temper and a pronounced
contempt for senior soldiers, Grey's attitude could be abrasive and even
petulant. Furthermore these were attributes to which Cathcart had fallen
victim in 1846. Grey had deemed him—since he was a military
man—unsuitable to continue as Governor General of Canada.[2] Cathcart's
feelings were not unique. Sir George Brown, Adjutant General from 1850
to 1853, described Grey as 'the last man in all England I wished to be
brought in contact with. His presence had . . . the effect of a wet blanket on

my spirits and conversational powers.'[3] Many soldiers felt that if he was not for them, Grey must be against them. Therefore he could be loosely bracketed with radicals, liberals and Cobdenites, men hell-bent on false economy in military expenditure and entrenched in doctrinaire views, untrammelled by the realities of national defence.

The truth is more complex. Henry Grey, Viscount Howick, was born in 1802, the eldest son of the second Earl Grey, of Reform Bill fame. Educated at Trinity College, Cambridge, he secured office in his father's government of 1830, as Under Secretary of State for the Colonies. The empire which he faced was very different from that which had existed before 1792. Britain's European rivals had been vanquished; during the Napoleonic wars she had acquired the strategic bases that were to give her a web of communications all over the world. In the fifty years after 1815 the empire expanded by about 100,000 square miles a year.[4] Commerce no longer remained at the heart of imperial logic. Britain's pre-eminence in world trade allowed Huskisson in 1825 to substitute preference for monopoly: he defended the empire on political, not economic, grounds. Thus the young Lord Howick became involved in colonial questions at a time when the administrative burdens the empire imposed had increased but when burgeoning productivity at home, and its concomitant, free trade, made the commercial rewards less evident. A fresh departure in colonial policy was required. Richard Cobden and his ilk espoused the traditional radical view that the colonies did little other than provoke war. Their solution was to abandon them. This, Howick was to write in 1849, 'I am old fashioned enough to believe wd be a national misfortune, & what is more a misfortune to the civilized world.'[5]

Cobden's attitude, however, was ceasing to be radical orthodoxy. Edward Gibbon Wakefield, friend of Ricardo and J. S. Mill, had applied the principles of the utilitarians to colonial development. Great Britain, he contended, was characterised by an excess of capital and labour in relation to its field of production. In the colonies the position was reversed. Systematic emigration and colonisation could therefore solve the 'condition of England' question. In Wakefield's scheme, self-governing colonies would engage in free trade and thus over the whole world there would arise a proper division of labour. In 1831 Jeremy Bentham gave Wakefield's thinking his imprimatur. Colonisation was work of the greatest utility, and radicals could now approach the problems of empire in a more positive spirit. In the same year Howick too fell under the spell of Wakefield. Already well versed in the thinking of the political economists, including the Mills, J. R. McCulloch and Nassau Senior, Howick introduced an emigration Bill and persuaded Goderich to experiment with Wakefield's schemes for colonisation in New South Wales. Later, in 1844, as chairman of the select committee on New Zealand, he was to espouse Wakefield's thinking more openly, preferring the latter's New Zealand Company to the rights claimed by the Crown under the Treaty of Waitangi. But privately Howick remained critical, and, while accepting 'systematic colonisation', did not see it as the solution to Britain's domestic problems, since he argued that any outflow of labour would simply be compensated by a rise in the birth rate.

Nor does the relationship between Howick and Lord Durham provide a comprehensive guide to the former's views on empire. In 1838 Howick enthusiastically supported the appointment of his brother-in-law to the governorship of Canada and equally enthusiastically embraced his report advocating self-government. But there is no direct causal chain between the report and Howick's progress towards self-government from 1846. In 1840 he favoured a paternalistic and conciliatory approach at home as the path for future colonial administration. Not least was this the case because of the third, and dominant, consequence of his exposure to radical views—his ardent advocacy of free trade. An independent Canada would be more likely to adopt protection to guard its nascent industry; a united empire would spread the gospel of *laissez faire*. His 1842 motion on the budget, attacking the principle of colonial preference, therefore stemmed from his conviction that free trade would strengthen the colonial ties. However, Canada's strong desire to have its own party government simultaneously suggested that the selection of ministers would be removed from the hands of the Governor General and hence of the British Parliament. Howick became convinced by political arguments of the need for colonial self-government. But on the surface his conversion seemed to proceed from his acceptance of free trade: it was easy to argue that colonies in open competition in the world's markets should also be able to decide their own future. After 1840 he became the standard-bearer of the Colonial Reformers in government but he brought to colonial matters a less doctrinaire and increasingly realistic approach. The deeper, in consequence, was to be their disillusionment.[6]

But, before this divergence between Howick and his supporters became clear, he had gained further administrative experience. In 1835 the new Prime Minister, Melbourne, appointed him Secretary at War and he was elevated to the Cabinet. This was not the great state office it might appear. Theoretically his duties were confined to the preparation of the army estimates, the administration of army finance, the answering of questions in Parliament, and the drawing up of the Mutiny Bill and the Articles of War. For a man as impatient of bureaucracy as Howick the details of office, the form-filling and letter-signing, were infuriating. Furthermore, in his estimation, they conferred no real power. He felt himself at the beck and call of four great ministers of state: the Chancellor of the Exchequer retained a supervisory role in finance, the Foreign Secretary formulated the policy which the army might implement, the Home Secretary decided its distribution and employment at home, and the Secretary at War's direct superior, the Secretary of State for War and the Colonies, pronounced on similar affairs in the empire. But most frustrating of all was the position of the Commander-in-Chief, nominally independent of the Secretary at War, and with the right of direct access to the monarch. Although the Horse Guards staff was under no illusions as to its real status—financial control gave the Secretary at War a very real measure of power—Howick did not come to the same conclusion. 'I know too well,' he told his brother,

> how utterly powerless in the present state of things the unhappy occupant of this office is to carry anything to which the military people on the other side of the building are opposed, & I am consequently acting most rigidly upon the principle of doing as little as I can & of endeavouring to tide over every thing as quietly as I can. This wd not do permanently, but I have no idea of getting myself into hot water for nothing, I shall therefore try to preserve the status quo for the present, with the full determinatn. if I shd stay here of by & bye insisting upon such a change in my positn as wd give me some real control for that for which I am held responsible in the H. of C.[7]

But Howick was not a man to bide his time for long. His predecessor, Sir John Cam Hobhouse, had already in 1833 tried to make the Secretary at War 'a great state officer'.[8] The consequent committee, under the Duke of Richmond, had urged a measure of consolidation for the military departments. Thus the ground was already prepared when, in 1836, Howick convened a fresh committee. Its report, which he drafted himself,[9] and which was published in February 1837, proposed that the Secretary at War should always be in the Cabinet and should take on full responsibility for all military matters.[10] Although the Commander-in-Chief's powers stood nominally untouched, in practice his subordination to the War Office would be complete. William IV construed the report as an attack on the royal prerogative, and Lord Hill, the incumbent at the Horse Guards, had the support of the Duke of Wellington in his opposition. Howick tried to force the measure through by Order in Council, but without the backing of Glenelg, the Secretary of State for War and the Colonies, or Hussey Vivian, the Master General of the Ordnance, Melbourne could not encourage his maverick minister. As the scion of a great Whig household, Howick's espousal of the reform looked too much like open pursuit of his own ambitions and in particular an attempt to add to the already extensive scope of Grey patronage. Impatient with his colleagues as much as with his military opponents, he resigned his post in February 1839.

This experience hardened the divide between Howick and the Horse Guards. The fact that as Secretary of State for War and the Colonies he was in 1849–50 to attempt a similar measure of consolidation,[11] and once again to fall foul of Wellingtonian opposition, ensured that many other measures of military reform were to be blocked by the animosity between the two camps. Howick, on his side, concluded that 'every single improvement effected in the Army for the last 50 years had been forced on the professional soldiers by civil opinion',[12] a conclusion as untrue as it was indicative of his bellicosity. Although Hill and the Horse Guards collaborated on many of the improvements in conditions of service effected during Howick's period at the War Office, subsequently—as Secretary of State—he often had to proceed without the benefit of professional support and advice. For in 1842 Wellington succeeded Hill as Commander-in-Chief. Politically more astute than Hill, he was to add his weight to the cause of military conservatism.

Howick was not alone in his antipathy towards the Horse Guards. The frustrations of prolonged colonial service and of promotion blocked by a solid and immovable wedge of Peninsular heroes meant that there was a strong lobby of regimental officers dedicated to the reform of the army. Finding voice in a strident professional press, its principal concern in the 1830s was the amelioration of the lot of the private soldier. In 1836 the report of a commission on military punishments gave vent to much of the new orthodoxy: drunkenness and hence flogging would be reduced only by prevention, by rewarding the well conducted soldier and the provision of recreations as an antidote to the boredom of garrison life.[13] Howick was in direct touch with the views of these officers through his brother, Charles, who commanded the 71st Highland Light Infantry in Canada, and who, for example, consulted his sergeant major on Howick's proposed good conduct awards.[14]

The problems of adapting the army to its colonial responsibilities were much more dramatically served by the work of Dr Henry Marshall, an army surgeon, and Lieutenant A. M. Tulloch, a lawyer by training but a soldier by profession. In 1835 Marshall, who had for some time been amassing statistics on the health of troops abroad, published his findings in the *United Service Journal*. That such figures might provide an empirical basis for preventive medicine had long been a conviction of Sir James McGrigor, the Director General of the Army Medical Department, who had been collecting half-yearly returns on sickness since 1817.[15] Howick was impressed by Marshall's article, and commissioned him and Tulloch to collate the evidence amassed in the previous two decades.[16] The results were published region by region from 1837. Howick was convinced of the importance of Marshall's and Tulloch's conclusions as soon as he saw the first report.[17] They were to colour much of his subsequent thinking on the problems of imperial defence. Tulloch was to remain at the War Office, indefatigably compiling reports and statistics, and presenting an alternative version to that of the Horse Guards, until the Crimean war.

In many cases the reports confirmed suspicions: mortality in Gibraltar was 21.4 per 1,000 but only 13 (less than in Britain) if epidemics in 1828 and 1834 were discounted. By contrast Sierra Leone had a rate of 483 per 1,000, and in 1825 deaths had reached 783 per 1,000. The West Indies showed a varied pattern. Antigua and Montserrat (40.6 per 1,000), Barbados (58.8), Grenada (61.8) and St Vincent were distinguished as relatively healthy. Tobago (152.8), St Lucia (122.8), Dominica (137.4), the Bahamas (200) and Jamaica (128) pointed the contrast.[18] The withdrawal of garrisons from certain West Indian stations and their concentration in the healthy locations was a direct result of the report. The overall figures showed an average annual mortality of 15.9 per 1,000 in Britain, 21.1 in the temperate colonies (America and the Mediterranean) and 63.4 in the tropics.[19] Two main conclusions about foreign service were clear: that it was in the best interests of the men's health and therefore of a regiment's integrity that postings to tropical climates be kept short, and secondly that they be alternated with service in temperate stations, thus equalising the burden of duty.

Equipped with the first report, Howick immediately despatched memoranda to the Secretary of State on reducing the force in the West Indies, to the Board of Ordnance on the need to site barracks in healthy locations, to the Treasury on increasing the proportion of fresh food in the soldiers' diet and to the Commander-in-Chief on exercise and amusement. More complex were the problems of colonial reliefs. The cost of transport, and the fact that while they were at sea men were tied up uselessly, discouraged frequent moves. And yet now it appeared that stationary troops were just as expensive in terms of lives and pension bills. In 1836 seventy-six out of 103 battalions were stationed in the colonies and each could reckon on spending only about four of every thirty-four years at home. To reduce the time spent in the West Indies from ten to five years and in India from twenty to fifteen seemed eminently desirable, but totally impossible. Tulloch himself came to the rescue with an article in the *United Service Journal*.[20] Thirty-seven infantry regiments were, he calculated, at healthy stations, the same number at unhealthy ones, twenty-six at home and three at sea. He therefore urged three separate foreign tours, each totalling ten years abroad. The Atlantic circuit should be made up of four years in the Mediterranean, three in the West Indies and three in America. To the east, India should count as a complete ten-year tour in itself, and the remaining stations be divided into New South Wales three years, Ceylon or

Mauritius four, the Cape or St Helena three. Howick, with Horse Guards approval, implemented the Atlantic rotation immediately. He was to return to the difficulties of the eastern model when Secretary of State.[21]

Thus, by the time he resigned in 1839, Howick had begun to grapple with many of the problems of imperial garrisoning and had served a four-year apprenticeship in coping with them and, more particularly, with the Horse Guards. Although influenced by a number of theorists, actual administrative experience meant that theory and doctrine increasingly took second place to pragmatism. Indeed, there developed in him traits of rugged independence that were eventually to put Howick beyond party. However, in the short term the looser confederations of 1840s politics rendered such attributes less damaging.

In July 1845 he succeeded his father in the title of Earl Grey, and became the active leader of the Whigs in the House of Lords. His antipathy to Palmerston's holding the Foreign Office prevented Russell from forming a government in 1845. However, in 1846 he had little choice but to reconcile himself to the arrangement. Grey determined that he would not be the man to originate opposition to Palmerston's conduct of foreign policy. Indeed, when Prince Albert saw in the Cabinet a 'Grey' section which regarded the others—including Russell—as old women, he put Palmerston in the 'Grey' camp. But the Greys were not a party within a party; they were rather the self-conceived repository of intellectual and moral excellence.

By his own lights, Grey's relationships with his colleague were harmonious. This was partly, no doubt, because his sphere of responsibility was relatively self-contained and not in the mainstream of political debate.[22] He accepted the office for which his pedigree so obviously fitted him, that of Secretary of State for War and the Colonies. His administrative achievements in it were immense, but in consequence he broke completely with Wakefield and the Colonial Reformers. W. P. Morrell has called him by temperament an authoritarian, by conviction a reformer.[23] This judgement accurately reflects his patrician upbringing and his restless search for efficiency and economy—or even cost-effectiveness, attributes which made him a good administrator but a less astute politician.

His predecessors as Secretary of State had tended—naturally enough in time of peace—to concentrate on the colonial half of their duties. Indeed, it had been this, particularly with a superior as weak as Glenelg, which had allowed Howick so much latitude as Secretary at War. Those four years at the War Office meant that, although colonial problems were to be at the forefront of his mind throughout his period of office, they could be dovetailed into a strategy which for the first time since the peace gave a real sense of an evolving pattern of imperial defence. The unreformed nature of the office itself was ironically to enhance this aspect of Grey's work, since it gave him personal control of both areas without the irritation of negotiating with a second party. Governors of colonies had military powers but were appointed by him. He decided force strengths, and the policy that dictated their use rested with him.

The principal issue he faced in 1846 was colonial self-government. Equipped with Wakefield's theories, free trade nostrums and the Durham Report, Grey stood poised for new departures in imperial policy. That he did not achieve as much in this direction as perhaps he had hoped—so much so that he earned the unbounded wrath of Wakefield in *The Art of Colonization* (1849)—is a tribute to his own abilities as an administrator. He remained too sensitive to the advice of local bodies, of parliamentary committees and Colonial Office functionaries to carry through the theorists' panaceas. But certainly he confirmed that in future the link between the old colonies and the mother country would no longer be commerce. Free trade forced them as much as the mother country into the open market. Lacking any other exclusive rights, the appeal of Britain had to rest in vaguer concepts—liberty, race and culture.

The corollary of self-government was a greater share by the colonies in the burden of their own defence. Grey was prepared to accept that the British exchequer should meet imperial obligations, but the responsibility of policing, maintaining civil order or countering native insurgency should rest with the colony itself. Although insistent on the principle, he was responsive to the advice of Elgin, another relative and his replacement for Lord Cathcart in Canada. An immediate demand so soon after the introduction of free trade would divorce the colonies from the empire. Instead a cautious approach, allowing time for free trade to be accepted, would permit a gentle run-down of troops stationed in areas not faced by any immediate threat.[24]

In the event the publication in 1851 of Grey's ideas in relation to Canada did not drive her into the arms of the United States. By October 1852 the garrisons at eight military posts had been withdrawn and the total force cut by 1,400 rank and file. Grey planned to concentrate the remainder at Quebec and Kingston, thus enhancing the training and discipline of battalions previously scattered in small detachments. Improving relations with the United States took the edge off the argument that Canada would have no obvious enemy but for the British connection, and the Crimean war provided the excuse for a more rapid withdrawal.

However, full implementation of the model during Grey's tenure of office was confined to Australia. In 1846 New South Wales provided the troops to fight the Maoris in New Zealand, thus proving it could cope without the army. Its argument for imperial troops—that the convict settlement was the creation of the mother country—was thereby undermined. In 1849 Grey announced that the barracks and fortifications in Australia were to be handed over to the colonial government and in return for their upkeep a fixed number of imperial troops was to be provided. Even at the Cape a case for reduction could be made out. Sir William Molesworth contended that, since the Boer farmers did not themselves have to meet the cost of war against the Kaffirs, they were more reckless in incurring it.[25] Always, however, local factors predominated, and thus progress towards colonial self-defence proceeded slowly. In the year ending 31 March 1854 the colonies contributed only £378,253 to a total military budget of £3,968,599.[26] But Grey left as his testament that 'I think it will follow, that when this Country no longer attempts either to levy a commercial tribute from the Colonies by a system of restriction, nor to interfere needlessly in their internal affairs, it has a right to expect that they should take upon themselves a larger proportion than heretofore of the expenses incurred for their advantage.'[27]

The burden on the army of imperial garrisoning also attracted Grey's fervour for rationalisation. On 17 October 1846 he drew up a memorandum for his Cabinet colleagues on the subject of the army.[28] Knowing all too well that an appeal on the grounds of empire or army alone would strike few chords, he started by harping on the well established fears of French invasion. This was an issue which increasingly concerned the Cabinet in the winter of 1846–47, and on which even Wellington, in a famous letter of January 1847, was disposed to be alarmist. From the crises faced in the empire at the beginning of the decade—rebellion in Canada, war in Afghanistan and in China—the army by the end was preparing itself to meet a more traditional foe. And thus between 1840 and 1850 the forces in the colonies declined from 52,680 to 46,940, while those in Britain sprang from 28,277 to 52,460.[29] However spurious the real threat to the national coastline, in political terms it had to be taken seriously. To release troops from the empire, more effective methods of employing and distributing the army among the colonies had to be found.

> The policy [Grey advocated] upon which we ought to proceed in these days of easy communication by steam between different parts of the empire, is not to scatter our force more than can possibly be avoided, but to keep a large reserve in this country (our citadel, as it is well termed by Sir J. Graham), ready to be sent at a short notice wherever danger may threaten.

Most colonies by 1846 faced little serious internal threat, and insufficient regular troops could be maintained to guarantee their safety from external attack. Such a policy was wholly in accord with the drift to colonial self-defence and with the precepts of Tulloch and Marshall on the rotation of troops. Reliance should therefore be placed on the navy, and on a change in the description of force employed in the colonies.

All colonies, in Grey's view, should have colonial corps. 'These corps should be of two kinds: those in which both men and officers are of British origin and those of which the officers only, and sometimes not even the officers, are British.' The virtues of the latter category, of which existing examples were the West India Regiments, the Cape Mounted Rifles, the Ceylon Rifles and the Royal Malta Fencibles, were those highlighted by the Marshall and Tulloch reports. Natives proved more resilient to the ravages of local diseases. In the West Indies negroes succumbed at the rate of between 46.3 per 1,000 (St Kitts) and 28.4 (Grenada), and in West Africa at 30 per 1,000.[30] They were therefore cheaper in terms of transport costs and pensions. Furthermore in broken and wooded terrain their knowledge of the country and their hardiness could make them excellent irregular troops. The fighting virtues of the Maori—if only they could be harnessed—were regularly cited, and the Hottentots of the Cape Mounted Rifles were compared to the sepoys of India. But, like the sepoys, the loyalty of such soldiers could prove brittle, and in 1851 desertions and indiscipline among the Hottentots reached such epidemic proportions that they were replaced by Europeans.[31]

Pre-eminent in Grey's first category were the Royal Canadian Rifles. These were the fruit of his sojourn at the War Office. The Austrian example of creating military colonies on the Hungarian frontier, as a buffer against incursions from the Ottoman Empire, had attracted his attention and that of Sir Willoughby Gordon, the Quartermaster General.[32] In December 1835 Howick 'had ... a long conversation with George Grey about the possibility of forming colonial corps, & agreed with him that my favourite scheme of a militia settled on allotments of land & serving one or two days in the week might be tried with advantage in Canada'.[33] In addition to its specific military functions, such a force could develop land which had previously been neglected by settlers, and so, by conferring the economic benefits of stability and civilisation, curb the activities of marauders or semi-feudal societies. Herein was the fruit of Wakefield's emigration schemes.

In 1836 Howick proposed the organisation of a battalion, service in which would be a reward for at least fourteen years completed in the line. Its members were to be encouraged to farm, and were to be quartered by companies in villages, within a small enough radius to allow the battalion to assemble once a week. The pay proposed was 15d a day (as opposed to the usual shilling), so that membership would be a reward for good conduct. In the event earlier difficulties in settling retired soldiers meant that the regulations promulgated for the formation of the Royal Canadian Rifles smacked more of a regular corps than of a framework for a military colony. The pay was kept at 13*d* per day so that the surplus could go towards the purchase of land on the soldiers' discharge. Only twelve wives per 100 men were allowed, the officers formed part of the line and the men were liable for service anywhere in North America. The unit as formed had no permanent home, the reward was therefore minimal, and in consequence a second-rate line regiment had been created with no balancing compensations.[34] Wellington was wont to cite the American War of Independence as an example of the dangers of local armies.[35] Certainly the less hysterical arguments produced by the Horse Guards were applicable in the case of the Canadian Rifles: they were not available to reinforce other colonies, they did weaken the homogeneity of the regular army and their sedentary nature encouraged them to lapse into inefficiency.

In his 1846 memorandum Grey attempted to revert to the principles towards which he had originally been striving, 'to make admission to such corps a reward to good soldiers of the line, and at the same time to make them the means of increasing in the colonies the population of British origin'. In April the same year Wakefield had suggested the military colonisation of the Cape, Australia and New Zealand by regiments of married men.[36] In the event Wellington's opposition meant that Grey's original scheme became suffused in a second, also advocated in his memorandum.

In 1843 an Act had been passed to enrol and arm 10,000 military pensioners in Britain, to be paid only when called out for duty. In September 1846 Grey, reflecting Wakefield's views on emigration, proposed that similar bodies be sent out to the colonies.[37] Tulloch produced a memorandum, in which he urged the use of pensioners as military colonists. At home the pensioner was the first to lose his job, as he was unskilled, not elegible for poor relief, and old, and therefore tended to wander destitute round the country, a bad advertisement for the army, open to incitement and unavailable for reserved service. A body of men thus existed who might be ready to go out, and could be supplemented by a rotation system which brought a regiment to a suitable colony last before returning home and where free discharges might be given to those desirous to settle.[38]

New Zealand, so much the focus of Wakefield's schemes, was the departure point. Grey proposed that the pensioner should be employed on public works for the first year, after which the acre of land he received should be productive, and the pensioner's family established in the cottage provided. The pensioner would have an absolute right to the property after seven years if he drilled twelve days a year.[39] In October 1846 Russell[40] and Wellington[41] both approved the scheme in outline. Six hundred were required, and the offers of service proved so numerous that the upper age limit was reduced from forty-eight to forty-five.[42] Before their departure some elementary instruction in Maori warfare was provided.[43] However, newspaper reports suggested that the scheme had its imperfections: settled on the outskirts of Auckland, work proved hard to obtain and intemperance flourished.[44] Old soldiers, while well versed in the management of arms, lacked the resource, youth or skills required of good farming settlers.[45]

Nonetheless Grey received sufficiently favourable accounts to confirm him in his notions.[46] By March 1850 thirty pensioners had been settled in the Falkland Islands, 150 in Van Diemen's Land, eighty at Hudson's Bay and 140 in Western Australia.[47] Between Christmas 1849 and August 1850 1,157 went out to Australia as convict guards,[48] many going on to New Zealand, where there were 1,180 pensioners by November 1851. By the same date, 480 were in Canada.[49] In 1850 pensioners from the West India Regiments were enrolled in Gambia[50] and in 1853 were actually engaged in operations against the King of Keenung.[51]

A second and related scheme, floated by Grey in 1848, was for the formation of corps of military labourers. Men, preferably 'the semi-barbarians of Mayo & Donegal,'[52] should enlist for a seven- or even three-year period, and during that time should spend three months on public works for every one month on military duties. Thus, of a body of 16,000 in Canada, 4,000 could relieve a similar number of regular troops, while the remaining 12,000 built the railways. On their discharge they would settle and serve on the same basis as the enrolled pensioners. 'What I shd like,' wrote Grey, 'wd be to send out some of the many thousand emigrants who now go annually to America under the restraint of Military discipline to be employed not merely as soldiers but as pioneers to prepare some of the neglected lands of Canada for settlement.'[53] However, the idea only promised well as a solution to the Irish problem. Canada was not short of labour, and it was felt that the men themselves might be regarded as socially inferior, thus giving rise to disciplinary problems.[54]

Similar reactions greeted the same proposal for the Cape, where Grey thought the construction of roads[55] might be a precursor to the pacification of the Kaffirs. Sir Harry Smith, the Governor, pointed out that officer procurement had proved the great stumbling block to the pensioners' efficiency, and this problem would bedevil a corps of labourers. 'Example, precept, honour, good officers and non-commissioned officers' were the binding force in a regiment, and Smith felt that pensioners alone might be so imbued with these military qualities as to remain of some use in an extended colony if attacked. Grey was forced to agree.[56] Thus in 1848 all men whose regiments were due to leave the colony were allowed to take their discharge and settle.[57] They were, however, to point the limitations to Grey's hopes, even for the pensioners. Most of these old soldiers were established in four villages on the Cape eastern frontier. On Christmas Day 1850 they were surprised and massacred, almost to a man.[58]

In essence, because of their own failings and the lack of officer settlers, pensioners could never be a front line against a native uprising. The 522 pensioners in Van Diemen's Land were a valuable barrier between the convicts and the recently discovered gold; those in New Zealand had relieved 800 regular troops; and 600 enrolled in Canada had enabled the Royal Canadian Rifles to be reduced by four companies. Thus they might form a colonial militia, but they could not bear the brunt of major fighting.

In any case, Grey had another problem. If the pensioners were to fulfil a significant role in imperial settlement there would have to be a constant and sizable flow of fit men from the army. This could only be maintained by an increased rate of discharge, and an improved rate of enlistment. However, recruitment was for an indefinite period, and discharge was granted for good, not bad, conduct. For many commentators this arrangement highlighted the contrast between the army and the civilian society from which it was drawn. It equated military service with bondage and denied it any comparability with other working-class occupations. If service was confined to a limited period, it was argued, hope would be restored to the men, recruiting would be encouraged and the pool of pensioners created from which reserve corps could be established.

In 1846 Grey proposed that enlistment should be for a ten-year period. Marshall had reckoned that the average length of service before a soldier was invalided out was no greater,[59] and Charles Grey thought that about half the strength of every regiment had served under seven years.[60] In 1839 Sir Hussey Vivian urged on Grey the virtues of a set period of enlistment, both to attract a better class of recruit and to allow discharge at an age when a new trade could yet be acquired.[61] Thus Grey told his Secretary at War, Fox Maule,

> I have always been for limited enlistment; and what is more for practically short service from our soldiers. Limited inlistment wd make the service most popular, & if the men served but a short time, say 10 years, you wd have these gt advantages–1st An army always young & vigorous—2d great relief from the heavy burthen of the out pension list—3d the maintenance of a reserve force both at home & in the colonies of a very cheap & most effectual kind.[62]

On 14 December 1846 he wrote officially to Wellington. The ten-year period would be extendable for two years if the troops were on active service and for one year if abroad. On discharge the soldier would serve in a reserve until aged fifty-five and qualified for a pension. Those now serving were to have the benefit of limited service, provided that no regiment lost more than twenty-five men in the case of the infantry or ten for the cavalry.[63] To the Master General of the Ordnance he proposed terms of twelve years for the Royal Artillery and fourteen for the Royal Sappers and Miners, in view of their more extended training.[64]

The Duke's reaction was determined and hostile. At the moment, Wellington argued, those of over ten years' service amounted to 12,000 cavalry and infantry at home alone. The settled rhythm of military life would be upset, 'the most intelligent, the most efficient' men would be lost, and those eligible but debarred by the limitation of numbers from taking their discharge immediately would become discontented. He suggested, by way of compromise, that the experiment be limited to recruits only. Grey suspended the part relating to serving soldiers,[65] and thus in effect met the Duke's objections. With his customary lack of tact, however, he tried to suggest that the Duke's prognosis was wrong. After fourteen years' service a man was already entitled to apply for a free discharge (which in practice he proved reluctant to take), and therefore the futures of only 6,798 soldiers were being discussed—that is, those of more than ten but less than fourteen years' service.[66]

Wellington was not to be pushed, and even threatened to tender his resignation to the Queen.[67] Both Grey [68] and Lord John Russell [69] hastened to reassure him that they would not adopt the plan of discharging soldiers then in the army without consulting him, and that they would only progress with a Bill for prospective ten-year enlistment. On this basis a Bill was introduced in the Commons. In his winding-up speech on the third reading Russell reflected a wider spirit of reform: 'It is not an answer to us to say that there was a good Army thirty or forty years ago, in the Peninsula or at Waterloo, for we must make all the different institutions of the country conform to the general spirit of the times and the advancement of the day.'[70] In the Lords, Grey, facing the phalanx of now ennobled Peninsular heroes, explored the same vein. The Bill, he urged, must be seen as 'part of a course of policy and of a series of measures which for the last twenty-five years had been passed with the object of raising the character of the Army, and improving the condition of the soldier'.[71]

The measure was carried, but in the event its efficacy was marginal. In the choice between short service and a large reserve or long service and no reserve, a compromise had been reached which ensured neither. The time devoted to training, despatching troops to the colonies and acclimatisation meant that a two- or three-year term on the Continental model was impossible for an army with imperial obligations. A really large reserve for European war was therefore incompatible with a continuing colonial commitment. The possibility of attracting recruits in the boom years of the

1850s and '60s was doubtful, but in any case the offer of a ten-year commitment to induce a young man to take the Queen's shilling can have been little more persuasive than the former one of unlimited service. As Wellington's insistence on retaining old soldiers had been carried, the Act failed completely to ensure a reservoir for the indigenous colonial militias.

Part of the reason why Grey's anxiety to create a reserve was not treated with the urgency it deserved was that some sort of reserve system for colonial service already existed. Conceived by Wellington in 1825,[72] the arrangement was for a battalion going to any foreign station other than India to take six service companies abroad and leave four depot companies at home. This meant that 556 other ranks and twenty-six officers were kept in the field by 242 other ranks and thirteen officers.[73] The depots remained behind in order to supply the regiments overseas with trained recruits and officers, and at the same time to offer a haven for soldiers incapacitated by disease, climate or wounds. They also provided units to aid the civil power. Eighteen thousand men, divided into sixty-two depots (the position in 1854),[74] and composed of the unfit and the untrained, met the needs of the '20s and '30s but could not be rapidly collected into a manageable body to counter a French invasion. Nor apparently did the depot system furnish the most efficient method of garrisoning the colonies. In terms of men, 60.3 per cent of the infantry of the line was abroad in 1820 and 61.9 per cent in 1839. But owing to the low service strength of the regiment after the introduction of the depots in 1825, 56.7 per cent (fifty-five of the ninety-seven infantry battalions) abroad in 1820 had grown to 75.7 per cent (seventy-eight of the 103) in 1839.[75] In that year 32,064 soldiers were at home and 34,004 in the colonies, excluding India, but the proportion in terms of regiments was twenty-four to fifty-nine.[76] In 1853 it was calculated that if entire regiments served together only twenty-five need be abroad at any one time, as opposed to the forty-nine then in colonies other than India. Furthermore a rotation of six years at home to four away would be possible.[77]

The alternative to the four-company depots favoured by the military press was their reduction to one or two companies and their incorporation into so-called provisional battalions. These would have a permanent staff, be grouped according to the areas in which the respective service companies were stationed, would permit a much fuller scheme of instruction for recruits and would create stronger battalions abroad. The model was derived from Chatham, where since 1830 the depot companies of the East India Company's European regiments and the Queen's troops in India and New South Wales had functioned on just this system. In 1836 the *Naval and Military Gazette* repeated rumours of the extension of provisional battalions to regiments in the West Indies (to be at Cork), the

Mediterranean (at Plymouth), and to Ceylon, the Cape and Mauritius (at Portsmouth).[78] And in 1838 Charles Grey told Howick that, if the 71st went to Canada, he would apply to leave no depot. He objected to the breaking up of his regiment and to the fact that it prolonged rather than diminished foreign service.[79]

Howick proposed that battalions be formed of ten companies, eight of which would be for foreign service and two (totalling 139 men) should form part of a provisional battalion of five or six regimental depots. In consequence, forty-nine battalions would be abroad for ten years at a time, and thirty at home for four years eight months.[80] The provisional battalions, he suggested to Wellington, might be formed of regiments recruited in the same part of the kingdom and stationed accordingly, that for the Scottish regiments, for example, being in Edinburgh.[81]

Hill and Wellington opposed on the grounds that provisional battalions would provide an alternative system to that of the regiment, and the recruit would therefore still have much to learn on joining the service companies.[82] The only result of this sally was a redistribution in favour of the service companies (200 to 600), but in other respects Russell agreed to retire the government defeated.[83]

However, the colonial demands of 1842 caused nine regiments of foot to be increased to twelve companies, divided into two battalions, called the first and the reserve. The transformation left those regiments with depots of only 120 rank and file.[84] In this instance so small was the unit that the Horse Guards had little choice but to accept the provisional battalion organisation. The reduced establishment of each and the collective capability of the whole meant too that all those unfit for foreign service were weeded out,[85] so that the battalion was as effective as possible. By 1848, partly owing to the withdrawal of troops from the colonies, only thirteen four-company depots were left, as opposed to sixty a few years before.[86] Although the reserve battalions were reduced in 1849, Wellington was so converted to the idea of the provisional or depot battalions that at his request its demise was stayed two years until 1851.[87]

The example of the depot battalion reinforced the convictions of other more inventive minds. By 1848 Charles Grey had drafted a comprehensive scheme of infantry organisation under which the four-company depots, the recruiting districts and the militia staff should all be replaced by provisional battalions of reserve companies (100 rank and file each). Permanent barracks should be built for each battalion, in areas chosen with reference to the counties in which the regiments were originally raised and to which they should in future confine their recruiting. The depot would become an effective organ of administration and instruction.[88] Moreover such an organisation dovetailed neatly into Lord Grey's preference for local militia, which he envisaged as feeding a second home-service battalion for each regular regiment, officered by the first battalion and from which volunteering into the first or foreign service battalion would be encouraged.[89] Although Tulloch doubted whether in peacetime sufficient volunteers would be forthcoming,[90] there was no reason why the other end of Grey's scheme should not work. He proposed that, after serving the ten years of limited enlistment, a soldier could qualify for a deferred pension by signing on for eleven more years of regular service or enlisting in the reserve.[91]

This scheme embodied three important principles. The first was that of encouraging local connections, which with the example of the Highland regiments most commentators took to encourage better discipline. The second was an integration of the militia with the line. This, as several military observers noted, was the natural extension of giving battalions local links, with the reserve acting as the funnel through which willing and well conducted recruits would pass. Thirdly it gave the army a comprehensive and uniform structure, which recognised its two main strategic roles—home defence and imperial garrisoning. The depot would be a permanent centre for the regiment, a good school for recruits and, in Lord Seaton's words, 'a kind of home'[92] for the troops stationed abroad.

The most important convert to these ideas was Prince Albert, whose private secretary Charles Grey was from 1849. As a soldier, Charles Grey was diffident about trumpeting his scheme, particularly as it might involve collision with the Commander-in-Chief. Prince Albert therefore took his ideas in hand. He emphasised the creation of a trained reserve through the offer of deferred pensions and in February 1852 sent Grey's proposals and his own memorandum to Russell and Lord Hardinge,[93] who in that month became Master General of the Ordnance. The Prime Minister duly passed it on, with his blessing, to Wellington.[94] The consequences were predictable. The Duke asked the Military Secretary, Fitzroy Somerset, and the Adjutant General, Sir George Brown, for their views. Fitzroy Somerset replied that Grey's system 'would be entirely subversive of the existing arrangement as regards Regiments and Battalions—diminish the influence and pride of the Commanding Officer and put an end to esprit de corps'.[95] The Adjutant General refuted each of the criticisms which the proposed changes implied, point by point.[96] What they said was what the Duke wanted to hear. Above all else, Wellington disliked the proposals as enshrining the 1847 enlistment Act. Charles Grey had realised that the only really efficient way to form a reserve was to make discharge after ten years' service obligatory, except for NCOs.[97] The Duke's worst fears would be realised, and the line would be deprived of its most experienced men. This objection was enough to destroy the entire edifice.

The Grey brothers' ideas on regimental organisation were to surface again after the death of Wellington. But by that time Russell's government had fallen, and after February 1852 Grey—although he lived on until 1894—never again held office. Even had he continued it is doubtful whether he could have worked as successfully in tandem with Hardinge as did Sidney Herbert, the Secretary at War from 1852 to 1855. For Grey's insensitivity to others was the greatest bar to the achievement of his schemes. The issue of regimental reorganisation is a perfect case in point. As a solution to the problems of imperial defence it had much to recommend it. But implicit in it was a new system of training, which the new depots would provide. By trespassing on to such specifically military issues as musketry training and field manoeuvres he was treading on professional toes already bruised by his attempts at consolidation. In February 1852 Wellington wrote to Prince Albert, 'It is stated that the British Infantry cannot march—that the cavalry cannot ride—that the officers are ignorant—that the soldiers do not know the use of and cannot use their arms! ... Field Marshal the Duke of Wellington has qualified these opinions as unjust prejudices however high the official quarters in which entertained.'[98] The target of his barbs did not need identifying.

Only in one area was the worth of Grey's achievement openly acknowledged by his military contemporaries. His renewed attempts in 1846 and 1849 at imposing a rotation system in the eastern hemisphere included the idea that regiments might go from India to Australia, the Cape or New Zealand, with a view to encouraging men to take their discharge and settle in those colonies. The scheme could only be unacceptable to Wellington when—as with limited enlistment—its purpose was to deprive the army of its old soldiers.[99] However, the general trend of Grey's idea was adopted. The Duke always maintained the ideal of a ten-year maximum whatever a regiment's station.[100] Although not uniformly achieved, by 1848 no regiment had been abroad for more than twelve years,[101] and a proportion of ten years abroad and five at home for the 'inner service' was matched by fifteen and seven and a half for India and the more distant colonies.[102] The results could be seen in the dramatically improved health of the army. For the years 1851–52 mortality in Jamaica stood at 44 per 1,000, and for the rest of the West Indies at 22.1. The average in India for the previous thirty years had been 74.2, but it had now sunk to 48.5. Even the temperate zones had registered an improvement, the American colonies falling from 21.2 in the Marshall and Tulloch report to 14, and the Mediterranean stations from 23.5 to 12.7. On a worldwide aggregate in 1847, this was reckoned to be equivalent to the saving of a whole battalion a year.[103]

For the rest—and this was partly Grey's own fault—the conflict with the Horse Guards too often either blocked reform or moderated its effects. Alternatively, the solutions that he proposed were too far-seeing in their implications for hasty implementation. He did not, therefore, reap the harvest he had sown during his own tenure of office. But in so many directions he had pointed the way. Cardwell, who has regularly received the credit for shaping the army to meet its imperial obligations, was implementing ideas which had been mooted or brought to life under Grey. Furthermore Grey's emigration schemes and hopes of self-reliant colonial militias were—on a more extended reading—to produce the Dominion forces in the world wars. The two-battalion regimental structure, and its linking to the auxiliary forces, were to be sunk only temporarily by the demands of the Crimean war, and were finally to be carried out in 1881 by Childers. And Grey it was who introduced examinations for first commissions (1849) and promotion (1850)—surely the beginning of the end for purchase? Cardwell's so-called short service enlistment Act of 1870, introducing a period of six years with the colours, bore more relation to Grey's original intentions in the 1847 Act than to any Continental model.

However, the continuing insolubility of this very problem—that of recruiting—suggests that both he and Grey were seeking a chimera. Continental orthodoxy was working towards mass armies, based on short service and large reserves, and administered in brigades, divisions and even corps. The transport and acclimatisation problems meant that a long-service force was obligatory for the colonies, and the detached and isolated nature of the job meant that the regiment or battalion remained the administrative unit, and increasingly the soldier's home. Any compromise, therefore, between the twin demands of imperial and home defence would force a deviation from one or other of the models. The imperial commitment was the more realistic one, since it was in the colonies that the army actually fought. But the fear of invasion was the key to parliamentary coffers, and meant that never could the army be totally structured on the basis of the colonies alone.

Grey's contribution in all this was to draw the threads together, to pick up the problems of the post-Waterloo army, to listen to the grievances without the ear-trumpet of Wellington's Horse Guards. To those wedded to the Continental orthodoxy of the Peninsula his switch to the colonies was destructive. For many, economy and efficiency existed in separate compartments or were even contradictory, and they failed to see that for Grey they were related. His achievements in defence policy have consequently gone for too long unheralded. In particular they fell foul of the Crimean war, which cast so much dirt and smoke over the British army of the 1840s, but which was in truth a departure from the strategic mission

Grey had assigned it. Ironically the pressures of 1854–55 were to throw up a Secretary of State with responsibility for war alone—the office which Grey had coveted twenty years previously. But the relationship between Horse Guards and War Office was not at the same time redefined and the division in council between civil and military authorities was never fully overcome, not even by Cardwell, while the office of Commander-in-Chief continued to exist.

Notes

1   Sidney Herbert papers, in the possession of the Earl of Pembroke, III B (112)(a).
2   Grey to Elgin, 26 December 1848, in Sir Arthur G. Doughty (ed.), *The Elgin–Grey Papers, 1846–1852*, Public Archives of Canada, 1937, p. 266.
3   G. A. Wetherall papers, National Army Museum, 6210/93/7, [Brown] to Wetherall, 18 September 1858.
4   A. G. L. Shaw (ed.), *Great Britain and the Colonies, 1815–1865*, Methuen, London, 1970, p. 2.
5   Grey to Elgin, 22 August 1849, in *Elgin–Grey Papers*, p. 448.
6   J. M. Ward, *Colonial Self-government: the British Experience, 1759–1856*, Macmillan, London, 1976, pp. 62, 65, 72, 212–3, 231, 247, 250, 268, 270, 287. On colonial policy in this era see also Shaw, *op. cit.*; W. P. Morrell, *British Colonial Policy in the Age of Peel and Russell*, Oxford, 1930; Bernard Semmel, *The Rise of Free Trade Imperialism*, Cambridge, 1970; R. L. Schuyler, *The Fall of the Old Colonial System*, Oxford, 1945; J. M. Ward, 'The colonial policy of Lord John Russell's administration', *Historical Studies, Australia and New Zealand*, XI, 1959–61, pp. 244–62.
7   Grey papers, Department of Palaeography and Diplomatic, Durham University, Howick to Charles Grey, 16 December 1835.
8   Lord Broughton, *Recollections of a Long Life*, Murray, London, 1910–11, IV, pp. 276–7.
9   Grey papers, Howick to Charles Grey, 29 August 1836.
10 Parliamentary Papers (hereafter PP) 1837, XXXIV, *Report . . . into the Expediency of Consolidating the Different Departments connected with the Civil Administration of the Army*.
11 PP 1850, X, *Report from the Select Committee on Army and Ordnance Expenditure*, pp. 698–700, 715–24.
12 Royal Archives E 44/24, Grey to Charles Grey, 14 November 1852. Quoted by gracious permission of HM the Queen.
13 PP 1836, XXII, *Report . . . into the System of Military Punishments in the Army*.
14 Grey papers, Charles Grey to Howick, 24 April 1836.
15 *Autobiography and Services of Sir James McGrigor*, Longman Green, London, 1861, pp. 376–80.
16 WO 43/688, f. 128.
17 Grey papers, C 3/2, Grey's journal, 25 May 1836.
18 *United Service Journal*, 1838, Part III, pp. 306, 468; 1839, Part I, p. 371, and Part III, p. 87; 1840, Part I, p. 509.
19 *Naval and Military Gazette*, 21 June 1845, p. 3.
20 *United Service Journal*, 1836, Part III, p. 289; attributed to Tulloch in *Naval and Military Gazette*, 22 December 1838, p. 816.
21 WO 43/656, *passim*.

22 Donald Southgate, *The Passing of the Whigs, 1832–1886*, Macmillan, London, 1962.

23 Morrell, *Colonial Policy*, p. 201.

24 Doughty, *Elgin–Grey Papers*, pp. 217, 267, 272, 559–61.

25 On colonial self-defence under Grey see Morrell, *Colonial Policy*, pp. 286, 293, 474–8, 490, 498; R. L. Schuyler, 'The recall of the legions', *American Historical Review*, XXVI, 1920–21, pp. 18–36; W. C. B. Tunstall, 'Imperial Defence, 1815–1870', *Cambridge History of the British Empire*, Cambridge, 1940, II, pp. 808–9, 811–13; C. P. Stacey, *Canada and the British Army, 1846–1871*, Longman Green, London, 1936; Doughty, *Elgin–Grey Papers*, pp. 78, 144, 185–9, 217, 249, 267, 272, 448, 554, 559–61, 701–2, 716, 721; J. Mackay Hitsman, *Safeguarding Canada, 1763–1871*, University of Toronto Press, 1968, pp. 154–5.

26 Schuyler, 'Recall of the legions', p. 24.

27 Earl Grey, *Colonial Policy of Lord John Russell's Administration*, Bentley, London, 1853 (2nd ed), I, p. 18, also pp. 43–9.

28 Copies are to be found in many sets of papers. The one worked on here is from the Panmure papers, Scottish Record Office, GD 45/8/21.

29 PP 1850, X, pp. 770–3.

30 *United Service Journal*, 1839, Part I, p. 371; 1840, Part II, p. 509.

31 Grey papers, Harry Smith to Grey, 18 and 19 August 1851; Panmure papers, GD 45/8/87 and 99.

32 Grey papers, Gordon to Howick, 7 August 1837.

33 Grey papers, C 3/1B, journal, 21 December 1835.

34 WO 43/745, ff. 63–156, 207–46.

35 Grey papers, Wellington to Russell, 11 November 1846.

36 WO 1/598, ff. 747–50; WO 4/268, p. 332.

37 Panmure papers, GD 45/8/21, Grey to Fox Maule, 13 September 1846.

38 Grey papers, Tulloch to Grey, 25 September 1846.

39 Panmure papers, GD 45/8/115.

40 Grey papers, Russell to Grey, 30 October 1846.

41 Grey papers, Wellington to Grey, 23 November 1846.

42 WO 43/853.

43 *United Service Magazine*, 1847, Part II, pp. 482–3.

44 *British Army Despatch*, 15 February 1850, p. 150.

45 *Naval and Military Gazette*, 9 February 1850, p. 89; J. Rutherford, *Sir George Grey*, Cassell, London, 1961, pp. 93–4.

46 WO 43/876, f. 277; PP 1849, IX, pp. 479–482.

47 PP 1850, X, pp. 173–4.

48 Grey papers, Tulloch to Grey, 28 August 1850.

49 Sir George Brown papers, National Library of Scotland MSS 2849, f. 212, distribution of army, 27 November 1851.

50 WO 43/925.

51 J. E. Caulfield, *One Hundred Years' History of the 2nd Batt. West India Regiment*, Forster Groom, London, 1899, pp. 74, 84.

52 Doughty, *Elgin–Grey Papers*, pp. 222–3.

53 *Ibid.*, pp. 126–7.

54 *Ibid.*, pp. 1436–457.

55 Grey papers, Grey to Smith, 20 April 1848.

56 Grey papers, Smith to Grey, 28 June and 7 November 1848, and reply, 20 January 1849.

57 A. Gordon-Brown (ed.), *The Narrative of Private Buck Adams*, Van Riebeeck Society, Cape Town, 1941, p. 258.

58 R. P. Dunn-Pattison, *The History of the 91st Argyllshire Highlanders*,

Blackwood, Edinburgh, 1910, pp. 111, 144.

59   Henry Marshall, *Military Miscellany*, John Murray, London, 1846, p. 103.
60   Grey papers, Charles Grey to Howick, 6 November 1836.
61   Vivian papers, National Army Museum, 7709–6–14, p. 121, Vivian to Howick, 11 April 1839.
62   Panmure papers, GD 45/8/21, Grey to Maule, 13 September 1846.
63   WO 43/827, ff. 185–8; WO 30/112, Grey to Wellington, 14 December 1846.
64   WO 6/127, p. 297.
65   WO 30/112, memorandum by Wellington, 15 December 1846, and Grey to Somerset, 22 December 1846.
66   Grey papers, Grey to Wellington, 20 January 1847.
67   Wellington papers, Wellington to Russell, 23 January 1847; Wellington to Queen, n.d.
68   Grey papers, Grey to Wellington, 28 January 1847.
69   Grey papers, Russell to Grey, 27 January 1847.
70   Hansard, third series, XCI, cc. 864–5.
71   *Ibid.*, cc. 1316–33.
72   *Despatches of Arthur, Duke of Wellington*, edited by his son, John Murray, London, 1867–80, II, pp. 378–9; Peel papers, British Library Add. MSS 40474, f. 42, memo by Hardinge, 24 January 1842.
73   *King's Regulations and Orders for the Army*, 1837, p. 165.
74   Royal Archives E 3/52, Hardinge to Newcastle, 22 March 1854.
75   WO 1/595, pp. 74–81.
76   *United Service Journal*, 1839, Part II, p. 108.
77   *United Service Magazine*, 1853, Part I, pp. 608–11.
78   *Naval and Military Gazette*, 22 October 1836, p. 680; 5 November 1836, p. 720; 30 December 1837, p. 825; 13 January 1838, p. 25.
79   Grey papers, Charles Grey to Howick, 14 February 1838, 23 April 1838, 13 May 1839, 19 August 1839, and Howick to Charles Grey, 24 January 1839.
80   WO 1/595, pp. 82–94; WO 43/693, ff. 311–30.
81   Grey papers, Howick to Wellington, 27 June 1839; copy in Wellington papers dated 28 June 1839.
82   Wellington papers, Normanby to Wellington, 17 June 1839, and reply; Howick to Wellington, 28 June 1839, and reply, 30 June 1839; WO 1/595, pp. 97–114, 195–207, 227–55.
83   WO 6/127, pp. 55, 58; WO 1/595, p. 221.
84   Horse Guards circular, 7 May 1842.
85   WO 3/106, p. 81.
86   *Naval and Military Gazette*, 30 September 1848, p. 633.
87   WO 6/128, pp. 58, 67; WO 1/600, p. 203; WO 3/112, pp. 94, 104.
88   Grey papers, Charles Grey to Grey, 24 January 1848.
89   Grey papers, Grey to Tulloch, 11 November 1847.
90   Grey papers, Tulloch to Grey, 14 January 1848.
91   Panmure papers, GD 45/8/21, Grey's memorandum, 17 October 1846, pp. 8–9.
92   Seaton papers, in the possession of J. E. Colborne Mackrell, unsigned and undated memorandum, ?1853.
93   Grey papers, Charles Grey to Grey, 10 February 1852; Royal Archives E 43/24, Albert to Russell, 14 February 1852; Theodore Martin, *Life of H.R.H. the Prince Consort*, Smith Elder, London, 1876, II, pp. 433–7.
94   Royal Archives E 43/27, Russell to Albert, 15 February 1852.
95   Wellington papers, memorandum by Somerset, 17 February 1852.
96   Wellington papers, memorandum by Brown, 17 February 1852.
97   Grey papers, Charles Grey to Grey, 10 February 1852.

98   Herbert papers, II Add., Wellington to Prince Albert, 20 February 1852.

99   WO 43/876; WO 30/112, memorandum of 11 July 1849; Grey papers, Tulloch to Grey, 25 September 1846, and Gordon to Grey, 28 May 1849.

100 WO 1/599, pp. 93, 245; Panmure papers, GD 45/8/20.

101 *Naval and Military Gazette*, 30 September 1848, p. 633; Hansard, third series, XCVII, c. 1156.

102 *Ibid.*, CXV, c. 749; PP 1851, VII, p. 9.

103 *Ibid.*, XCI, cc. 1326–7; CIII, c. 976; CXXIV, c. 677.

2

EDWARD CARDWELL AND THE ABOLITION OF PURCHASE

ANTHONY BRUCE

Edward Cardwell's achievements as Secretary of State for War (1868–74) in Gladstone's first administration have been the subject of thorough re-examination by contemporary historians.[1] The uncritical admiration of his closest associates, particularly his biographer and private secretary, Sir Robert Biddulph,[2] has been called into question by recent research which suggests that the effects of his major reforms were much more limited than had previously been supposed. His period of office is no longer seen as a turning point in the history of the British army. There is little doubt, however, that in his radical approach to army matters Cardwell was unlike any other nineteenth-century Secretary for War. Even before his appointment to the War Office he had prepared an important paper on the army's main deficiencies.[3] These included the disorganised state of central military administration, the anachronistic purchase system, severe recruiting problems and the absence of a reserve. Cardwell translated his preliminary thoughts into positive proposals with the help of his most trusted professional advisers, and for the first time a comprehensive and logical plan of army reorganisation was adopted. His most controversial measure was the abolition of the purchase system, which produced the most bitter and prolonged conflict of the period, both inside and outside Parliament. It illuminates many of the difficulties which civilian heads of the army faced in their attempts to plan and introduce major reforms.

Edward T. Cardwell was born in 1813, the son of a prosperous Liverpool merchant.[4] He was educated at Winchester and Balliol College, Oxford, where he gained a double first, and was called to the bar in 1838. However, his main ambition was a political career, which ample private means enabled him to pursue. He entered Parliament in 1842 as a free-trade Conservative. Sir Robert Peel, with whom he became politically closely associated, was clearly impressed with Cardwell's abilities, and appointed him Secretary to the Treasury at the age of thirty-two. Cardwell's political beliefs were essentially conservative, and were a reflection of the outlook of the increasingly important middle class of which he was a member. He had no enthusiasm for any further extension of the franchise, shared Peel's deep respect for legally constituted authority, and considered that government's role in society was a strictly limited one.

During the long period of political instability that followed the repeal of the Corn Laws Cardwell was a leading member of the Peelites. The group began to lose its separate political identity when six of them, including Cardwell, joined Aberdeen's coalition government in 1852. Cardwell became President of the Board of Trade, an appointment which his financial ability and administrative talents seemed fully to justify. His close political colleague Gladstone, Chancellor of the Exchequer, relied heavily on his financial advice, particularly in preparing his budgets. Cardwell was in fact offered the Treasury in 1855 by Aberdeen's successor, Lord Palmerston, after he had resigned from the government along with his Peelite colleagues. However, loyalty to his political friends would not permit him to accept, and for the next four years Cardwell waited for the right moment to join one of the two main parties.

Although he had serious reservations about Palmerston's foreign policy, Cardwell entered his second administration in 1859 as Chief Secretary for Ireland, his first seat in the Cabinet. His brief term of office did nothing to enhance his reputation; and his period (1861–64) as Chancellor of the Duchy of Lancaster perhaps indicates a low point in his political fortunes, although he again worked closely with Gladstone on financial matters. In 1864 a return to favour was marked by his appointment as Colonial Secretary, his most important post so far. During his term of office he played a major role in formulating proposals for the federation of British North America, and the Act, passed later, creating the Dominion of Canada owes much to his efforts. He was much involved in colonial military problems, including the planning of operations, which provided a useful background to his later work at the War Office. Finally, Cardwell implemented the agreed policy of promoting imperial self-defence by withdrawing troops from the colonies whenever the opportunity arose. When Russell assumed the leadership of the Liberal Party on the death of Palmerston in 1865, he considered appointing Cardwell Secretary for War, because the War Office was 'a great office of expenditure'.[5] However, Cardwell remained at the Colonial Office until the government resigned in 1866. In the general election of 1868 he campaigned vigorously to defend his Oxford seat, and one of the issues he raised was army reform: radical changes were, he said, necessary so that 'an army of the people of England' could be created.[6]

Contemporary opinion thought that Gladstone was likely to appoint Cardwell Chancellor of the Exchequer in the new Liberal government.[7] It was a post he had been offered before and was of an importance appropriate to a politician of his seniority and influence. The fact that Gladstone seems first to have thought of appointing Lord Hartington Secretary for War is further evidence that Cardwell was originally not destined for this less important post.[8] However, Hartington unexpectedly lost his seat and Gladstone turned to Cardwell. He informed Queen Victoria that the War Office required a 'cautious, conciliatory and experienced man', qualities which Cardwell seemed to possess.[9] More important was the fact that he fully endorsed the Liberal call for retrenchment in military expenditure. He had already said that a review was necessary 'of the two great spending departments, the army and the navy; with a view at once to increased efficiency and to diminished expenditure'.[10] The Cabinet's main military interest was in the size of the army Estimates, which at that time accounted for as much as 30 per cent of government expenditure. For Gladstone this was a fundamental issue which helped to determine the administration's position in Parliament, and the extent to which it could rely on radical support. Every year, except for a brief period during the Franco-Prussian war, he and the Chancellor, Robert Lowe, pressed for large reductions in total manpower.[11] Their correspondence with Cardwell became increasingly acrimonious, and when Cardwell refused to reduce the Estimates for 1873–74 Gladstone said he now had to decide 'under what terms can I hold my ground'.[12] He was in fact forced to make that decision early in 1874. During 1873 he became convinced that a promise to abolish income tax, which required substantial reductions in the army and navy Estimates for 1874–75, was the only possible way of reviving the government's declining popularity. Both Cardwell and Goschen, First Lord of the Admiralty, consistently refused to comply with his wishes, on the grounds that military expenditure was 'reduced last year . . . to the lowest level'.[13] For this reason among others the Cabinet, which was already seriously divided, resolved on a dissolution. Gladstone hoped that an election victory would give him the authority to overrule both ministers.

In contrast Cardwell's army reform plans, including the abolition of purchase, all seem to have met 'with general approval from his colleagues'.[14] Cabinet ministers' concern about army expenditure did not generally reflect a deep knowledge of or interest in the substance of military issues, apart from an ill defined doubt about the value of a large standing army. Their indifference to military questions was normally overcome only when a War Office proposal had direct implications for another government department.[15] Cabinet discussions on military policy tended, therefore, to be confined to general principles, and informed comment could be expected only from the few ministers, like Lord Hartington, who had a working knowledge of military affairs. A further reason for the relative ease with which Cardwell secured the Cabinet's agreement to his plans was perhaps its understanding of their likely adverse effect on the influence of the Crown and on the privileges of the upper classes. For this reason, for example, the Earl of Kimberley said of the abolition of purchase that 'nothing which this government has yet done has cost so great an effort, and nothing was more worthy of such an effort, not even the disestablishment of the Irish Church'.[16] The anti-privilege argument rallied the Cabinet in support of Cardwell when he was attacked by conservatives in the press and in Parliament, or when Queen Victoria demanded, as she did more than once, his removal from the War Office.[17]

Cardwell's personal qualities also helped him to secure acceptance of his plans. He was a 'most useful and considerate colleague' and had 'rather a sententious, but nevertheless modest way of expressing himself'.[18] In addition he was one of Gladstone's closest and most trusted advisers, perhaps second only to Lord Granville. In spite of their differences over military expenditure the Prime Minister had considerable confidence in his judgement, giving him maximum autonomy in his own department, and was the first to acknowledge his capabilities as a war minister: 'it is impossible to speak too highly of [his] indefatigable and assiduous attentions . . . to these difficult subjects'.[19] The fact that the Queen herself on two occasions had mentioned Cardwell as a possible Chancellor of the

Exchequer indicates that he maintained his political standing in the Cabinet and seemed destined for a more general political career. Indeed, by 1874 Cardwell was thought by many leading Liberals to be the most suitable successor to Gladstone if he were to retire as leader. His seniority in the party, his achievements at the War Office and his close connections with the Prime Minister were the main reasons for their support.[20] However, soon after the general election Cardwell unexpectedly indicated to Gladstone that he would like a peerage: five years at the War Office had exhausted him physically and mentally. He entered the House of Lords as Viscount Cardwell of Ellerbeck and occasionally participated in debates, but his active political career was effectively over.[21] He was not included in Gladstone's second administration in 1880, for by then he was beginning to suffer the effects of the brain disease which caused his death in 1886. It was the result, according to Lord Wolseley, 'of the worry, work, abuse and anxiety he ... underwent at the hands of men who did not understand modern warfare or its requirements'.[22]

Cardwell's influential position in the government had little direct connection with the status of the office to which he had been appointed. It was one of the least attractive senior ministerial posts and was normally 'regarded as a mere stepping stone to higher office'.[23] Its unpopularity may partly be explained by the circumstances which gave rise to Cardwell's demand for the removal of 'all reservations express or implied from the authority of that officer' and for the as yet absent 'principle of plenary responsibility to Parliament on the part of the Parliamentary head of [the War] Department'.[24] These defects were a product of the hasty reorganisation of army administration following the disasters of the Crimean war, when the functions of thirteen separate and largely unco-ordinated military departments were amalgamated and centralised. The Secretary for War was head of the civil administration of the army and was responsible to Parliament for all military matters. However, an exemption to his patent continued to give the Commander-in-Chief, who held office at the pleasure of the Crown, more or less unrestricted control over all matters of command, discipline, appointment and promotion.[25]

The creation of two rival departments, each with its own separate headquarters and with overlapping responsibilities, reflected the absence of full parliamentary control and the continuing influence of the Crown. Queen Victoria, who had a special interest in the army, aimed to preserve as far as possible the Crown's ancient prerogative powers, one of which was 'the *direct communication* with an immovable and non-political officer of high rank' about military business.[26] An extreme conservative in army matters, she invariably intervened in opposition to the activities of a reforming Secretary for War. The Queen had the full support of the

Commander-in-Chief, the Duke of Cambridge, her first cousin, and his senior officers, who wished to maintain the army's special connection with the Crown partly to protect the appointment and promotion of officers from political interference and partly to ensure that civilian involvement in technical military questions was kept to a minimum. Thus radical reforms approved by Parliament normally had little chance of being effectively implemented unless they were acceptable to the Duke of Cambridge. Other factors further weakened the position of the Secretary for War. The Duke's tenure of office was unlimited, and from his appointment in 1856 onwards his prestige and authority gradually increased. On the other hand the succession of politicians appointed to the War Office for brief periods lacked detailed military knowledge and were at an obvious disadvantage in their negotiations with the military authorities. The Secretary for War himself was charged with numerous responsibilities, any one of which would 'be sufficient to occupy the whole time of a man of first rate industry, ability and knowledge'.[27] Moreover the internal organisation of the new War Office was itself at a formative stage. Precedents were being established and in the light of experience there were frequent changes in the titles and functions of senior permanent officials, who apparently often disagreed about the division of their responsibilities. It was an office 'in which the minister's intentions can be entirely negatived by all his sub-departments and those of each of the sub-departments by every other'.[28]

The 'chaos' that characterised army administration and the constraints on the political head of the army were the first major issues Cardwell tackled as Secretary of State. Legislation was introduced which among other matters aimed to resolve the unsatisfactory position of the Commander-in-Chief.[29] For the first time he was subordinated to the Secretary for War, who in theory now had direct and immediate control of every branch of army administration, assisted by two under-secretaries of state and three executive officers, who were directly responsible to the Secretary for War for the work of the department. The Commander-in-Chief was the principal military adviser and was responsible for all strictly military functions connected with the regular and auxiliary forces. The Surveyor General of the Ordnance was responsible for all civil administrative duties, including transport, supply and munitions, while the Financial Secretary was concerned with the Estimates and with the accounting and checking of expenditure. Further changes were made to emphasise the ultimate political responsibility of the Secretary for War and of the Cabinet. The Duke of Cambridge was forced after a determined resistance to move his office from the Horse Guards to the War Office, then at Buckingham House, Pall Mall. In addition, a five-year tenure was, with the exception of the office of Commander-in-Chief, imposed on all senior staff appointments, including the Military Secretary, who became more directly responsible to the Secretary of State, and the Adjutant General, the Duke of Cambridge's unofficial deputy.[30]

In constitutional terms control of the army had finally been removed from the Crown to the Cabinet and to a responsible minister. In practice, however, the basic problems of divided power and limited civilian control remained unresolved. One major difficulty was the favourable terms on which the Duke had been allowed to remain in his post. He was to be exempt from the five-year tenure rule, although it was to apply to his successors. The Cabinet kept the option of removing him from office at any time, a possibility with which, as will be seen, he was to be threatened during the struggle to abolish purchase. The Duke also preserved his main executive powers—particularly those relating to the exercise of patronage and to discipline—subject only to the general responsibility of the Secretary of State. This represented a major dilution of the original aims of Cardwell's reorganisation, and reflected 'the efforts which the government has made to meet your Majesty's desires and to avert any undue shock to the existing ... Commandership in Chief'.[31] Contemporary opinion was also impressed with the argument that officers' appointment and promotion should be above any suspicion of 'supposed political partiality',[32] a not unimportant consideration in view of the proposed introduction of promotion by selection following the abolition of purchase. Also lacking in the reorganised War Office was a body of senior officers responsible collectively to the Secretary for War for advice on military policy and planning and which might have enabled him to assert more civilian control over professional matters.

Cardwell, who like his predecessors was overburdened with too many responsibilities and had only a sketchy knowledge of technical questions, was heavily dependent on the availability of professional advice and its quality.[33] Primary responsibility for this task was given to the Commander-in-Chief, who was charged 'with the duty of rendering such assistance as may be required of him by the Secretary of State'.[34] The specialist committees which co-ordinated War Office business were a useful source of information, and the Secretary of State chaired regular general meetings at which he discussed current issues with senior officials, but Cardwell had difficulty in obtaining independent advice from individual staff officers at the War Office. The Duke's role as principal military adviser and as supreme military head of the army seems to have inhibited his immediate subordinates from tendering their own views direct to the Secretary of State. The complex command, administrative and planning functions of the Commander-in-Chief helped to confuse the degree of priority he was expected to give to his advisory role. Like the Secretary for War, he tended to be excessively burdened with routine administrative tasks.[35] Cardwell's relations with the Duke had been coloured almost from the beginning by his plan to subordinate the office of Commander-in-Chief, which created a thinly disguised antagonism between them. Moreover the Duke's strong conservatism and his known views on the major issues of the time—the level of military expenditure, the abolition of purchase, short service and localisation—were apparently inflexible and were not in accordance with Cardwell's aim of reconstructing the army on new principles. Finally, the frequent public attacks on the Duke as a barrier to progress and the apparent weakening of his position as a result of War Office reorganisation did not make him completely compliant to his political masters. He was more circumspect in his opposition to them, but he could still, for example, try to render the Secretary of State's plans inoperative by appealing direct to the Queen for her support.

Cardwell had the sole initiative and responsibility for asking his subordinates for their advice. He was not required to consult them, and decision-making was his function alone. Cardwell tended to involve the Duke of Cambridge in policy discussions only when he thought it was prudent, with the result that the Queen commented, 'the only way to secure ... harmony [between the civil and military heads of the army] is by freely consulting the Duke of Cambridge on all military matters, and Mr Gladstone should never cease impressing this on Mr Cardwell'.[36] The Duke is said sometimes to have first learned of major policy changes in the military press, and it was following his request to know more about the measures being taken that Cardwell convened a weekly War Office council in order, he claimed, to increase 'the weight and influence of [the Duke's] opinion in regard to the matters on which it is necessary for me to take decisions on the part of Her Majesty's government'.[37] Cardwell's real motive was probably that he wished to involve the Duke more closely to reduce the possibility of misunderstandings arising and to encourage his more willing co-operation.

An appreciation of the limitations of his official advisers led Cardwell to turn elsewhere for the assistance he required. Lord Northbrook, as Under Secretary of State, a post he had held before, became his principal adviser and confidant.[38] He worked closely with Cardwell on all his reforms, and his advice and frank criticisms contributed much to the development of his ideas. Cardwell and Northbrook realised that they would need help from individuals not closely identified with the military hierarchy and whose minds were 'emancipated from the traditions of a past no longer possible'.[39] They turned to members of the 'new army school' which had emerged to revive public interest in military questions in the 1860s. Prominent among the group were Sir Patrick MacDougall, who chaired the committee on the localisation of the army, and Garnet Wolseley, a distinguished soldier who has been described as 'the mainstay and chief support' of the Secretary for War.[40] Less experienced junior officers, such as Evelyn Baring and George Colley, who had displayed special ability and were sympathetic to the idea of reform were brought to Lord Northbrook's attention and quickly given wide responsibilities. Also involved were civil servants, of whom Ralph Knox was the most important, and Cardwell's private secretary, Sir Robert Biddulph.

During the period 1870–72 each major issue was thoroughly investigated and discussed, and papers were prepared by Cardwell's advisers on the conclusions reached. At War Office conferences the reformers, assisted and protected by Cardwell, expressed their opinions openly and contradicted the known views of the Duke of Cambridge. The resulting antagonism between progressives and conservatives created a major division in the army which Cardwell was able to use to his own advantage. The Duke was no longer able to present a single military viewpoint with which to confront a reforming Secretary for War. However, the fact that Cardwell's advisers formed an *ad hoc* group outside the formal structure indicated a serious practical limitation on the value of their advice. They had no control at all over the implementation of the measures they helped to devise: 'they could, by virtue of the authority of the Secretary of State, get orders issued; they could not get the system which was to work them established and well understood'.[41]

The major task of the Secretary for War's advisers was to plan the various interconnected measures—short service, the formation of a reserve, localisation, and linked battalions—which together constituted the 'Cardwell system'.[42] Designed to facilitate both the periodic replenishment and relief of imperial garrisons and the formation of a potential expeditionary force at home, they were a radical response to the weaknesses of the Wellingtonian long-service army which military developments on the Continent and changing British defence commitments had brought to light. The army's functions were wide-ranging. Periodic fears of a French invasion emphasised the importance of its primary function of defending the country from external attack. Following the Indian mutiny English military commitments in India had increased, and there was a continuing requirement to garrison widely scattered colonies. The army needed to prepare for small colonial conflicts and for the possibility, however remote, of military intervention on the Continent. In terms of its numerical strength and organisation it was unable to meet all or even a lesser combination of the conflicting calls upon it: for example, during the Indian mutiny, when demands for additional troops were also being made elsewhere, there were at one stage only fourteen infantry regiments left in England. Now established beyond doubt was 'the inability of the regular army of about 150,000 men to police an Empire of 3,000,000 square miles'.[43]

Britain also appeared to be increasingly powerless in relation to the major European states, and her ability to influence events by the credible threat of military intervention was negligible. One reason was that the size of European armies was becoming a vital factor in war: in 1866, for example, Prussia was able to mobilise 400,000 men. Manpower needs on this scale were not met by maintaining expensive standing armies but by substantial reserves created by the introduction of short service. The impact of events in Europe was reinforced by the increasing difficulty of recruiting, a situation which long service (a minimum of twelve years) and the army's poor public image helped to produce. By 1868 the establishment of the army had reached a new low, and various attempts to form a trained reserve had been largely unsuccessful.

As a first step Cardwell reduced the level of British commitments by continuing the established policy of withdrawing colonial garrisons, and by 1870 there were only just under 24,000 troops stationed abroad, excluding India. It had the advantage of facilitating reductions in the number of troops at home, it concentrated forces in England, and it helped to encourage colonial self-reliance. It was also, as Cardwell wrote, 'at the bottom of the whole question of army reform. As long as the period of foreign service bears so large a proportion to that of service at home, the discouragement to enlisting for the more reputable portions of the population must be very great'. It also meant that 'it will be difficult if not impossible to reduce the period of enlistment'.[44] Short service was introduced in 1870, initially in the infantry only: recruits spent six years in the regular army and six in the reserves. Men stationed in India were required to serve there for the full term of twelve years. Cardwell's aim of forming a large reserve of trained soldiers, which it was hoped would eventually amount to about 80,000 men, was the main reason for introducing short service. The planned reserve was to be called out only in times of national emergency to reinforce the regular army. Lesser problems—small colonial wars, for example—were to be dealt with, as before, by the regular army alone. However, whether the Prussian model could be successfully adapted for English use without conscription, which ensured a regular supply of recruits, and with overseas military commitments, remained to be seen. Short service would also lead to a substantial reduction in expenditure on pensions, and would make it less difficult for soldiers to find employment, as they would leave the army when still relatively young. Above all, it was hoped that short service would attract a greater number of recruits from a wider cross-section of the population. When it was combined with the restrictions on flogging and the prohibition on branding deserters, Cardwell believed that Britain's recruiting problems would at last be over.

Recruiting would also be assisted by the localisation of regiments in territorial areas, which would enable them to establish closer links with a particular locality.[45] The plan was to divide the country into sixty-six districts, each of which would contain a brigade depot. Attached to it would be two line battalions, two Militia battalions and Volunteers. Apart from helping recruiting, localisation would enable the line battalions to form much closer connections with the auxiliary forces, which were already organised on a territorial basis. One of the regular battalions was to be at home and the other abroad, and each was to have two companies based at the depot centre. Recruits received initial training at the depot, and were then passed to the line battalions serving in England, which provided drafts for the units stationed overseas, and which would eventually replace them. The authorised size of home corps, which varied from 520 to 820 rank and file, depended on their place on the roster for overseas service. This plan could be applied without difficulty to the first twenty-five regiments, which in 1857 had a second battalion added to them. For the remaining corps Cardwell did not create additional battalions but linked existing ones together.

The introduction of short service actually made recruiting more difficult by creating a much higher demand for men than long service had done. It seems that the reduction in the minimum period of service did not prove to be the major attraction that Cardwell had hoped. Voluntary enlistment was still unable to meet the army's needs, and there were regular crises, especially during periods of industrial prosperity.[46] Soldiers' pay remained low, the army continued to be generally unpopular, and genuine short service never really existed. There was also no real improvement in the quality of troops. Standards were in fact lowered in order to attract more recruits, who were generally young and physically immature. The experienced long-service soldier soon disappeared; the youthful short-service recruits were often unable to bear the hardships of colonial campaigns and their value in battle was widely questioned. Restrictions were soon placed on the overseas service of young soldiers, who became concentrated at home.

For other reasons as well regiments in England were to find it increasingly difficult to meet the constant demand for replacements from battalions overseas. The linked battalion system depended on a balance of regiments at home and abroad, with a generous margin of additional battalions in England to meet colonial emergencies. However, for financial reasons Cardwell's plan was based on the existing number and distribution of regiments, which meant that in 1872 there was a balance in favour of the home army of only one battalion. The assumption implicit in his plan that colonial military commitments were unlikely to change was falsified in the late 1870s. It became necessary to increase permanently the number of battalions serving overseas, which destroyed Cardwell's precarious balance and left several regiments without support battalions at home. Successive governments were unwilling to expand the home army in line with increasing colonial obligations, and the linked battalion system was unable to operate as had been planned. The likelihood of British military involvement in Europe seemed remote, and the home army, which had low establishments and a high proportion of ineffectives, was run down in order to maintain the efficiency and manpower levels of battalions overseas. In these circumstances the role of the reserve, which had been gradually built up to a strength of 80,000 men, was very different from that which had originally been intended. It could not be used to strengthen an already efficient army during the course of a war, but was needed, as in the South African war, to replace young or unfit soldiers at the beginning of a campaign. Britain's effective military forces were, as in the Crimean war, more or less fully committed at the outset, with no substantial source of reinforcements readily available to draw upon later. Little had changed in fifty years.

Cardwell's reforms also suffered from his failure to tackle several major issues. No agreed statement was drawn up of Britain's defence needs and priorities. There was confusion about military objectives, and difficulties emerged when the army was reorganised independently of them, on the basis of financial criteria or of the forces actually in existence. Army organisation was not directly related to the likely pattern of future military needs. No permanently embodied expeditionary force was available which could be sent to the colonies when needed, without disrupting the home army each time. No thought was given to the mobilisation of the army in the event of a major war, beyond Cardwell's notional plan for the formation of two army corps. Localisation was based on recruiting needs, and did not, unlike the Prussian version, bear any resemblance to the larger formations that would actually be needed in wartime.

Similar reservations were to be expressed about the limited effects of Cardwell's third major reform—the abolition of purchase.[47] Cardwell had displayed no interest in purchase reform in the 1860s, and his memorandum of December 1868 revealed a slightly ambiguous attitude towards the sale of commissions. However, he did consider that purchase was one of several military questions likely to be raised in Parliament which would require from him 'something more than a merely passive attitude'.[48] Cardwell may have been deterred from making a clear statement in favour of total abolition by its likely cost, which would amount to several million pounds. Apart from compensating officers for the sums they had invested in the commissions, there was almost certain to be a need to provide a pension scheme to maintain an acceptable rate of retirement.

Indeed, the supposed economy of purchase is one reason why it had survived for so long. Another was the fact that it had been elevated almost to the level of a constitutional principle because it was thought to have ensured the political compliance of the army.[49] Purchase had restricted recruitment to the officer corps largely to the same classes which controlled the machinery of government, and their common origins linked them closely together. Yet the arguments against purchase were becoming more and more compelling: purchase created powerful vested interests, it made any thorough reorganisation of the army almost impossible, and it helped to reinforce the separation and independence of individual corps from central authority. Since 1720 a regulation price had been officially determined for each commission, yet normally the rules were not complied with. Young officers with private means, but not necessarily with any merit, who were eager for advancement would pay large sums (known as 'over-regulation' amounts) in excess of those laid down to induce their senior colleagues to retire. Its most harmful effect was to dissociate merit from promotion and thus prevent the development of a professional officer corps.

This may have been the reason which prompted Cardwell to discuss purchase with the Duke of Cambridge in 1869. The Duke, who was asked for his views on the desirability of ending the sale of lieutenant-colonelcies, was predictably against 'any change in the system ... for however theoretically objectionable, I think it has worked favourably to the interests of the service'.[50] Cardwell did not pursue further these unproductive discussions, although not long afterwards the whole question of abolition was unexpectedly raised again. Ironically it resulted from his adoption of the plan of his Conservative predecessor, Sir John Pakington, to dispense with the lowest commissioned rank following a reduction in the number of cornets and ensigns. When Cardwell consulted the Duke of Cambridge about the idea he advised that the government should fully compensate officers for that part of their regulation purchase money which would be lost as a result of the change, but the Duke failed to alert him to the likely consequences of ignoring the over-regulation sums involved. These soon became clear when Cardwell announced his plan in March 1870. Both MPs and army officers strongly criticised it because they feared that 'if one step were abolished without a recognition of the claim for over-regulation, the whole of the money involved in the over-regulation system would be for ever lost'.[51] In the face of unexpected opposition, Cardwell hastily withdrew his proposal. He consulted the Cabinet, which was unwilling to give official recognition to an illegal practice or to provide further compensation without an official inquiry into it. The Royal Commission which investigated the subject was in favour of the officers' claim on the grounds that 'there has been a tacit acquiescence in the practice amounting in our opinion to a virtual recognition of it by civil and military authorities'.[52]

Cardwell's immediate reaction was to refer the report to the law officers of the Crown, who concluded that the War Office was powerless to prevent over-regulation payments under existing statute law. He refused to permit the flouting of the regulations to continue and said that 'as soon as Parliament meets the law must in some way be altered'.[53] In the summer of 1870, therefore, Cardwell discussed the problem at length with Lord Northbrook. It was at this time, according to Northbrook, that a definite decision was taken, for as he wrote later to Cardwell, 'I wish I could have a ride with you on the heather at Eastbury where we planned the abolition of purchase.'[54] The option of legalising over-regulation payments, which the logic of past official practice might have dictated, was ruled out. As Cardwell said, 'can we propose . . . to introduce a new vested interest more fatal to any scheme for improved organisation of the army than the present'.[55] He concluded that effective prohibition of over-regulation payments was the only acceptable answer. Yet the payment of illegal prices and the existence of the authorised purchase system were inseparable: it was impossible to prevent the first without abolishing the second. The growing need for a more professional officer corps, which was underlined by the Prussian army's performance in the war with France, and by the findings of the recent Royal Commission on military education, also argued for ending purchase. Cardwell was influenced in addition by Sir Charles Trevelyan's eloquent arguments against purchase.[56] The officer corps, like the reformed civil service, should be open to the educated middle classes, who would dedicate themselves to their profession and would help to change its prevailing ethos.

In September 1870 Cardwell informed Gladstone and the Duke of Cambridge of his plan to end purchase. However, he was aware of the Duke's views on the subject, and he revealed his further thoughts only to his most trusted colleagues. Gladstone was kept fully informed of their progress and occasionally gave advice. The first major task was to determine the likely cost of the measure. In view of the severe constraints on expenditure both Cardwell and Gladstone tried in different ways to define the principles of repayment as narrowly as possible. When consulted, Northbrook argued that to award officers compensation on terms less generous than their entitlement to sell commissions on the open market entailed a great risk of defeat in Parliament.[57] Cardwell eventually agreed to revise his proposal accordingly, and its net cost was now estimated to be about £8 million, of which only a proportion would be required immediately after abolition, the rest being paid out over many years as officers decided to retire. The level of annual expenditure would be controlled by a restriction on the number of permitted retirements each year. Cardwell found he was able to meet the estimated initial cost of abolition, and of a pension scheme from savings effected in other areas, without the need to raise additional funds by increasing taxation.

Gladstone had other reasons for giving his full support to the planned reform. He was aware that the continued existence of purchase was incompatible with the growth of political democracy and did not accord with the government's attempts to reduce the power of privilege in other areas of national life, for example in education and the civil service, and by the introduction of secret voting. In Gladstone's view purchase provided solid 'proof of the extent to which the government of this country has been worked in the spirit of class, and to the disadvantage of the mass of the community'. If purchase were not soon ended, Gladstone feared, 'the time is approaching for what may be termed a rather strict settlement of account'.[58]

Now that the basic problems had been resolved Cardwell sought specialist advice on formulating the new principles of appointment and promotion. He did not turn to the staff of the military department, who continued to remain on the periphery of the discussions, but to the few individual officers, mainly relatively junior, who were known to be sympathetic to abolition. For example, Major George Colley was asked to prepare a plan for the appointment of candidates to first commissions, which he submitted in November 1870. A much more senior officer, Sir William Mansfield, then Commander-in-Chief in Ireland, was in regular contact with Cardwell about the preparation of a new system of promotion. His advice was invaluable, as for instance when he helped Cardwell avoid too great a reliance on the principle of seniority in promotion, which might have permitted the covert reappearance of purchase.[59] Others regularly consulted included Hugh Childers, First Lord of the Admiralty, and Captain Vivian, Financial Secretary at the War Office.[60] These intensive consultations and the documents which Cardwell and his advisers had produced formed the basis of the draft regulations on appointment, promotion and retirement which Mansfield prepared. It was only at this relatively advanced stage that Cardwell fully involved the Duke of Cambridge by asking for his comments on Mansfield's document.[61] He made no major criticisms of it.

Cardwell also sought more general advice and information which he thought he might find useful as the Bill to give effect to abolition passed through Parliament. Evelyn Baring, for example, prepared a statement of the arguments for and against purchase,[62] while Sir Henry Storks, Surveyor General of the Ordnance, entered the House of Commons at Cardwell's suggestion, so that War Office representation there was strengthened. Wolseley attended the parliamentary debates on purchase, in case Cardwell required any immediate advice. Before the Army Regulation Bill, which dealt with purchase and several other matters, could be presented to Parliament, several final potential obstacles had to be negotiated. The Cabinet presented no real difficulty and apparently unanimously endorsed Cardwell's main proposals. Cardwell gave the Queen very little opportunity to criticise his plans by failing to send her a copy of the draft Bill until the last possible moment.

Cardwell expected widespread criticism of his proposal because purchase was an important symbol of the privileges of the wealthy and of the dominant position of the upper classes in the army. However, it is unlikely that he could have foreseen the extent of the opposition which it actually created. All those institutions—the conservative press, Society, the clubs and the Tory party—which upheld the *status quo* and with which purchase officers had close connections united in bitter condemnation of the measure. Opposition in Parliament was not directed by Disraeli, the Conservative leader, whose attitude to purchase was rather ambiguous, but by a group of former army officers known as 'the Colonels'. In the past MPs with military connections had often acted in concert to defeat army reform proposals, but their tactics on this occasion were unprecedented. They vowed in Parliament to oppose the Bill 'clause by clause, step by step, by every means which the forms of the House placed at their disposal'.[63] It is the first example of systematic obstruction in the Commons, a technique used later by Irish nationalists to much greater effect.

The Colonels achieved very little. Unable to secure the defeat of the government on the principle of abolition, during the committee stage they constantly pressed for more generous terms of compensation. They sought immediate repayment of the regulation purchase money, but were deliberately vague about the return of over-regulation sums, which gained them the support of several Liberal MPs who thought it might substantially reduce the total cost of the measure. This curious alliance of army officers and radicals was never able to command sufficient parliamentary support to defeat the government, which had decided at an early date not to abandon the measure however prolonged or determined the opposition to it.

The successful conclusion of the long and often repetitive debates in the Commons early in July 1871 did not mean the end of Cardwell's difficulties. Evidence emerged that leading Conservative members of the House of Lords were also planning to obstruct the Bill, and Cardwell became aware that three ministers, one of whom is known to have been Childers, were apparently opposed to abolition.[64] Although the Duke of Cambridge was unable to obstruct Cardwell's preparations for reform, there was a strong feeling 'in the House ... that the measure of Her Majesty's government, if not actually deprecated, is not cordially supported by Your Royal Highness'.[65] This impression may possibly have strengthened the will of the Colonels to prolong their battle in the Commons. The Duke had also permitted one of their number to contact commanding officers to discover what were the views of their subordinates. Armed with the results, which indicated almost total opposition to the proposal, the Colonels' authority was increased as self-styled spokesmen for the officers.

The Duke himself was forced to be circumspect in giving vent to his opposition to the proposals. In the past a variety of circumstances, including direct support from the Crown, official acceptance of his own position as supreme professional head of the army, and lukewarm government commitment to military reform, had together helped him successfully to resist change. These favourable conditions no longer applied to the same degree. Cardwell informed him that unfortunate consequences might result if he were not willing publicly to correct the prevailing view that he was not in favour of abolition. Demands for his removal from office were likely to be renewed with greater vigour. The government, he said, might itself again review the Duke's position and his exemption from the five-year tenure rule. The Cabinet discussed the matter and decided that no particular period should be specified because, as Robert Lowe explained, 'he ought not to retain office at all if his views were not in accordance with the ministry of the day, and that five years might be too long'.[66]

A disagreement followed about the extent to which the Commander-in-Chief was expected to express public support for the policies of the current party in power. The Duke objected strongly to Cardwell's suggestion that he should make a speech in the Lords in support of the Bill. It would inevitably draw the Commander-in-Chief into party politics and would be a significant departure from the established custom of his not being required to defend government policy in the Lords. His tenure of office would as a result be dependent on each change of government; it would become a political appointment and the army would be 'handed over ... to the Commons, instead of as hitherto looking mainly to the Crown for its rewards and honours'.[67] However, according to the government purchase was no longer a narrow party question: the principle of abolition had been agreed and the illegality of over-regulation prices had been officially determined, which meant that it was impossible for 'any executive government in any possible Parliament of whatever politics to tolerate it'.[68] What was now important was not so much the possible rejection of the Bill by the House of Lords, an action which could, Gladstone thought, if necessary be nullified, but rather 'the convenient or inconvenient manner of the abolition and the degree and certainty of care to be had for the interests of the purchase officers'.[69] For this reason the Duke would not be required to express his personal opinion or to cast his vote in the Lords. He would merely be expected to 'view the question with reference to the consequences of rejecting the measure now proposed'.[70]

The Duke's noncommittal speech had little effect on the outcome of the debate on the second reading. As the government expected, the Lords championed the interests of the upper classes and in effect rejected the Bill. However, the developing conflict between the Lords and the Commons was quickly ended when the government unexpectedly announced the abolition of purchase by royal warrant. This action, which Cardwell first suggested, was made possible by the Brokerage Act of 1809, which prohibited the purchase of commissions except in so far as it was permitted by official regulations. Parliament's agreement to the principle of abolition had not therefore been strictly necessary, although legislation had been required to provide compensation and for other reasons. To permit the Lords to delay the measure any longer was unacceptable: the Commons might not be so willing to agree to the repayment of over-regulation sums if it had to consider the question again. As a result there was a 'great risk of a serious disorganisation of the discipline of the army' which might produce a 'conflict between the army and Parliament'.[71] Now that the warrant had been issued the only effect of the Lords' continued refusal to pass the Bill would be to deprive officers of their compensation.

The government's victory in the parliamentary struggle did not mean that the Colonels abandoned the objectives they had been pursuing. Further battles were to be fought over the claimed inadequacies of the terms of compensation, which a Royal Commission eventually investigated. More important is the extent to which the conservatives were able to preserve unaltered the traditional connection between the landed classes and the army, and the social milieu which it created. All the evidence indicates that the disproportionate representation of the upper classes continued, and that it was not until the first world war and after that more radical changes began to take place.[72] All the essential features of a socially restricted officer corps were preserved. For example, regimental expenses remained high, and in the absence of improved officers' pay a private income was still required. It is not therefore surprising that criticism of the performance of officers was very similar to that expressed while purchase existed, and that interest in professional matters was still confined to a small minority.

The reasons why middle-class representation in the officer corps remained low are complex. The failure of successive governments to raise pay to an adequate level is one, while another is perhaps unfavourable public attitudes towards the army. More important were the informal methods used in addition to competitive entrance examinations to regulate admission to the officer corps. The Commander-in-Chief remained as before abolition 'the arbiter of the fitness of any gentleman for a commission', and 'no one would question his right to withold him from the competition'.[73] Acceptable social origins and a public school education were the main criteria for admission. The Duke's own predelictions were reinforced by the social exclusiveness which most individual regiments tried to maintain. The Duke also helped to ensure that Cardwell's new system of promotion, which was based on a combination of seniority and selection, was never fully implemented while he remained at the head of the army. Support for promotion by seniority became one of the new orthodoxies of the War Office, and the early promotion of officers on the sole ground of merit was almost as rare as it had been under purchase. The Duke objected to the introduction of confidential reports, an essential feature of an effective selection process, and promotion examinations do not always appear to have been taken very seriously.[74] All that the abolition of purchase meant initially was that the method of admission and promotion was no longer in itself a barrier to change. What was clearly lacking during this period was any willingness on the part of the military authorities to introduce and encourage acceptance of the further changes which logically followed on from abolition. It was not until the early years of the twentieth century, when there was greater official recognition of the fact that the uneducated gentleman officer was now more of a liability than an asset, that the potential benefits of abolition were more fully realised.

The claim that Cardwell revolutionised the British army exaggerates and misinterprets the significance of his work as Secretary for War. Although his proposals were bold and apparently complete, their actual practical results were limited, and did not accord with his own expectations. Cardwell himself underestimated the difficulties of implementing his reforms, of which the most important was the ability of senior officers to prevent or at least to postpone the full adoption of measures with which they were not in full sympathy. Only a partial answer had been found to the need for improved civilian control of the army. Continuing major weaknesses of Cardwell's arrangements were the maintenance in office without restriction of the Duke of Cambridge and the absence of a general staff. The main achievement of the Cardwell system—the creation of a reserve—was overshadowed by its failure to solve the recruiting problem or to reconcile the conflicting needs of home defence and of colonial garrisons. The inherent defects of the new arrangements were compounded by opposition within the military, by continuing financial stringency and by the failure to establish at the outset a national military policy which listed the army's functions in order of priority. This also explains the absence of preparations for mobilisation in the event of a major European war and of a special corps permanently available in England to meet any colonial emergencies which might arise.

Cardwell's achievements were in fact of a more limited order. He gave new impetus to the intermittent process of military reconstruction which had been set in train at the time of the Crimean war. He raised important questions about the organisation and purposes of a volunteer army, which continued to be debated in professional circles and among interested politicians during the latter part of the century. His one major irreversible achievement—the abolition of purchase—provides the most solid evidence for the claim that he was a great military reformer. The ending of purchase, even if it was limited in its immediate effect, was an essential precondition—along with the introduction of short service—of the eventual emergence of a modern professional army. The era when the British army was a loose amalgamation of more or less independent regiments organised mainly for the convenience of their officers was coming to an end. It was left to other military reformers, after the continuing weaknesses of the army were again revealed in the South African war, to complete and extend Cardwell's work.

Notes

1   See, for example, B. J. Bond, 'The introduction and operation of short service and localisation in the British army, 1868–92', unpublished MA thesis, University of London, 1962; W. S. Hamer, *The British Army. Civil–Military Relations, 1885–1905*, Oxford University Press, London, 1970; and A. V. Tucker, 'Army and society in England, 1870–1900: a reassessment of the Cardwell reforms', *Journal of British Studies*, II, 1963, pp. 110–41.
2   *Lord Cardwell at the War Office*, John Murray, London, 1904.
3   'The army', December 1868, in *ibid.*, pp. 249–54.
4   For his political career see A. B. Erickson, 'Edward T. Cardwell: Peelite', *Transactions of the American Philosophical Association*, XLIX, 1962, pp. 6–67; *The Times*, 16 February 1886, p. 7; Cardwell papers, PRO 30/48/8/54, 90–117.
5   MS, Note (October 1865) by Russell, Russell papers, PRO 30/22/15.
6   Quoted in Erickson, 'Edward T. Cardwell', p. 66.
7   *Ibid.*, p. 67.
8   Bernard Holland, *The life of Spencer Compton, Eighth Duke of Devonshire*, Longmans, London, 1911, I, pp. 73–4.

9   Queen Victoria, 'Memorandum', 3 December 1868, in G. E. Buckle (ed.), *The letters of Queen Victoria*, John Murray, London, 1926, I, p. 565.

10   'The army', December 1868, in Biddulph, *Lord Cardwell*, p. 249.

11   The fullest account of the debate is in Bond, 'The introduction and operation of short service', pp. 69 ff.

12   W. E. Gladstone to E. Cardwell, December 1872, quoted in Erickson, 'Edward T. Cardwell', p. 97.

13   Quoted in Lord Edmond Fitzmaurice, *The Life of Granville George Leveson Gower, Second Earl Granville, 1815–1891*, Longmans, London, 1901, II, p. 119.

14   Ethel Drus (ed.), 'A journal of events during the Gladstone ministry, 1868–1874, by John, First Earl of Kimberley', *Camden Miscellany*, XXI, 1958, p. 19.

15   One example is the disagreement over Cardwell's proposal to increase the proportion of the military expenditure for which India was responsible. See Duchess of Argyll (ed.), *8th Duke of Argyll . . . Autobiography and Memoirs*, Murray, London, 1906, I, p. 276.

16   Drus (ed.), 'A journal of events during the Gladstone ministry', p. 26.

17   See for example, Queen Victoria to W. E. Gladstone, 5 August 1873, in Philip Guedalla, *The Queen and Mr Gladstone*, Hodder & Stoughton, London, 1933, I, p. 420.

18   *Letters of the Rt Hon Henry Austin Bruce, Lord Aberdare*, published privately, Oxford, 1902, I, p. 291; Susan, Countess of Ardagh, *The Life of Major General Sir John Ardagh*, Murray, London, 1909, p. 48.
       W. E. Gladstone to Queen Victoria, 20 January 1871, in Guedalla, *The Queen*, p. 269.

20   Fitzmaurice, *The Life of George Granville Leveson Gower*, pp. 136–7.

21   For his last years see Erickson, 'Edward T. Cardwell', pp. 99–100.

22   Garnet J. Wolseley, *The Story of a Soldier's Life*, Constable, London, 1903, II, p. 256.

23   B. J. Bond, 'The effect of the Cardwell reforms in army organisation, 1874–1904', *Journal of the Royal United Service Institution*, CV, 1960, p. 523.

24   'The army', December 1868, in Biddulph, *Lord Cardwell*, p. 250.

25   For War Office organisation before 1870 see Hampden Gordon, *The War Office*, Putnam, London, 1935, pp. 53–7; Hamer, *The British Army*, pp. 1–7; Owen Wheeler, *The War Office: Past and Present*, Methuen, London, 1914, pp. 173 ff.

26   Quoted in F. Hardie, *The Political Influence of Queen Victoria*, Oxford University Press, London, 1935, pp. 180–1.

27   *Report of the Royal Commission on Warlike Stories*, PP 1887, XV, 5062, p. ix.

28   Florence Nightingale to Sidney Herbert, 18 November 1859, in Lord Stanmore, *Sidney Herbert*, Murray, London, 1902, II, p. 369.

29   There is a useful diagram of War Office organisation after the 1870 Act in B. J. Bond, *The Victorian Army and the Staff College*, Eyre Methuen, London, 1972, p. 118. The various issues which led to the reorganisation are discussed in *Reports of a Committee appointed to Inquire into the Arrangements in Force for the Conduct of Business in the Army Departments*, PP 1870, XII, 1.

30   Duke of Cambridge to E. Cardwell, 27 December 1869, in W. Verner, *The Military Life of H.R.H. George, Duke of Cambridge*, Murray, London, 1905, I, pp. 415–17.

31   W. E. Gladstone to Queen Victoria, 8 July 1871, in Guedalla, *The Queen*, p. 287.

32   Queen Victoria to W. E. Gladstone, 3 October 1871, in *ibid.*, p. 307.
33   This issue is discussed fully by Hamer, *The British Army*, pp. 39–58.
34   Order in Council, June 1870, PP XLII, 683, 164.
35   Hamer, *The British Army*, pp. 58–9.
36   Queen Victoria to W. E. Gladstone, 25 March 1871, in Guedalla, *The Queen*, p. 278.
37   E. Cardwell to the Duke of Cambridge, 12 April 1870, in Verner, *The Military Life of H.R.H. George, Duke of Cambridge*, I, p. 428.
38   B. Mallet, *Thomas George Earl of Northbrook: a memoir*, Longmans, London, 1908, p. 54.
39   W. F. Butler, *The Life of Sir George Pomeroy-Colley*, John Murray, London, 1899, p. 85.
40   'The War Office and the army', *Quarterly Review*, CLXXXIII, 1896, p. 191.
41   *Ibid.*, p. 196.
42   For a detailed account of the Cardwell system and its consequences see Bond, 'The introduction and operation of short service'. Also useful on the impact of short service is Tucker, 'Army and society in England', pp. 129–40.
43   B. J. Bond, 'Prelude to the Cardwell reforms', *Journal of the Royal United Service Institution*, CVI, 1961, p. 231.
44   Quoted in B. J. Bond, 'Edward Cardwell's army reforms', *Army Quarterly*, LXXXIV, 1962, p. 109.
45   Sir R.Whigham, 'The Cardwell reforms—a retrospect', *Army Quarterly*, VII, 1923, pp. 21–2.
46   There is a good brief discussion of the recruiting problem in A. R. Skelley, *The Victorian Army at Home*, Croom Helm, London, 1977, pp. 253 ff.
47   For a detailed history of purchase see my PhD thesis: 'The system of purchase and sale of officers' commissions in the British army', Manchester University, 1974; Biddulph, *Lord Cardwell*, pp. 73 ff.; and Gwyn Harries-Jenkins, *The Army in Victorian Society*, Routledge & Kegan Paul, London, 1977, pp. 59–102.
48   'The army', December 1868, in Biddulph, *Lord Cardwell*, p. 253.
49   See, for example, Duke of Wellington, *Memorandum on Military Governments*, 7 March 1833, PP VII, 650, 274.
50   Duke of Cambridge to Edward Cardwell, 24 November 1869, Cardwell papers, PRO 30/48/3/12, 150.
51   Edward Cardwell, 'Military organisation', 1870, Gladstone papers, Add. MS 44615, p. 33.
52   *Report of the Commissioners appointed to Inquire into Over-regulation Payments on Promotion in the Army*, PP 1870, XII, 201, 63, pp. xxiv–xxv.
53   E. Cardwell, 'Military organisation', p. 33.
54   Lord Northbrook to E. Cardwell, 8 July 1872, Cardwell papers, PRO 30/48/4/21, 13.
55   E. Cardwell, 'Military organisation', p. 33.
56   Sir C. E. Trevelyan, *The Purchase System in the British Army*, Longmans, London, 1867.
57   Lord Northbrook to E. Cardwell, 30 September 1870, Cardwell papers, PRO 30/48/4/19, 96–8.
58   W. E. Gladstone, Memorandum, 5 October 1871, quoted in T. F. Gallagher, ' "Cardwellian mysteries": the fate of the British Army Regulation Bill, 1871', *Historical Journal*, XVIII, 1975, p. 348.
59   Lord Northbrook to E. Cardwell, 23 December 1870, Cardwell papers, PRO 30/48/4/19, 156–8.
60   Spencer Childers, *The Life and Correspondence of the Rt Hon Hugh C. E. Childers, 1827–1896*, Murray, London, 1901, I, pp. 187–8.

61   'Proposed method of appointments, promotion and retirements after the abolition of purchase', Gladstone papers, Add. MS 44617, 67–8.

62   'The arguments for and against the purchase system', Granville papers, PRO 30/29/68.

63   *P. Debs.*, third series, CCVI, 451.

64   E. Cardwell to W. E. Gladstone, 7 June 1871, Cardwell papers, PRO 30/48/2/8, 90–1.

65   Same to Duke of Cambridge, 3 June 1871, *ibid.*, PRO 30/48/4/15, 181–2.

66   Robert Lowe, Memorandum, 12 July 1871, Gladstone papers, Add. MS 44760, 61.

67   Duke of Cambridge to Queen Victoria, 6 July 1871, in Verner, *The Military life of H.R.H. George, Duke of Cambridge*, II, p. 14.

68   W. E. Gladstone to Duke of Cambridge, 9 July 1871, in *ibid.*, II, p. 15.

69   *Ibid.*

70   Sir T. Biddulph to Duke of Cambridge, 9 July 1871, in *ibid.*, p. 16.

71   Drus (ed.), 'A journal of events during the Gladstone ministry', pp. 24–5.

72   See Tucker, 'Army and society in England', pp. 122–9; and C. B. Otley, 'The origins and recruitment of the British army elite, 1870–1959', unpublished PhD thesis, Hull University, 1965.

73   *P. Debs.*, third series, CCXVI, 1218.

74   Sir J. Edmonds, 'The abolition of the sale and purchase of army commissions', *Journal of the Royal United Service Institution*, XCIX, 1954, p.592.

3

H. O. ARNOLD-FORSTER
AND
THE VOLUNTEERS

IAN BECKETT

It would appear generally true that the Secretaries of State for War most praised by contemporaries have been those who entered the War Office either unwillingly or without any preconceived ideas of the policy they would follow once in office. By contrast the Secretaries of State who appeared most suited by background and experience to fill the office have frequently been those most vilified by their contemporaries and even now may lack a balanced reassessment. In this latter category might be numbered Hugh Oakley Arnold-Forster, who became Secretary of State in October 1903. Arnold-Forster is interesting not only because his undoubted failure was that of a man so apparently well qualified but because he entered office at a time when Britain's military and strategic affairs were in disarray in the wake of the South African war and the constitutional position of the office was itself peculiar as a result of the recommendations of official inquiries into the conduct of the war.

The shocks of a war so confidently undertaken, not least the eventual deployment of over 450,000 regular, auxiliary and colonial troops to defeat barely 50,000 Boers, provoked profound reassessments of Britain's military, strategic and foreign policies. In terms of foreign policy, the war had only emphasised the uncomfortable realities of an isolation that had lost its splendour. Even before the war the government had been compelled in 1896 to abandon the traditional concern for the independence of the Ottoman Empire and the freedom of the Straits. Britain's increased weakness during and after it was indicated by concessions to the United States over the Venezuelan episode in 1901, the tentative negotiations with Germany in the same year, and the conclusion of a treaty with Japan in 1902. In strategic terms, the country was still faced with the threats posed by the Franco-Russian alliance of 1894: a French invasion of the United Kingdom or a Russian assault on India. Whilst dismissing the practicalities of full-scale invasion in 1902, the newly formed Committee of Imperial Defence devoted some or all of over fifty of its eighty-two meetings between 1902 and 1905 to the defence of India. As yet few politicians' minds had turned to the challenge of Imperial Germany, though by 1902 the Admiralty was beginning to assess the threat from Tirpitz's navy and, in the War Office, Sir William Robertson had already warned that Germany should be regarded rather as a potential enemy than as a potential ally.

In military terms there were the consequences of defeat so narrowly avoided. The first official inquiry—the Dawkins Committee—reported as early as May 1901 on the mutual recriminations between soldiers and politicians over the lack of preparation for war. In September 1902 a Royal Commission under the chairmanship of Lord Elgin set out to investigate the defects of the army's administration. The commission concluded in its report of July 1903 that the Commander-in-Chief, Lord Wolseley, had failed to perform his duties in advising the Cabinet on the basis of the intelligence available but, equally, that politicians had failed to consult the soldiers sufficiently. However, whereas Dawkins had suggested a new War Office Board to resolve civil–military differences, the Elgin Commission recommended no fundamental reforms. It was largely in order to remedy this shortcoming that the War Office Reconstruction Committee, chaired by that éminence grise of Edwardian politics, Lord Esher, was established in November 1903. The recommendations of the Esher Committee would not only place Arnold-Forster in a highly unusual position as Secretary of

State but would lay down policies which he would be required to implement. A further inquiry was undertaken in March 1903—a Royal Commission on the Militia and Volunteers chaired by the Duke of Norfolk. This, too, would inhibit the freedom of the Secretary of State whilst the results of its deliberations were awaited.

With respect to the wider issue of army reform, Arnold-Forster took office following the failure of the ambitious scheme advanced by his immediate predecessor, St John Brodrick, who had attempted to undertake major reforms whilst the South African war was still in progress. His plans to increase the size of the army through short-service enlistment and better pay, and the creation of six Army Corps of 40,000 men each, were opposed not only by the Treasury but by the War Office Council. When the scheme also attracted the opposition of a group of disgruntled Unionist back-benchers Brodrick found himself unable to command the support of the House.[1] With the government torn by the tariff reform issue it was essential to find a strong minister to restore credibility and resolve the now long-standing problem of army reform. This was the challenge that faced Arnold-Forster.

The formative influences on the politician who entered the House of Commons as Unionist MP for Belfast West in 1892 were conflicting. Born in 1855, Arnold-Forster was the son of an officer in the Indian Army and a grandson of Dr Arnold of Rugby. Orphaned at three, he was taken under the protection of his father's sister and her husband—the Liberal MP and Quaker W. E. Forster, whose surname he adopted. Following Rugby, Oxford and the bar it seemed natural to stand as Liberal candidate for Devonport in 1883. In fact Arnold-Forster was already increasingly drawn towards the Conservative cause. His wife later suggested that the break from the Liberals resulted from his experience as Forster's secretary in Ireland,[2] but he had also become honorary secretary of the Imperial Federation Committee. With his views on Ireland and empire diametrically opposed to party policy he left the Liberals. In 1886 he stood unsuccessfully as Unionist candidate at Darlington and at Dewsbury in 1888. By this time he had built a career as journalist, author and businessman, having joined Cassell's, the publishers, in 1884. He was also an acknowledged authority on defence.

Arnold-Forster's early interest in defence centred on naval rather than military matters. He was closely involved with W. T. Stead of the *Pall Mall Gazette* in promoting the naval scare of 1884, adding his own contribution to the vogue for alarmist invasion literature with *In a Conning Tower* in 1888. He became associated with Sir Charles Dilke, Spenser Wilkinson and Sir George Chesney in 1894.[3] The extent to which he shared Dilke's views on the need for a dual army system in preference to Cardwell's scheme of linked battalions was indicated in his pamphlet *Our Home Army* (1897) and his *Army Letters* (1898). A fuller statement of his ideas was published in 1900 as *The War Office, the Army and the Empire*. His first ministerial appointment was as Parliamentary Secretary to the Admiralty in 1900; he was still at the Admiralty when offered the post of Secretary of State for War.

Arnold-Forster was not, however, the first choice to succeed Brodrick, and this had a crucial bearing on his position within the Cabinet. In all, nine men were considered for the War Office, of whom five refused. Two of those who refused were the candidates most acceptable to the King, who maintained a close interest in army affairs, and to the Prime Minister, Balfour. These were the Unionist chief whip, Akers-Douglas, and Esher. Esher had once offered Brodrick his services as permanent under-secretary at the War Office but had long since resolved to prefer power to responsibility. His influence had already been damned by Brodrick. When Akers-Douglas learned that Esher was to head a small committee to examine the structure of the War Office he too refused the post.[4] The circumstances in which Arnold-Forster entered the Cabinet could hardly have been less conducive to gaining his colleagues' confidence in his ability to solve an almost intractable problem. He was a junior and inexperienced minister within a Cabinet in which sat two former Secretaries of State whose policies he was now proposing to reverse—Landsdowne at the Foreign Office and Brodrick at the India Office. Arnold-Forster also nursed something of a grievance against his former superior at the Admiralty, Selborne, whom he believed to have taken the credit for the establishment of the Committee of Imperial Defence when Arnold-Forster had drafted the original memorandum suggesting such a body to the First Lord in October 1902.[5] Arnold-Forster's task would have been difficult enough in the face of such embarrassments without the additional defects of his own personality and state of health.

Brodrick had been considered tactless and over-sensitive when in office but opinions of Arnold-Forster were universally worse. One problem was the fact that most of his views on what was required in army reform had been crystallised long before. This was not lost on Lord Roberts, who wrote to Balfour in July 1904:[6]

> perhaps the fact that he long ago formed very decided opinions as to the way in which it should be dealt with has led him to formulate a scheme in accordance with these opinions, without his having sufficient knowledge of the Army to enable him to appreciate the consequences of the changes he proposes.

Virtually all accounts by colleagues and subordinates record impressions of dogmatism, irritability and priggishness. Leo Amery, who was one of his closest collaborators, recalled that Arnold-Forster's 'zeal' outran his patience in dealing with senior officers, who complained 'not altogether without reason, that he was too apt to lecture them and too little inclined to listen'. Balfour wrote to Esher in July 1904 of Arnold-Forster's habit of regarding arguments against his ideas as personal attacks and of his conveying the impression that everyone to whom he had talked agreed with him, 'so that he is perpetually quoting eminent soldiers to me as being among his supporters, though I suspect they look with coldness on many parts of his scheme'. Balfour's influential secretary, Jack Sandars, complained to Esher in October 1905 that 'the disease of egotism is more developed in him than I have ever seen it. His language about his own achievements and about his own correctness and his own infallibility beggared description.' The view from the opposition benches was similar, Campbell-Bannermann recording of Arnold-Forster's performance at the dispatch box in April 1905 that his 'metallic voice, sour visage and dogmatic egotism bored when it did not irritate'.[7]

Yet, for all that Arnold-Forster may not have been the most engaging of personalities nor the most amenable of colleagues, he was the victim not only of considerable duplicity from those whose support he was entitled to expect but of open social prejudice. He remained an outsider; a Liberal Unionist by conviction rather than a Conservative by upbringing. He was to find no place within the inner circle of the party. Indeed, he had written to Balfour in October 1903 that he lacked 'prestige, wealth or position' and would need the support of the Prime Minister. While Admiral Fisher wrote to Esher merely that Arnold-Forster was 'not one of us', Sandars recorded that the Secretary of State's visit to the King at Balmoral had evidently 'given him no polish' and that his manners remained 'atrocious'.[8]

A further contributory factor to Arnold-Forster's irritability with his Cabinet colleagues and certainly to his determination to push forward his reforms was ill health. In 1903 he had severely strained his heart whilst riding and had accepted Balfour's offer only after consultation with his doctor. He was well aware of the risks he ran:[9]

> It is particularly trying to me after so many years of active life to have
> to give up almost all forms of exercise, to think twice before I do
> anything, and to know that the most important part of my machinery
> may play me false any day.

He was often ill, and on one occasion Leo Amery was called in by Mary Arnold-Forster on account of her husband's collapse to assist in the preparation of an important policy statement to be presented to the House on 14 July 1904. Though they might disagree with his policies, most recognised his courage, as Guy Fleetwood-Wilson, Director of Finance at

the War Office wrote: 'in feeble health and in frequent pain he never
flunked. His devotion to his work and his dogged determination,
notwithstanding his disability, commanded respect and admiration.' Most,
but not all—Esher, for one, inclined to believe Arnold-Forster's frequent
recourse to bed more moral than physical collapse.[10]

The scheme unveiled to the Cabinet by the Secretary of State between
December 1903 and June 1904 was influenced by three basic factors.[11]
Firstly, Arnold-Forster wished to harness efficiency with economy.
Secondly, there was the serious depletion in foreign drafts due to the
introduction of three years' short-service enlistment by Brodrick and the
fact that only 20 per cent of the infantry were prepared to extend their
service beyond three years, instead of the 75 per cent confidently expected.
Thirdly, as an adherent of the 'Blue Water School', Arnold-Forster
accepted the decision of the Committee of Imperial Defence, re-emphasised
in June 1904 and February 1905, which gave the defence of India priority.
He proposed to end the old Cardwell scheme of linked battalions and to
utilise fifteen larger depots to supply drafts to groups of battalions whilst
abolishing the remaining fifty-four depots. More important, he proposed to
create two separate armies—a long-service army of 112 regular battalions
enlisted for nine years with the colours, which would provide foreign
garrisons and a striking force; and a home or short-service army of thirty
regular battalions enlisted for two years with the colours and providing
drafts for the long-service army in time of war. A further fourteen regular
battalions would be disbanded. The Militia, for which Arnold-Forster had
no great regard, would, in the final version of the scheme, contribute thirty
battalions to the home army and a further twenty-four battalions would be
entirely disbanded. The Volunteer force would also be considerably
reduced and divided into two classes of efficiency. Arnold-Forster also
proposed to reorganise the cavalry, to build better barracks and to improve
the employment prospects of ex-soldiers.

Most of the basic elements of the scheme had been outlined in *Our Home
Army* in 1897. Arnold-Forster had sent Balfour a copy at the time of
publication, and the Prime Minister had received a memorandum
reiterating these views in May 1903. The likely plans of the new Secretary
of State were thus not unknown to Balfour, nor was the concept of two
separate armies enlisted under different conditions unique to Arnold-
Forster. Dilke and Roberts held similar views; such a scheme having been
proposed by John Holms MP in 1875, and more recently by Leo Amery in
a series of articles in the *Times* attacking Brodrick's scheme in January and
February 1903.[12] With the notable exception of the Militia plans, the
opposition in the Cabinet appears to have been concerned with
practicalities rather than Arnold-Forster's principles.

One source of opposition was Brodrick. Sir George Clarke, soon to be secretary of the Committee of Imperial Defence, wrote to Esher in March 1904 that Brodrick was still 'fighting for his Army Corpses'. There was an early embarrassment over Brodrick's continuing interest in the War Office when he sought unsuccessfully to appear before the Treasury Committee established by Balfour in January 1904 to investigate the financial implications of Arnold-Forster's scheme. In July 1904 Arnold-Forster suspected Brodrick not only of leaking information on the Militia plans to the press but of encouraging Lansdowne to make a particularly damaging speech in the House of Lords implying that he lacked Cabinet support.[13]

The Treasury had proved a formidable opponent of Brodrick's reforms. Once more a Chancellor of the Exchequer, now Austen Chamberlain, sought to raise major objections to the cost of reform. Arnold-Forster maintained that the reduction in regular battalions and depots and in the establishment and actual front-line strength of the army represented a considerable saving. The Cabinet Treasury Committee confirmed his costings in March 1904, but Chamberlain described the reductions 'as wholly inadequate, both to the expectation of the public and to the real necessities of the situation ...'. Arnold-Forster could only retort that his attempted economies found no favour with his Cabinet colleagues: 'They bid me economise and reform. If I could do as I please I could accomplish this feat; but every man who says "Economise", cries "Hands Off" directly I touch his particular preserve.' Thus the Foreign Office refused to allow troops to be withdrawn from Egypt; the Admiralty refused to take over more overseas defence responsibilities; the Colonial Office refused to press the Dominions into assuming more defence responsibilities; and Milner refused to contemplate withdrawal of troops from South Africa.[14]

But the issue that brought the most powerful opposition within the Cabinet was the intended reform of the Militia. For long a competitor with the regular army for recruits, the Militia had become merely an adjunct passing most of its best men directly to the army. In 1904 it was 39,000 short of establishment, with 42 per cent of its rank and file having less than two years' service and 73 per cent being under twenty years of age. In short, as the Norfolk Commission concluded in October 1904, it was 'unfit to take the field' for the defence of the country. Yet the 'Old Constitutional Force' had considerable support in Parliament. Arnold-Forster was to complain bitterly of 'all those old women who look upon their regiments as a sort of honorary addition to their positions as County Magnates or as leading figures in some dull, ineffective society'. Even Balfour supported the Militia, because, according to Arnold-Forster, 'Jim Cranborne [the Lord Privy Seal] and Selborne are good fellows and good Militiamen and naturally stick up for a force they have worked so hard to save from decay'. It was only by the threat of a resignation the government could not afford that Arnold-Forster persuaded the Cabinet to allow him to make his long overdue statement to the House of Commons on 14 July 1904.

There is little doubt that the details of the Militia plans were deliberately leaked to the *Daily Express* and the *Standard* prior to the Commons debate in order to ensure a hostile reception. If the Commons had any doubt at all that Arnold-Forster lacked Cabinet backing, the matter was made clear in the Lords on 21 July 1904. The Under Secretary, Earl Donoughmore, confused matters by describing the scheme as one of the 'Army Council' but indicated it had Cabinet approval. Lansdowne flatly contradicted the idea that Arnold-Forster had full Cabinet backing. The damage was done by the time Selborne announced in the Lords on 29 July that the 'Army Council' scheme did in fact enjoy Cabinet support. Before another important statement by Donoughmore in the Lords in February 1905 Arnold-Forster took the precaution of writing to Lansdowne to ensure that he did not again contradict the Under Secretary of State.[15]

Arnold-Forster's relationship with his Cabinet colleagues was never one of mutual confidence. The frequency with which he had to threaten or offer his resignation in order to make any progress at all was probably without parallel. He first threatened to resign as early as February 1904 if the commitment to army reform was not upheld. It was threatened in June 1904 when Balfour delayed setting a date for the Commons statement and twice in July 1904, once, as related, before the statement and again after Lansdowne's speech. It was offered in April 1905 and again in June 1905. Each time he was persuaded to remain, in the interests of preserving what little credibility the government still enjoyed. On the last occasion he managed to gain the concession of Cabinet agreement to opening recruitment for fourteen home service battalions, but only as an experiment, and even this was subsequently reduced in scope to eight battalions.[16] The Cabinet was prepared to concede only what it confidently expected the Commons to reject: a case, perhaps, of collective cowardice rather than collective responsibility. But then, the structure of defence administration itself was far from clear.

Balfour was served not by one Secretary of State but by three— Arnold-Forster, Esher and Sir George Clarke—of whom the actual Secretary of State was the least influential.[17] A condition of Arnold-Forster's appointment was that Esher should undertake a major review of War Office organisation. Arnold-Forster fully expected to be included on the War Office Reconstruction Committee but this was not what Esher or, indeed, the King intended. Ironically, one of the reasons for Esher's belief in the need for an organisation at the War Office resembling the Board of Admiralty was that it would restore the influence of the Secretary of State.

Brodrick had established a War Office Council in 1900 to express the collective civil and military opinion of the War Office, but it fell far short of the kind of professional Minister of National Defence advocated in the 1890s by Wolseley, Dilke and Arnold-Forster himself. The Elgin Commission had little to suggest in terms of a higher War Office administration, and it was left to Esher to seize the opportunity to suggest radical reform. His committee, consisting of himself, Fisher and Clarke, enjoyed unprecedented executive powers not only to recommend a new organisation but to appoint the first professional heads of that organisation. The report, which was produced with extraordinary speed in order to throw military opposition off balance, recommended an Army Council of three civil and four military members. The first military member would be designated 'Chief of the General Staff' and the Secretary of State would be elevated to the standing of the First Lord of the Admiralty on the equivalent naval board. The report also recommended the establishment of a permanent secretariat for the Committee of Imperial Defence. The recommendations were adopted without submitting the report to the approval of Parliament or its nominations to the military positions on the Army Council to the Secretary of State. Indeed, some of the measures had already been carried into effect by the time the committee dissolved itself in May 1904.[18]

The proceedings of the Esher Committee had thus been conducted without reference to the opinions of the Secretary of State, who was now required to implement its recommendations. Esher had every intention of retaining a close interest in his creation, and maintained close touch with Balfour through Sandars and with the King through the latter's private secretary, Knollys. Arnold-Forster warned Knollys in March 1904 that 'I was quite sure that if the King wished to communicate his wishes to a Principal Secretary of State in charge of a very important office, he would not do so through the channel of an unauthorised person communicating with my Private Secretary . . .'. Again in October 1904 Arnold-Forster noted 'this constant interference on the part of an unauthorised and irresponsible person', and his bitterness was such that in 1908 he suggested to Dilke that the matter of Esher's continuing membership of the CID be raised in Parliament.[19]

Clarke, who became first secretary of the CID in April 1904, had a much more formal position in the structure of government and began to subject Balfour to a stream of memoranda on every conceivable military subject. Clarke favoured Arnold-Forster's plans for larger depots and a long-service army but wanted the home army organised in such a way as to provide two divisions for a striking force. He also supported the retention of the Militia as the 'second line' largely because he believed it too deeply entrenched to be destroyed and useful as the only part of the Crown's military forces theoretically liable to compulsion. He therefore actively encouraged both Balfour and the Army Council to resist Arnold-Forster's scheme.

The culmination of this intrigue against the Secretary of State was the establishment in January 1905 of a sub-committee of the CID, suggested originally by Sandars, to consider Arnold-Forster's scheme in conjunction with an alternative proposal based on retention of the Militia put forward by Balfour at Clarke's instigation. The sub-committee was to consist of Balfour as chairman, Esher, Clarke and Sir George Murray of the Treasury. As Murray and Balfour were usually absent, the work devolved on Esher and Clarke. Arnold-Forster, who never appeared before it, was appalled not only by the inclusion of Clarke, whose motives he rightly suspected, but by the way in which the committee undertook its task:[20] 'I repeat that I speak without accurate knowledge of what is going on; my subordinates know far more than I do, and I think that fact is proof of the falseness of the situation.'

Not surprisingly, the committee endorsed Balfour's plan. There were then attempts by Esher and Clarke to prevent Arnold-Forster's comments on the Balfour plan from reaching the Cabinet and by Arnold-Forster to prevent details of the plan reaching the Army Council. In sending his comments on the committee report to Balfour in March 1905, Arnold-Forster acidly noted in his diary, 'I suppose he will now hand it over to Clarke who will hand it over to Esher, who will hand it over to Acourt [Repington] who will write about it in the *Times*.' With complete justification he had written to Sandars in January that the War Office was a 'perfect caravanserai, where everybody has turned in at any casual moment to talk with all my subordinates about what is my business'.[21]

The additional problem was that those subordinates were bitterly opposed to his scheme. Throughout his term of office there was utter discord between minister and professional advisers. The relationship had got off to a bad start with the original incumbents of the War Office at the time of Arnold-Forster's appointment. The Adjutant General, Kelly-Kenny, was reported as early as October 1903 as attacking Arnold-Forster's policies, 'of which he knows, and can know, nothing whatever'. Charged with removing the established professional heads of the army in accordance with the recommendations of the Esher Committee, Arnold-Forster chose to do so in a particularly tactless manner. The C-in-C, Roberts, and the rest of the War Office Council were simply informed by letter on a Sunday afternoon that the new Army Council would commence its work the following day and that they were all dismissed. The Inspector General of Auxiliary Forces, Sir Alfred Turner, escaped 'Black Monday' but was soon removed after making 'disloyal' comments to the press on the Secretary of State's Volunteer policies in April 1904.[22]

It was intended by Esher that all decisions in future should be those of the Army Council collectively and that it would share with the Secretary of State responsibility to Parliament. Members would be colleagues and must acquiesce in collective decisions or resign. The new military members of the Army Council who were to carry out this bold departure from previous practice reflected badly on the judgement of the Esher Committee. The only member in whom Arnold-Forster had any confidence was the Quartermaster General, Herbert Plumer. The Master General of the Ordnance, Sir James Wolfe-Murray, was as indecisive as his later nickname, 'Sheep', would suggest, offering and withdrawing his resignation three times in his first six months of office. The Adjutant General, Sir Charles Douglas, was dismissed by the Secretary of State as a 'fool'. The Chief of the General Staff, however, earned even more opprobium: Sir Neville Lyttelton's inefficiency was the one thing on which the King, Esher, Clarke and Arnold-Forster could happily agree. In December 1904 Lyttelton went as far as to admit publicly that there was friction between himself and Douglas and that he did not understand the workings of the Army Council system. This extraordinary speech directly contravened Arnold-Forster's strict enjoinder to the military members in July 1904 that they should not make controversial statements in public. Arnold-Forster determined to be rid of Lyttelton, but the CGS had powerful friends and the advantage of having his brother, Alfred, sitting in the Cabinet as Colonial Secretary. Unable to force Lyttelton's resignation, Arnold-Forster resorted to intrigue. In May 1905 he tried to get Lyttelton to accept the Gibraltar command and, when he refused, attempted to force resignation over the report of the Butler Committee into irregularities in the sale and refund of army stores to contractors while Lyttelton had been C-in-C, South Africa. Lyttelton again rode the storm and in November 1905 held out against Arnold-Forster's suggestion that he accept the Scottish command. At one stage in the summer of 1905 Arnold-Forster was conducting negotiations with the former Director of Military Intelligence, Sir William Nicholson, as a possible successor on condition that he accepted Arnold-Forster's army scheme. In the meantime Esher, who feared the threat posed to the Army Council concept by Lyttelton's incompetence, had also offered the post to Kitchener, who had declined.[23]

The Army Council began with reasonably constructive comments on Arnold-Forster's scheme, but gradually their attitude hardened against the proposals as it became obvious that the Cabinet did not support the Secretary of State and that he was giving the impression that he had their support. Thus, after Selborne's statement in the Lords in July 1904

referring to the 'Army Council' scheme, Lyttelton immediately sought to
dissociate himself and his colleagues from Arnold-Forster. The latter was
prepared to acknowledge in his diary that the scheme was certainly not of
the Army Council's making:[24] 'I have been yearning for suggestions, and
... for all these weeks I have had nothing but trivial criticism and no
suggestions at all.'

In particular, Lyttelton, Wolfe-Murray and Douglas feared that the
simultaneous recruiting of men on long- and short-term enlistments would
inevitably jeopardise the long-service army as well as causing considerable
disruption in itself. The Army Council as a whole would have infinitely
preferred conscription for the home army. Their opposition to short-service
recruiting came to a head in March 1905 when, following Donoughmore's
announcement in the Lords that short service would be temporarily
postponed, they wrote a formal letter to Arnold-Forster which he tried
unsuccessfully to keep from the Cabinet:[25]

> We therefore desire to place it upon record that we cannot acquiesce
> in any mere postponement of the system, and that we decline to be
> pledged in any way to its subsequent introduction; and that in order
> that all possibility of misconception of our position regarding this
> important matter may be removed, we respectively desire that this
> statement of our views may be laid before the Cabinet.

When the Cabinet subsequently conceded the beginning of short-service
enlistment in June 1905, Clarke was dispatched to explain the situation to
the recalcitrant military. Clarke reported that the Army Council was 'sore'
with Arnold-Forster:[26]

> He has blocked administrative questions in a wholesale fashion and
> they cannot get him to give decisions, or to allow their questions to be
> discussed. At the same time he causes it to be widely understood he
> would have carried out a series of beneficial reforms. Thus the Army
> and the Press is beginning to believe that they are useless and
> obstructive persons, which naturally galls them much. They are all of
> them earnest and hardworking, and in other hands they would have
> been perfectly capable of doing all that is required in administering the
> Army. In fact the Army Council scheme might have proved
> conspicuously successful, but for the advent of the fatal scheme.

His experience of working with the Army Council could hardly have
convinced Clarke that they were the paragons his memorandum implied.
He also conveyed the subsequent threat of the Army Council to Balfour
that they would resign if short service was introduced, but Balfour
negotiated a compromise by which they agreed to the experiment without
implying support for a larger scheme of short-service recruiting.

The Army Council were essentially dishonest in never openly stating their opposition. Indeed, in November 1905 Arnold-Forster compelled the military members to remain after a council meeting to record matters agreed and action to be taken in order to 'obviate tiresome confusion' resulting from subsequent dispute over the minutes.[27] High-handedness on the one side and indecisiveness on the other was not the best means of achieving the collective responsibility envisaged by the Esher Committee. The Army Council scheme simply did not work, and it is arguable, in view of Haldane's later limited consultation with the council, that it was the system itself rather than the personalities involved which failed.

There was little enough in terms of achievement that Arnold-Forster could set down either in his report to the King on leaving office or his apologia, *The Army in 1906*. Those of his reforms actually implemented such as the short-service enlistment experiment and the plans for new barracks did not long survive the advent of his successor. Other 'achievements' were, in fact, the recommendations of others which he had merely implemented, such as the establishment of the Army Council, the decentralisation of the War Office Finance Department and the establishment of the General Staff. This latter measure was the most enduring legacy of his period of office but here too the drive had come from other sources. The survival of the concept amid War Office disunity, Balfour's lack of interest and the Treasury's suspicion was due almost entirely to the determination of Clarke and, to a lesser extent, Esher and Henry Wilson. A series of articles in the *Times* by Repington in May 1905, consciously aimed at Arnold-Forster's sense of his own destiny, prompted the Secretary of State to take a more active interest than hitherto in the General Staff. Under the tutelage of Wilson, Arnold-Forster moved towards his memorandum of November 1905 which formally created a General Staff. Another lasting achievement was the rearming of the Royal Artillery with thirteen-pounder guns for the horse artillery and eighteen-pounders for the field artillery, but again the Equipment Committee to consider rearmament had been constituted in January 1901. Arnold-Forster had been confined to participating in the subsequent dispute over the merits of the eighteen-pounder and it would appear that the casting vote on the scheme was actually that of Balfour.[28]

The only other lasting achievements of varying importance were the ordering of the short-magazine Lee Enfield, the holding of joint army/naval manoeuvres in Essex, the ending of flogging in military prisons and the reduction of some colonial garrisons. In terms of the overall strategic orientation of the state, Arnold-Forster saw his dual army as a solution to the problem of finding drafts for India. His vision, like that of Balfour, did not extend to Europe. In so far as revolutionary strategic decisions were about to be made, these lay in the hands of Clarke and Esher. In October

1905, for example, Esher, Clarke and Sandars arranged military discussions on the implications of a renewed Anglo-Japanese treaty without Arnold-Forster's knowledge. This was an ominous forerunner of the process by which secret staff conversations were begun with the French under the auspices of the Committee of Imperial Defence in the interval between the Unionist government's resignation and the assumption of office by the Liberals.[29]

Arnold-Forster's Volunteer policies, which have gone largely unremarked, are a microcosm of his wider problems in the War Office. His plans for the Volunteer force were the most judicious part of his entire scheme. By 1903 the Volunteers were sorely deficient in both training and equipment and over 100,000 short of establishment. To a large extent their deficiencies had resulted from the way in which they had been allowed to evolve in the localities without any regard to a coherent plan. When it was revived in response to a French invasion panic in 1859 the government of the day had intended that the force should satisfy public opinion at absolutely no cost to the state, since units would be entirely self-supporting. In fact this had never been a reality and a capitation grant had been recommended for 'efficient' Volunteers by a Royal Commission in 1862 even before the change in the force's social composition which saw a predominantly middle-class organisation transformed into dependence upon the artisan classes of society. With the change in membership and concurrent decline in financial support from members and public, the state's financial contribution had grown steadily from barely £3,000 in 1860 to £627,200 by 1897. The price of that increased aid was ever higher proficiency requirements which threatened to upset the delicate relationship between a Volunteer and his civil employer over the amount of time which he could devote to military training. Few soldiers in 1859 had considered that Volunteers would be anything other than useless in the event of invasion, a view shared by many politicians. However, mutual suspicion between Volunteers and regulars was eased to some extent by closer co-operation after the Cardwell reforms. There was also an increasing official need in the last quarter of the nineteenth century for additional manpower and a viable 'second line' for home defence. Thus Volunteer units were incorporated into the mobilisation scheme of 1886 and 1888, and at the time of the South African war, the government was forced to admit that in the absence of the regular army the Volunteers represented the main defence against possible raids on the British coast. However, an attempt in December 1901 to raise efficiency requirements by instituting compulsory summer camps brought widespread hostility and declining numbers.[30] Declining numbers resulted inevitably in declining capitation income, which further damaged confidence and military capability. Thus the key to

Arnold-Forster's problem was basically finance.

Arnold-Forster considered that the only way in which more money could be made available for the Volunteer force would be through a reduction in numbers from 364,000 to 200,000. The Committee of Imperial Defence had pronounced that the Volunteers' *raison d'être*—invasion—was improbable and thus a reduction in numbers would also be compatible with the size of force required to defend the country against raids alone. The actual field strength of the Volunteers would be reduced to 180,000 men, of whom 60,000 would be on higher efficiency conditions and receive higher allowances. The distinction would not be between 'good' and 'bad' men but between those who could afford to give their time and those who could not. The estimated saving of £380,000 would then be ploughed back into the force to provide such necessities as transport. Precisely how the reduction was to be achieved was not clear, and in January 1904 Arnold-Forster resolved to await the report of the Norfolk Commission.

The commission had been established by Brodick as much to muzzle discussion as to cure the ills of the auxiliary forces. The difficulties encountered by the members in obtaining reliable figures on which to work from the War Office, the Admiralty and the Committee of Imperial Defence lent additional support to the suspicion that little importance was attached to its findings. The commission concluded that neither Militia nor Volunteers were fit to take the field against trained Continental troops. Recommendations were made, in the case of the Volunteers, for increased camping allowances, training 'in situ', fourteen-day camps, state aid for ranges and transport and a separate Volunteer Department at the War Office. But since both the commissioners themselves and the majority of the witnesses continued to believe in the possibility of invasion, they concluded that the only means of defeating an invasion without Regular support would be by a home defence army raised by conscription. On publication in May 1904 Arnold-Forster at once rejected the report as a 'tiresome thing which never ought to have been created'. In his subsequent Commons statement on 14 July 1904 he merely outlined his owns plans to reduce the Volunteer force without giving any details of how it was to be effected. By this time Arnold-Forster had already clashed with the Volunteers over a decision to dismantle a separate Volunteer Department at the War Office. When Parliament was prorogued in August the Volunteer MPs were already suspicious of the minister's attitude towards the force.[31] In view of the powerful vested interest which the Volunteers still represented in the House of Commons, this was a serious development.

The Volunteers in Parliament had by the 1890s developed from a loose assortment of MPs of varying political persuasions to a highly organised group concentrated almost exclusively within the Unionist Party. The Volunteers had displayed their new-found determination and organisation by voting against their own government in 1885 and 1886 and by supporting the cordite vote against the Liberal government in 1895. Arnold-Forster could hardly afford to incur the animosity of over forty Volunteer MPs, but he was in fact confident that he could sway them to his own point of view. He was to be sadly mistaken, for on 22 and 23 February 1905, almost as soon as Parliament had reassembled, the Volunteers obstructed the debate on the address. After five hours of disruption on the first day Arnold-Forster commented:[32]

> A stranger coming into the House would never have realised that we have any Regular Army, that we live on an island, or that there is such a thing as the Royal Navy. The whole idea is that there are so many existing Volunteers and that these Volunteers must be paid to go on existing, simply to please themselves and to oblige their Commanding Officers.

He was able to allay some fears by announcing that he no longer intended to create two classes in the force but his new proposals, evolved during the winter, would have much the same effect. Discussions on how to reduce the force had begun in September 1904 between Arnold-Forster, Douglas and the Director of Auxiliary Forces, Mackinnon. It had been decided to effect the reduction by means of a gradual raising of physical standards and by the amalgamation or abolition of inefficient units. Arnold-Forster now proposed to reduce establishment to 230,000. It was hoped that this would allow 60,000 Volunteers to camp for fourteen days with raised allowances. The capitation grant would remain at 35s for those who went to camp, but non-campers would earn only 20s. It was also proposed to increase transport and create a divisional staff as an experiment. All this, however, was conditional upon a reduction in numbers providing the necessary money.[33]

These ideas were outlined by Arnold-Forster on 28 March, but the debate 'degenerated, as usual, into the ordinary drivel about Volunteers...'. Arnold-Forster was increasingly critical of Volunteers 'who take not the slightest interest or concern in the Army as a whole, and seem to regard the Regular Army rather as a necessary evil, than as the principal land defence of the Empire'. Balfour refused to allow the Volunteers to discuss the proposals outside the Estimates but the Volunteers then disrupted the Pay Vote on 4, 5 and 6 April 1905 to press their points. The crux of their argument, enunciated principally by Sir Howard Vincent, was that the Volunteers were still vital to home defence. Much to Arnold-Forster's annoyance, Balfour replied that the CID had considered invasion unlikely under existing conditions, one of which was the existence of the force, so that the necessity of the Volunteers and the improbability of invasion were not mutually contradictory.[34] The Secretary of State still claimed that most Volunteers in the country supported him, but this appeared somewhat optimistic. The true attitude of the Volunteer force as a whole was, however, soon to be tested by the so-called 'June circular'.

At the meeting of the Army Council on 13 April 1905 it had been decided that little could be done to reduce the Volunteers in the current year with the exception of obtaining reports from GOCs with recommendations on units which might be disbanded or amalgamated on the grounds of inefficiency or lack of numbers. It was decided to ask GOCs at the same time for information on the number of Volunteers fit to serve abroad. A circular was accordingly drawn up after consultation between Mackinnon, Douglas and the DADG, Army Medical Services. Arnold-Forster approved the circular on 6 June and it was issued on 20 June 1905. Unfortunately the wording was ambiguous, and when the contents were revealed in the press on 4 July it appeared that the government was introducing a severe medical requirement designed to reduce the force. Donoughmore insisted in the Lords that the government merely required to know how many men were fit for active service and that no action was contemplated, but on 5 July the Liberal and former Unionist MP J. E. B. Seely attempted to move an adjournment debate in the Commons on the circular. There was in fact only one day left for discussing Supply, and, at the instigation of Campbell-Bannerman, Balfour agreed to allot this day—13 July—to the Volunteers.[35]

Although many provincial and some national newspapers supported the idea of the circular, there was considerable criticism of Arnold-Forster, notably in the *Standard*. As a result of the press and parliamentary opposition both Douglas and Mackinnon attempted to dissociate themselves from their own circular. Mackinnon threatened to resign when Arnold-Forster pointed out that he had in fact drafted it. Mackinnon then appealed to Roberts, still a member of the CID, claiming that he had told Douglas that he disapproved, that he had only drafted an Army Council resolution and that he did not have sufficient access to the Secretary of State. Douglas claimed that he had disapproved of the circular as well, drawing from Arnold-Forster the comment that there was no record of Mackinnon's alleged dissension and that he could not accept that Douglas was not responsible:[36]

> Every member of the Army Council is responsible for all its decisions. I see the AG's initials on the minutes of the proceedings of the 13 April. We all know perfectly well that the reasonable precautions we are now taking are necessary. I have heard no word of this disapproval until now.

A new circular was issued on 11 July clearly setting out the purpose of the medical inquiry, but the Commons debate went ahead on 13 July. The Secretary of State defended himself against the charge that he was aiming at reduction by stealth, and some Volunteers, including Vincent, were sufficiently impressed by his speech to vote with the government. As a result the motion was narrowly defeated by 232 to 206 votes, but the debate continued in the country. It would appear that there was substantially less criticism of the circulars in the provinces than in Parliament. Most COs naturally considered the best means of asserting the fitness of their men would be through medical examination. There was press encouragement, again notably in the *Standard*, to refuse the medical, and isolated cases where it actually occurred. The Deputy Judge Advocate General ruled that the men concerned could not be held guilty of disobedience, since the examination was based on foreign service requirements which were not legally part of a Volunteer's duty. All the military members of the Army Council, with the exception of Plumer, now wanted to withdraw the circulars but Arnold-Forster considered that 'few corps will care to write themselves down as manifestly unfit, which they certainly would do if they deliberately declined to supply the information asked for'. Only in the Midlands and Wales was it reported that men had refused to come forward because of press incitement, and Arnold-Forster believed himself justified:[37]

> Despite the most frantic appeals in newspapers whose editors forgot that politics and soldiering have nothing to do with each other; despite deliberate incitement to insubordination, and invitations to officers and men to behave in an unsoldierly and disgraceful fashion, the Volunteers have with exceptions so few as to be quite unimportant, behaved admirably.

In the Commons, however, the Volunteers had taken up nine days allotted to Supply. The debate on 13 July 1905 was the last occasion on which any of Arnold-Forster's plans were debated in the Commons.

Although the session had ended, Arnold-Forster still hoped to effect some Volunteer reforms. On 28 July 1905 he met forty-two Volunteer commanding officers at the Commons to hear their views on a wide range of problems and he believed that real progress could now be made. However, on 26 September Douglas insisted that the policy of reduction must be abandoned:

> I fear that any attempt to reduce numbers or capitation grant would, in the present temper of the Volunteers, be doomed to failure; it would increase the unrest, it would have a bad effect on the Country, and would further weaken the position of the Army Council.

It was more than likely that Douglas's decision was influenced by a speech made by Balfour on 9 September in which he maintained that the regular army could only be sent abroad 'so long as the patriotism of this country will provide us with a sufficiency of trained Volunteers, to deal with any emergency that may arise'. This was followed by a speech at Liverpool on 29 September in which Sir George White called for four times as many Volunteers and by a speech by the King to Scottish Volunteers in October in which he urged more men to enlist in the force. Arnold-Forster was also made aware by the government whips of the likely reaction in the Commons to a continued policy of reduction: 'I cannot conceal from myself, that in the opinion of our Whips, the policy of reduction is exceedingly unpopular and likely to be resented.'[38]

In the circumstances he saw little alternative but to accept the suggestions of Douglas, Fleetwood-Wilson and the rest of the Army Council that Parliament must be asked for more money for the Volunteers. Proposals agreed by the Army Council on 6 November were submitted to the Cabinet on the 11th. A two-guinea capitation grant was to be paid to those camping for fifteen days, £1 18s 6d for eight days and £1 for non-campers. It was proposed also to reorganise the Volunteer force into brigades and create an experimental division. All this would add £170,000 to the estimates. Lyttelton, Wolfe-Murray and Douglas then attempted to cancel their own proposals on 25 November because they did not want the Volunteers to be given preference over the Militia, but the Cabinet had already signified its approval. On 23 November Arnold-Forster secured the reluctant agreement of the Army Council to a field artillery experiment for two Volunteer units to be rearmed with Ehrhardt quick-firing guns. On 11 December 1905 the government resigned. At the first meeting of the Army Council under Haldane's chairmanship it was decided to continue the reorganisation of Volunteer brigades and the other experiments as temporary expedients, but in January 1906 the experimental division was suspended. At the next meeting of the council the field artillery experiment was also abandoned.[39]

In twenty-six months of office Arnold-Forster had conspicuously failed to implement his Volunteer policies owing to the intransigence of Volunteer MPs, the Army Council and his own colleagues. The Volunteer plans had been virtually the only ones accepted by the Cabinet, but there is a strong suspicion that Balfour knew their likely fate in the Commons. The force as a whole was by no means entirely opposed to Arnold-Forster's policies, which were in many ways a sensible solution to its financial problems. He was also justified to a large extent in believing that Vincent and his fellow Volunteer MPs were unrepresentative of the force as a whole. However, those MPs consistently refused to accept reductions of any kind and destroyed the policies by their obstruction. Some Volunteers welcomed

Arnold-Forster's departure, but he himself noted after meeting his successor, Haldane,[40] 'The "talkin" Volunteers, who are always silly, are already rejoicing because they think they are going to squeeze more money out of him, in return for less work. My impression is they may have a rude awakening.'

On that at least Arnold-Forster was correct. He had suffered considerably from his brief period at the War Office. In 1906 he gave up his Belfast seat to save the strain of travelling and became MP for Croydon. He devoted his energies to opposing Haldane's reforms, producing a series of articles published as *Military Needs and Military Policy* (1909). But his health was failing, and he died in March 1909. To the end he remained firm to the principles of army reform which brought about his own failure in office and the confinement of an instructive period of civil–military relations to the back room of history.[41]

Notes

1   L. J. Satre, 'St John Brodrick and army reform', *Journal of British Studies*, XV, 1976, pp. 117–39.

2   Mary Arnold-Forster, *The Rt. Hon. H. O. Arnold-Forster: a Memoir by his Wife*, Edward Arnold, London, 1910, p. 38.

3   Papers concerning their joint letter are to be found in Ogilby Trust, Spenser Wilkinson papers, OTP 13/9.

4   A. V. Tucker, 'The issue of army reform in the unionist government, 1903–5', *Historical Journal*, IX, 1966, pp. 90–100; Viscount Chilston, *Chief Whip*, Routledge & Kegan Paul, London, 1961, pp. 313–20.

5   Arnold-Forster papers, Diary, 2 August 1904, Add. MSS 50339.

6   Balfour papers, Roberts to Balfour, 11 July 1904, Add. MSS 49725.

7   Leo Amery, *My Political Life*, Hutchinson, London, 1953, I. p. 209; Balfour papers, Balfour to Esher, 30 July 1904, Add. MSS 49718; Esher papers, Sanders to Esher, 16 October 1905. E/10/32; Campbell-Bannerman Papers, Campbell-Bannerman to Haliburton, 7 April 1905, Add. MSS 41218. A typical incident is recorded in Field Marshal Lord Grenfell, *Memoirs*, Hodder & Stoughton, London, 1925, pp. 171–2; Austen Chamberlain, *Politics from the Inside*, Cassell, London, 1936, pp. 60–1; and General Sir Neville Lyttelton, *Eighty Years Soldiering, Politics and Games*, Hodder & Stoughton, London, 1927, p. 273.

8   Arnold-Forster papers, Diary, 5 October 1903, Add. MSS 50335; Esher papers, Fisher to Esher, 5 August 1904, quoted J. Bertie, 'H. O. Arnold-Forster at the War Office, 1903–5', unpublished PhD thesis, Liverpool University, 1974, p. 84; Balfour papers, Sandars to Balfour, 12 October 1904, Add. MSS 49718.

9   Arnold-Forster papers, Diary, 6 October 1903, Add. MSS 50335; Mary Arnold-Forster, *A Memoir*, p. 225.

10 Amery, *My Political Life*, pp. 210–22; Sir Guy Fleetwood-Wilson, *Letters to Somebody: a Retrospect*, Cassell, London, 1922, p. 135; Balfour papers, Esher to Balfour, 17 June 1904, Esher to Sandars, 27 July 1904, and Balfour to Esher, 30 July 1904, Add. MSS 49718.

11 H. O. Arnold-Forster, *The Army in 1906*, Murray, London, 1906, *passim*.

12 Balfour papers, Arnold-Forster to Balfour, 15 June 1897, Add. MSS 49722;

Arnold-Forster papers, 'Notes on the present system of army organisation and some suggested changes', Add. MSS 50301; John Holms, *The British Army in 1875*, Longmans, London, 1875; Satre, 'St John Brodrick', pp. 117–39.

13   Esher papers, Clarke to Esher, 5 August 1904, quoted Bertie, p. 85; Balfour papers, Wyndham and Sandars to Balfour, 23 February 1904, Add. MSS 49726; Arnold-Forster papers, Diary, 19 July and 25 July 1904, Add. MSS 50339.

14   PRO, Chamberlain memoranda, Cab. 37/70, No. 61, and Cab. 37/74, No. 21; Arnold-Forster papers, Diary, 1 May 1904, 3 June 1904, 13 June 1904 and 3 November 1905, Add. MSS 50338, 50342 and 50352; Mary Arnold-Forster, *A Memoir*, pp. 254–5.

15   Arnold-Forster papers, Diary, 12 July 1904, Add. MSS 50339; Peter Fraser, *Lord Esher: a Political Biography*, Hart-Davis & MacGibbon, London, 1973, pp. 108–21; Arnold-Forster papers, Diary, July 1904, *passim*, Add. MSS 50339; Bertie, p. 190.

16   Mary Arnold-Forster, *A Memoir*, pp. 279–83; Balfour papers, Arnold-Forster to Balfour, 22 June 1905, Add. MSS 50309; PRO, 'Army reorganisation', 9 June 1905, Cab. 37/78, No. 106.

17   Tucker, 'Army reform', p. 94.

18   On the Esher Committee generally see W. S. Hamer, *The British Army: Civil–Military Relations, 1885–1905*, Oxford University Press, London, 1970, pp. 223–54, and John Gooch, *The Plans of War: the General Staff and British Military Strategy, 1900–1916*, Routledge & Kegan Paul, London, 1974, pp. 32–61.

19   Arnold-Forster papers, Diary, 7 November, 4 March and 17 October 1904, Add. MSS 50341, 50337 and 50340; Hamer, *British Army*, pp. 226–7.

20   PRO, Arnold-Forster to Balfour, 3 February 1905, Cab. 37/74, No. 10, which reproduces the Arnold-Forster–Balfour exchange of correspondence on the CID sub-committee. For the CID generally see J. P. Mackintosh, 'The role of the Committee of Imperial Defence before 1914', *English Historical Review*, LXXVII, 1962, pp. 490–503; and N. D'Ombrain, *War Machinery and High Policy: Defence Administration in Peacetime Britain, 1902–1914*, Oxford, 1973. For Clarke in particular see John Gooch, 'Sir George Clarke's career at the Committee of Imperial Defence, 1904–1907', *Historical Journal*, XVIII, 1975, pp. 555–69.

21   Arnold-Forster papers, Diary, 5, 7, 14 and 27 February 1905, Add. MSS 50344; Diary, 28 March 1905, Add. MSS 50345; Balfour papers, Arnold-Forster to Sandars, 24 January 1905, Add. MSS 49723.

22   Arnold-Forster papers, Diary, 26 October 1903, Add. MSS 50335; Sir Alfred Turner, *Sixty Years of a Soldiers's Life*, Methuen, London, 1912, pp. 310–11.

23   Arnold-Forster papers, Diary, 8 and 12 July 1904, Add. MSS 50339; Diary, December 1904 and November 1905, *passim*, Add. MSS 50342 and 50352; Gooch, *Plans of War*, pp. 68–9, 77–9, 86.

24   Arnold-Forster papers, Diary, 13 July 1904, Add. MSS 50339.

25   Balfour papers, Arnold-Forster to Balfour, 16 March 1905, Add. MSS 49723.

26   Balfour papers, Clarke to Balfour, 1 July 1905, Add. MSS 49701.

27   Arnold-Forster papers, Diary, 2 November 1905, Add. MSS 50352.

28   Gooch, *Plans of War*, pp. 62–92. Maj. Gen. John Headlam, *History of the Royal Artillery*, Royal Artillery Institution, London, 1937, II, pp. 71–6. E. M. Spiers, 'Rearming the Edwardian artillery', *Journal of the Society for Army Historical Research*, LVII, 1979, pp. 167–76.

29   Gooch, *Plans of War*, pp. 278–95; S. Williamson, *The Politics of Grand*

Strategy, Harvard, 1969; N. W. Summerton, 'The development of British military planning for a war against Germany, 1904–1914', unpublished PhD thesis, London University, 1970; Bertie, p. 249.

30   George Wyndham, 12 February, 1900, *Army Debates*, 1900, I, 1178–85; I. F. W. Beckett, 'The English Rifle Volunteer movement, 1859–1908', unpublished PhD thesis, London University, 1974, pp. 325–9.

31   For the Norfolk Commission generally see Beckett, pp. 334–9; Howard Moon, 'The invasion of the United Kingdom: public controversy and official planning, 1888–1918', unpublished PhD thesis, London University, 1968, I, pp. 197–200; M. Allison, 'The National Service issue, 1899–1914', unpublished PhD thesis, London University, 1975, pp. 1–41; Beckett, pp. 344–7.

32   Arnold-Forster papers, Diary, 22 February 1905, Add. MSS 50344.

33   Arnold-Forster papers, Diary, 12 October 1904 and 17 January 1905, Add. MSS 50340 and 50343; Arnold-Forster to Douglas, 23 December 1904, Add. MSS 50312; Balfour papers, Arnold-Forster to Balfour, 15 September 1904; Add. MSS 49722; PRO Cab. 37/74, No. 7; Arnold-Forster, 10 March 1905, *Army Debates*, 1905.

34   Arnold-Forster papers, Diary, 28 March and 14 April 1905, Add. MSS 50345 and 50346; Balfour, 3 and 5 April 1905, *Army Debates*, 1905, 898, 1076–8; Arnold-Forster papers, Diary, 5 and 6 April 1905, Add. MSS 50346.

35   Arnold-Forster papers, 'Papers relating to the origin of the circulars', Add. MSS 50312, section 23; Diary, 13 April 1905, Add. MSS 50346; PRO, Minutes of the Army Council, 13 April 1905; WO 163/10; PP 1905 [Cd 2437], XLVI, 905; Donoughmore, 4 July 1905, Seely, 5 July, and Campbell-Bannerman, 6 July, *Army Debates*, 1905, 821–3, 1873–75, 1886.

36   Correspondence between Roberts, Mackinnon and Douglas can be found in Roberts papers, NAM 7101–23 R4/61–7, and correspondence between Arnold-Forster and Douglas in Arnold-Forster papers, Add. MSS 50312, section 23 and 50. Arnold-Forster papers, Diary, July–September, 1905, *passim*, Add. MSS 50349 and 50350.

37   Reactions to the circulars can be traced in Arnold-Forster papers, Add. MSS 50312, sections 23–54, and results of the examinations in sections 27 and 28; Diary, 31 July 1905, Add. MSS 50349; Arnold-Forster to Walker, 30 October 1905, Add. MSS 50312, section 51.

38   Arnold-Forster papers, 'Correspondence with the AG', Add MSS 50312, section 50; Diary, 11 and 30 September and 19 October 1905, Add. MSS 50350 and 50351; PRO Cab. 37/80, No. 170.

39   Arnold-Forster papers, Diary, 30 September, 10 October, 2, 6, 11 and 23 November 1905, Add. MSS 50350, 50351 and 50352; Add. MSS 50312, sections 10, 11 and 17, for correspondence on the artillery experiment; PRO, 'Reorganisation of volunteer infantry brigades', WO 32/6378; Minutes of the Army Council, 19 December 1905 and 22 February 1906, WO 162/11; Arnold-Forster, *Army in 1906*, pp. 540–8.

40   Arnold-Forster papers, Diary, 16 December 1905, Add. MSS 50353.

41   Quotations from Crown copyright records in the PRO appear by permission of HM Stationery Office. For making papers available and for permission to quote the author wishes to thank the British Library Board, the National Army Museum and the Army Museums Ogilby Trust.

4

HALDANE
AND
THE 'NATIONAL ARMY'

JOHN GOOCH

In 1896 the celebrated caricaturist Spy included among his series of famous lawyers in *Vanity Fair* a study of Richard Burdon Haldane, whom he labelled 'A Hegelian Politician'. Another decade had still to pass before Haldane took up the seals of Secretary of State for War, and subsequently piloted his scheme for the reorganisation of the regular army and the creation of the Territorial army between the shoals of political and military conservatism and on to the statute book. Yet it is not too much to say that without his personality and background the 'National Army' might never have come into existence at all. The mixture of philosopher and politician was to produce a mind uniquely shaped both by principle and by expediency, and to make of Haldane a minister whose achievements at the War Office were never surpassed.

Haldane was born in Edinburgh in 1856 into a comfortable Scottish background but unlike many of his fellows did not travel south to be educated in England: he stayed in Edinburgh until his twenty-first year, attending first the Academy and then the University, where he read philosophy. During his days as an undergraduate he paid a brief visit to Germany, studying for four months at Göttingen under the metaphysician Hermann Lotze. This brief exposure to German culture was to stimulate both a profound and lasting interest in philosophy and also a respect for German methods which he afterwards voiced with vigour and conviction, and which was ultimately to cost him the Woolsack. In his later years he liked to emphasise the Hegelianism he had absorbed then, and reportedly remarked to the Army Council in 1905 that he wished to create a Hegelian army—a concept which, not unnaturally, temporarily deprived them of the powers of speech; however, it is possible that this strand of his intellect has been somewhat overemphasised, and certainly during his first visit to Germany it was Goethe, not Hegel, who captured his imagination.

Haldane graduated with first-class honours in 1876 and the following year departed for London to read for the bar, to which he was called in 1879 and from which he took silk eleven years later. The law did not provide full employment for his powerful intellect, nor did it satisfy his interests in social and educational reform, so that there was a certain inevitability about his decision to stand for East Lothian in the parliamentary elections of 1885, in which he was successful. A generous host, an entertaining guest and a man of undoubted intellectual gifts, Haldane soon became a member of a wide circle of political acquaintances which included Balfour, Asquith, Grey and Sidney and Beatrice Webb. On the eve of the great Liberal victory of 1906 he was an experienced lawyer with an outstanding record in educational issues, having taken a hand in the reform of London University, the creation of Liverpool University and the reorganisation of the Irish universities, as well as having helped to create both Imperial College and the London School of Economics.[1] It was precisely because this was not the stuff of which most of the War Office's civil masters were usually made that he was to achieve such success. That success, however, was less uniquely his own than he afterwards chose to claim; at one point, indeed, he came very close to abandoning the most important provisions of his scheme for the reserve portion of the 'National Army'. Without powerful encouragement, and the assistance of a number of young and intelligent soldiers newly brought into the War Office to speed reform, Haldane's achievements would have been no more noteworthy than those of many another occupant of what Campbell-

Bannerman liked to call 'the kailyard'.

As well as being gifted, Haldane was also fortunate—and luck plays as much a part in a war minister's reputation as in a general's. The aftermath of the Boer war had seen a series of reforms which had swept away the confused and unstructured system by means of which military advice was offered to the Cabinet, and had replaced it with the Committee of Imperial Defence as the forum where military service experts and Cabinet ministers could confer together, away from political hurly-burly and public scrutiny, on the detailed issues of imperial defence. As a result of the recommendations made by a committee on War Office reform chaired by Lord Esher, the CID was provided with a secretariat which saw to the production of papers and the keeping of minutes. The same wave of reform had produced an Army Council, dividing up the various professional responsibilities of the War Office for supply, training, planning, administration and financial control among seven members.[2] Though the system was far from perfect, it meant that Haldane had at his disposal a machine designed to provide the political head of the War Office with specialist military advice on all the various technical aspects of organising a modern army, and allowed him freedom from the pressures of a single fount of military advice in the shape of a Commander-in-Chief—a post which Esher's committee had shrewdly abolished. Haldane thus had room to manoeuvre within his administrative machine, and he used it to the utmost. He also had the CID, in which the pressing defence problems of the day might be discussed and by which authoritative policy decisions could be taken. This was to make it somewhat easier for him to relate the structure of the army to its assumed purpose.

In later life Haldane liked to claim that when he became head of the War Office, after earlier plans to send Campbell-Bannerman to the house of Lords (which meant the Foreign Office for Grey, the Exchequer for Asquith and the Lord Chancellorship for himself) had foundered on their leader's downright refusal to make the planned ascension, he knew little of military affairs and was wholly ignorant of army organisation.[3] In this he was being less than honest, for he had been appointed a member of Rayleigh's committee on smokeless propellants in May 1900, and that same September had harangued the electors of East Lothian on the necessity for reform of the War Office on the grounds that it was at present on a highly unbusinesslike footing. What was true was that he had no specific preconceived ideas about an ideal of military organisation, belonged to no recognised faction in such matters, and could adopt the useful pose of the disinterested outsider who would weigh up the rival claims of the experts before reaching his decision. Haldane was to play skilfully on this pose, with such success that he was bombarded with advice by those who thought they could exert a decisive influence on him during the time he was drawing up his scheme for the 'National Army'.

Haldane's was not the only name discussed for the War Office in the dying weeks of Balfour's government: Tweedmouth and Dilke were also mentioned as possible incumbents. However, Esher was far-sighted enough to have a long talk with him on War Office matters early in October, during which he put the Crown's objectives. After the failure of the Relugas compact he was offered the War Office on 7 December and accepted it the following day.[4] His appointment came as a surprise to many in the military world—and no doubt to not a few outside it—but his courtesy and good humour contrasted so strongly with his predecessor's uncertain temperament that he soon made a good impression; one member of the War Office noted in his diary, 'On the whole I took a great fancy at first sight to Mr. Haldane, his courteous manner was a pleasing contrast to the ways of his abrupt predecessor.'[5] He was immediately a prey to pressure, for Esher was particularly concerned to establish the machinery of the CID as an 'Imperial General Staff' and to create a proper General Staff to work under the Chief of General Staff, a post which he had devised. He accordingly arranged for the secretary of his committee, Colonel Gerald Ellison, to become Haldane's private secretary, recording jubilantly, 'Of course nothing could indicate more clearly the "nobbling" of Haldane by our Committee.'[6] Ellison went at once to Scotland and at the end of the year tutored the incoming Secretary at length on military affairs, the pair talking until late at night and walking 'backwards and forwards in a big billiard room, Mr. Haldane on one side of the table, smoking the best cigars procurable, I on the other'.[7] Esher may have miscalculated in this move: propounding his views on the development of the General Staff, he had urged that Britain could not slavishly imitate the German model, yet Ellison was already an admirer of the system developed in Germany, having attended manoeuvres there in 1888, 1889 and 1895. Esher it was who first put to Haldane the idea of a volunteer army capable of expansion in time of war.[8]

Haldane proved well capable of resisting the early pressures, both subtle and unsubtle, that people sought to bring to bear on him. His tidy legal mind appreciated the need for a brief by which to acquaint himself with the current state of affairs, and accordingly a week before Christmas he commissioned a complete survey of the army as a whole.[9] Armed with this, and appreciating the reckless manner in which Arnold-Forster had launched schemes without fully consulting his officials, leaving Pall Mall in a chaotic state, he settled down to work out the pressing questions of the day: what was the army for, and how could it be organised to meet its tasks whilst at the same time offering the Liberal Party the economies it would demand?

One of the strongest shackles which had bound Haldane's predecessors in considering the purpose for which the army existed, and therefore the organisation it should adopt, was the fear of invasion—at first from France, latterly from Germany. Haldane was the first Secretary of State for War to be offered relief from this incubus. In February 1903 a special sub-committee of the CID had been set up under the chairmanship of the Prime Minister himself to examine the likelihood of invasion, and it had soon reached the conclusion that there was no serious danger from that direction. To stand any chance of success an invading force must consist of at least 70,000 men, a force which would require 200 boats in order to undertake the twenty-hour crossing and which under ideal conditions would need at least forty-eight hours to disembark; the necessary procedures of transportation and landing offered more than sufficient time for any attempt to be completely disrupted by the action of the Royal Navy. All in all, Balfour concluded, the difficulties attendant upon such an operation were so great that it could not succeed.[10] This analysis was confirmed by experience on manoeuvres, and the official seal was set on the invasion preoccupation when, on 9 March 1905, the defences of London were officially abolished.

If there was no significant likelihood that Haldane would have to prepare an army to fight a major engagement on English soil, there were many other locations where a striking force might be required. One of the first reports made by the Director of Military Operations after Haldane's arrival indicated that, as well as possibly having to deploy a force of upwards of 100,000 men in India in the event of war with Russia, Britain might also have to deploy major forces to contend with a Boer rising in South Africa, war with France, war against Germany in alliance with France and war with the United States; in addition any one of a number of small wars might occur, including a native rising in South Africa and operations in Abyssinia, China, Lower Egypt and the Sudan. To meet these varied requirements Arnold-Forster had left behind him a force of some 90,000 men organised as one army corps and six divisions.[11] There were in addition immediate concerns which Haldane had to bear in mind when devising his new scheme of army organisation.

On 8 January 1906 the Foreign Secretary, Sir Edward Grey, had written to Haldane informing him of persistent rumours that the Germans were planning to attack France and warning him that he had better be thinking about what might be done, as Sir John Fisher already was for the navy. Four days later Grey met Haldane in Northumberland and revealed his wish that the British and French General Staffs enter into military conversations with one another to explore possible co-operation. Campbell Bannerman agreed, and on 14 January Haldane instructed the Chief of the General Staff to initiate talks with the French military attaché, General Huguet.[12] In fact he was lagging somewhat behind events, for conversations of a sort had already begun: a group of CID and service officials centred around Esher was already in contact with Huguet by the end of December, using as their intermediary Colonel Repington, the military correspondent of the *Times*.[13] It was to avoid any confusion in French minds that Grey, knowing of these approaches, had sanctioned their conversion into provisional and noncommittal talks.

In later life Haldane gave the impression that it was the Agadir crisis and its aftermath of technical staff conversations which held the key to his military reforms. Called on by Grey to consider the military implications of French proposals for such conversations (his version ran), and particularly the need to produce 100,000 men to guard the French frontiers with Belgium, he had realised that the British army was almost completely inadequate for the purpose and had accordingly initiated a complete military revolution at home. That revolution was determined by the need for an expeditionary force of sufficient size and mobilising power to be able to assist the French army in the event of an attack on the north or north-eastern parts of France.[14] Historians have subsequently fastened on Haldane's explanation of his reforms and transformed it into an orthodoxy which has been more or less unanimously accepted ever since. In a number of respects it was highly misleading.

One of the guiding principles behind Haldane's creation of a 'National Army' was economy. Campbell-Bannerman had sounded the call for financial retrenchment shortly after taking office, and it was soon clear that Haldane's first task was the reduce army Estimates below £28 millions, to satisfy his party. His first Estimates, for 1906–7, were some £1,976,000 above the line, but by the following year, thanks to some prudent financial management, he had achieved his aim. It was within this restrictive financial corset that plans for a more efficient system of military organisation had to be developed.[15] In terms of converting such aspirations into real reform of the regular army, Haldane had to take account of a strong current of opinion already existing within the War Office to the effect that Britain needed an efficient striking force which might be used anywhere. As early as July 1904 the Director of Military Operations, Sir James Grierson, had argued for flexibility in military organisation, since it was 'impossible to foretell whether our field army will be employed in India, Canada, South Africa, or elsewhere'.[16] Then in March 1905 Grierson had challenged an attempt to restrict the force available for service anywhere abroad to the three divisions of the Aldershot army corps and to equip the remaining six divisions primarily for reinforcing India on the North West Frontier. War with India was not the only operation the War Office was prepared to undertake, he remarked brusquely; it was merely the largest.[17] On the eve of Haldane's arrival the War Office had for some months been working secretly to stockpile modern equipment for all nine divisions in order to form them into the elements of a general striking force, though any active operations would have been severely hampered by the fact that there was only one set of General Mobilisation Regulations—for home defence.

The Moroccan crisis therefore demonstrated to Haldane the truth of two of the contentions that the War Office had been pressing for some months before his arrival. Firstly it demonstrated the force of Grierson's argument that the defence of India was not necessarily the call most likely to be made upon the army. The fact that in February 1906 Haldane was deeply immersed in considering a plan of campaign in the event of war with Germany, whilst three months later he was facing the possibility of having to send a division to Egypt as a consequence of the Tabah incident, underscored the truth of this point.[18] In the second place the crisis pointed up the critical defects in the existing arrangements for mobilising the army. A test carried out on 16 January demonstrated that all four cavalry brigades could be mobilised, but only two of the three army corps.

The problem of reconciling the organisation of the army with its purpose was thus thrown by chance into high relief just at the moment when Haldane entered office. The central question with regard to the regular army was posed succinctly by the Adjutant General, Sir Charles Douglas: 'Why one Army Corps [as a striking force]? For small wars it is unsuitable, for a large war it is insufficient. We should organise either in Army Corps or in divisions.'[19] Within the War Office there were a number of people who felt that in the circumstances organisation ought to be based upon a campaign in Europe as the most likely contingency to be faced, and who believed that intervention in such a campaign would have to be rapid if it was to be effective. The logical corollary of these two assumptions was that the army corps was the most suitable form of organisation for the regular army.

To challenge these two contentions there appeared the formidable figure of Sir William Nicholson, newly arrived, at Haldane's express wish, as Quartermaster General and subsequently to become the first Chief of the Imperial General Staff. Nicholson began by questioning the belief that effective intervention in Europe necessarily meant rapid mobilisation, despatch and concentration of the home army. 'History teaches us,' he argued, 'that the crises of war on a large scale do not always—I might say, do not generally—occur at the beginning of a campaign.' The idea that the primary object of Britain's military organisation was to be ready at the shortest notice to take part in a war on the Continent involved an entirely new concept of the functions of the army, one which Nicholson was not prepared to accept.

> In view of the uncertainty as to the demands likely to be made on the British army [he continued,] I am hardly prepared to admit that our war organisation should be based on one contingency only, namely, a possible intervention in a continental struggle, or that it would be wise closely to imitate the war organisation of Continental armies, the peace organisation of which is fundamentally different from that of our Regular Forces, being based on universal service, and the territorialization of units.[20]

Nicholson therefore put his weight behind a divisional organisation: divisions were more convenient and more flexible, it being easier to combine them together into corps than to reverse the process; they offered a large number of intermediate commanders if the army found itself operating large forces; and they made better provision for the varied nature of possible future military operations.

The issue was thrashed out by the Army Council, the governing administrative body, in May and June 1906, with Haldane remaining neutrally in the chair, and resolved itself into a choice between three army corps and six 'great' divisions, each of 18,000–20,00 men rather than the 10,000 of an old-style division. The majority favoured the new division as being both more suitable to the size and requirements of the army and more flexible. The argument that the corps would provide its own permanent staff, whereas combining divisions would demand an improvised staff, was not thought compelling in the light of Nicholson's assertion that it was easier to combine than to divide. The 'great' division was favoured by most members of the Army Council as being 'more flexible for tactical purposes, and also more analogous with the organisation of the Indian army'.[21] On 21 June 1906 the Army Council duly instituted the new-style division as the organisational basis of the regular army.

Haldane published his own intentions to the Cabinet some three days before the final decision on the organisation of the regular army was taken by the Army Council, and the new structure figured large in his scheme for producing an army of 150,000 men, composed as six infantry divisions and four cavalry brigades, which should all be mobilisable troops. Behind them, for purposes of expansion and home defence, were to stand the Yeomanry and Volunteers, their administration decentralised into County Associations under the leadership of Lords Lieutenant. The two elements were to make up what Haldane later referred to as a 'National Army', and their purpose was to replace an inefficient force with an efficient one: 'Broadly, the Government's proposal is that effort shall, in the future, be mainly concentrated on the production of an expeditionary force immediately available for use overseas in war, with a territorial organisation behind, capable of supporting and expanding it.'[22] The regular element had been shaped less by himself than by his professional advisers, and his calculated failure to indicate where it might be used was not a tacit admission that it had but one destination; nor was it the consequence of a push imparted by Grey to military organisation in order to ensure that Haldane's reforms produced an organisation which was 'the necessary complement to the direction which he was imparting to Britain's foreign policy.'[23] Rather it was the logical conclusion of what both Haldane's predecessors had sought to achieve, and what his professional advisers recommended. Much greater originality was to be found in the second-line Territorial force, over which Haldane's scheme nearly foundered.

By the beginning of February 1906 Haldane had publicised his idea of a territorial reserve force, managed by specially organised local associations, which would be capable with little delay of becoming an effective force with which to defend the empire should danger threaten. This was to be the germ of the Territorial army. It was, however, an instrument whose precise purpose remained shrouded in mystery. On the one hand, Haldane was wont to explain it in the first weeks in somewhat mystifying Hegelian terms: it was to be a complement to the regular army, a force not separated from the people but regarded by them as their own. On the other, it had in practical terms to replace the traditional Militia, Yeomanry and Volunteers—the former strongly entrenched in social custom and national tradition, the latter strongly entrenched in Parliament—and overcome the shortage of manpower that these two guardians manifested. There was a good practical case for reconsidering the position of the existing reserve forces, not least because of the three only the Militia had its members fixed by Parliament—in the annual Appropriation Act. Also the Militia was some 40,000 under strength in 1906, and in any case not liable for service overseas, the Volunteers 100,000 under strength and fiercely jealous of their independence at a time when their military efficiency was under attack.[24] The questions at issue were whether the new force could marry its Hegelian and pragmatic requirements, and whether it could carry the day against strongly entrenched interest groups.

To give the new proposals the seal of acceptability a special committee was set up of some four dozen prominent men, all of whom, Esher reassured the King, were by birth, political conviction and education opposed to the Liberal government and who could therefore be relied upon to countenance no reform which would diminish the authority of the

Crown over all the armed forces of the kingdom, regular or auxiliary, since they were 'opposed absolutely to anything in the shape of what is generally understood by the term "citizen army"'.[25] The committee were convinced that Haldane's idea of breaking up the Volunteers into counties would have a beneficial effect, but excluded their own force—the Militia—from this conclusion. They realised all too clearly that the proposed County Associations would be the main instruments by means of which the new force could attain an independent existence, and moved carefully to block this eventuality by securing the place of vested interests on the new bodies. Thus they recommended that the County Associations should consist of *ex officio*, elected and co-opted members—thereby denying the War Office the chance to put its own nominees into critical positions—and wanted to give the associations direct power over command and training. The resulting bodies, as both they and Haldane realised, would not differ very much from the existing reserve forces and would be every bit as independent of central control. This was not at all what Haldane had in mind. There was in addition the problem of how the new system would produce the drafts needed to support an expeditionary force in the field. In April a General Staff study demonstrated that in the first six months of European war an expeditionary force of 140,000 men would require up to 50,000 drafts, which had to be trained and ready when the striking force mobilised.[26] The survival of Haldane's scheme was ultimately to depend on how this circle could be squared, since the Territorials could never fulfil the requirement. It also depended on whether Haldane could stand up to the pressure to weaken his County Associations.

Esher's support for Haldane's proposal was crucial, and he was particularly alert to the question of the need for continual re-supply of men: in March he had reminded Campbell Bannerman of his predecessor's concern with the enormous problem of the manpower necessary for an Indian campaign and of his failure to get an army organisation which could meet it.[27] His support for the new Secretary of State was not entirely disinterested; he was himself a firm believer in the need for compulsory military service, and saw Haldane's County Associations as a means by which it might be gained. If Haldane's scheme failed, and Esher thought it might, then he could see no other way to expand the regular army to the necessary extent except conscription.[28] At the War Office, Colonel Henry Wilson also supported conscription, and found it difficult to imagine a more clumsy and unworkable scheme than the one his civilian master was now proposing, recording in his diary, 'I think Haldane will prove a greater failure than any previous War Minister unless he mends his ways.'[29]

Haldane presented his scheme for the County Associations to the Cabinet early in July, already aware of the weight of opposition against it, and was instructed to avoid committing himself to details 'as to the more speculative portions of the organisation and constitution of the County Committees' when making his statement.[30] Shortly afterwards he left for Germany to attend the summer manoeuvres, first visiting the Hotel Weimar in Marienbad so that the King could instruct him on how to comport himself. The trip was of considerable value, for as a consequence of it Haldane learned a lot about the organisation of the German army and War Office, and in the course of it he met the Chief of the General Staff, Helmuth von Moltke. Von Moltke approved of the reorganisation of the regular army into divisions which had just been effected by his guest, and strongly disclaimed any interest in a war against England. 'A war with England would be for them, as for us also,' reported Haldane, 'a fearful calamity because it could not be short, whichever won,and would mean slow exhaustion while America helped herself to the trade of both of us.'[31] Esher, who regarded Germany as the *point noir* on the European horizon and saw a conflict with her as all but inevitable, heartily disliked this and other signs of Haldane's German proclivities.

On his return Haldane began a round of dinners and speeches in which he sought to explain the merits of his Territorial army, but soon showed signs of caving in under pressure from the Volunteer commanding officers, who simply refused to be administered by the County Associations, leaving his stillborn protégés with no real financial independence and few functions beyond that of acquiring manoeuvre areas.[32] He admitted to Esher that he was not ready to make a frontal attack on the entrenched interests which stood against him over the County Associations and preferred to find a turning manoeuvre;[33] his attempt to achieve this by keeping the Militia in being in order to allow his expeditionary force to mobilise and keep the field for six months would have completely destroyed the unity of his original concept of the Territorial army.

Aware as a result of his many contacts of the pressure Haldane was under to retain the Militia and to reduce the County Associations to little more than advisory bodies, Esher came to the rescue of the original scheme. He forcefully urged Haldane to stand out against the Volunteer commanding officers and retain powerful and not emasculated County Associations; only in that way, he argued, could Douglas Haig's scheme for the Territorial army, which aimed at placing an army of 900,000 in the field after twelve months and keeping it there for five years, be realised.[34] On the eve of this exhortation Haldane had been contemplating the fact that he might have to resign, in which case he thought that Winston Churchill or Seely might succeed him. Esher's arrival at his side was decisive: three days later he had swung away from the idea of keeping the Militia in existence and back to that of giving the County Associations the financial independence they needed if they were to escape from the control of the Volunteers.[35]

Esher supported Haldane's original scheme because he too was searching for a turning movement; in his case, however, the target was not the Volunteers but the whole idea of a voluntary system of military organisation. He wished by this means to complement the head-on attack being mounted by Lord Roberts and his supporters on the voluntary system, and their attempts to introduce conscription. Should the County Association fail to produce an adequate volunteer army, Esher argued, 'they would be the most likely machinery to be accepted by the English people, for turning out a compulsory Army'.[36]

Professional support for Haldane's scheme was clearly essential if the Volunteers were to be outmanoeuvred. An idea first mooted by Repington in September that a committee of generals be formed to give the scheme professional backing was now revived. The committee, chaired by Esher, and consisting of General Sir Neville Lyttelton (Chief of the General Staff), Major General Spencer Ewart (Director of Military Operations), General Sir John French (commanding the Aldershot army corps), and Sir George Clarke (secretary of the CID), set to work on 28 November to find arguments to support Haldane's scheme. It very nearly foundered on the central weakness of that scheme, one of which Haldane's critics were keenly aware: that there was no way in which the territorial force envisaged could produce the drafts necessary to sustain the expeditionary force during the first six months in which it was at war. This crucial dilemma was resolved by Ewart, who suggested retaining the Militia depots as seventy-four reserve battalion cadres, which could on mobilisation becomedraft-producing battalions for the regular army. The idea was clearly put to the committee in a very diplomatic form: Haldane later wrote, 'The effect of General Ewart's suggestion about carrying to its completion Cardwell's scheme of a third battalion has worked like magic with the generals.'[37] This was the germ of the 'Special Reserve', the third element in Haldane's 'National Army', and the one which saved his scheme—and helped to confound Esher's. The sub-committee then quickly approved the scheme for County Associations and the Territorial force as 'a practical test of the limits of the voluntary system'.[38] It was presented to the Cabinet on 21 December 1906, and at once gained the approbation of Campbell-Bannerman and Morley. The greatest obstacle had been overcome.

Haldane presented the details of his Bill on 4 March 1907, having sagaciously prepared the way two weeks earlier by presenting army Estimates on which a saving of £2,036,000 had been effected. Clarke, who favoured the continued existence of the Militia, expected the new associations to meet with success in some counties, failure in others, and difficulties in all.[39] He wrote before he heard Haldane's presentation of his case in the Commons, and was unaware of the care with which Haldane and his advisers had devised a scheme which reconciled military efficiency with democratic control. The key lay in the new role perceived for the Territorial forces: instead of producing drafts for service overseas, their function was now switched to that of home defence. The defects of the existing system of reserves were confronted boldly. 'We realised,' said Haldane, 'that the state of things in the Auxiliary Forces was such that no one who had the military military interests of the country at heart could be really content with it, and we saw that a great transition into another state of things would be necessary if the Auxiliary Forces were to be put upon a satisfactory footing.'[40] He then unveiled a system of County Associations over the membership of which the Army Council was to have large discretionary powers, and which would have nothing to do with command or training, which was to be directed from the War Office in conformity with the most up-to-date policies and doctrine. The Army Council would appoint to the associations representatives from the county councils, borough councils and universities—something to which a democratic House could scarcely object—and Haldane made it quite plain that the government expected the traditional leaders of county society to fall in line, remarking that in future Deputy Lieutenants would be chosen only from among those who had 'done good work in the organisation of the local forces of the country'. He was careful to reassure the House that it would exercise direct control over the calling out of the new Territorial forces, since it would have to vote the necessary money, and he repeatedly emphasised the primary purpose of the new force as the defence of Britain's shores.

Esher clearly sensed defeat in the new organisation, for he soon took steps to counteract a voluntary system, suggesting to Lord Roberts that a secret fund be set up to pay writers and lecturers to support compulsion 'with an appearance of independence'.[41] However, residual political opposition was rapidly scotched by the King, who called all the Lords Lieutenant to Buckingham Palace on 21 October and instructed them to throw their weight behind the scheme; and the opposition of the compulsory service lobby was stripped of any force when the second invasion inquiry—which Roberts and Repington had worked to stimulate—found that there was no danger of invasion coming as a 'Bolt from the Blue', and added that two of the six regular divisions should stay behind if the expeditionary force was despatched overseas until such time as the Territorial forces were fit to guard against raids in their stead.[42] This finding was confirmed by a third invasion inquiry in 1913.

There remained one possible threat to Haldane's 'National Army'.

Focus was sharpening on Continental military action, and Ewart for one felt that the liability to undertake military operations in Belgium represented one of the most serious calls that could be made on the resources of the empire. There was thus some opposition within the War Office to money being given to a stay-at-home force, the Territorials, when Britain's greatest need was for a striking force and its supports.[43] The radical wing of the Liberal Party would never have countenanced any increase or change in military expenditure for this purpose, and some feared that the radicals—led by Lloyd George, Churchill and McKenna—might cut the regulars and boost the 'comparatively useless' Territorial Army. The strategic problem disappeared in 1909, when a special sub-committee of the CID concluded that, subject to Cabinet approval at the time, four divisions of the regular army would go to the French left wing in the event of a war between France and Germany, regardless of whether or not Belgian neutrality had been violated. At the same time it established the conviction that the early land battles would be critical, thereby placing a premium on rapid arrival rather than on overwhelming numbers over a longer period of time.[44] A week before the final meeting of the sub-committee which reached this crucial decision, Haldane had become convinced of what, after the Great War, he was to give the impression of always having believed: that the expeditionary force must be organised to support France and Russia against Germany and perhaps against Austria.[45]

As well as presiding over the creation of his 'National Army', Haldane had other tasks to attend to, of which perhaps the most important was the need to complete the work done by Esher's War Office (Reconstitution) Committee in 1904 by creating a General Staff. Esher had created the post of Chief of the General Staff and had selected Sir Neville Lyttleton as the first incumbent—an unfortunate choice, as he lacked drive. Arnold-Forster had begun to move towards completing this aspect of Esher's work before his departure, but further work was necessary—in which the leading parts were taken by Esher, Haig, Ellison, Nicholson and Edward VII himself—before the Army Order published on 12 September 1906 established the new body and confirmed its place in army organisation. Towards the end of his life Haldane was prone to take the lion's share of the credit for this innovation, but in reality he depended heavily on the work of the professional advisers—as he had in bringing into being the 'National Army'. The best summary of his role was given later by Repington: 'Pieces of the framework of a General Staff had been juxtaposed awaiting the arrival of someone to fit them together.'[46] Haldane grasped the opportunity, with the help and advice of others.

At the Colonial Conference of 1909 Haldane extended the new body by creating an Imperial General Staff, though he was careful to emphasise that local primacy would be maintained in regard to the educational programmes undertaken and the solutions devised to overcome local defence problems. This reflected an interest in imperial organisation which Haldane maintained until the war, though its anti-centralist tone created considerable opposition; Milner recorded of a speech by Haldane on the matter that it was 'all *blather*'.[47] His later suggestion to Asquith that the Imperial General Staff might provide a basis on which to remodel the entire system of Dominion and imperial relations was far too optimistic, and the loose framework of the Imperial General Staff never amounted to very much.

Haldane also did much work on the numerous sub-committees spawned by the CID; one such body he chaired in 1909 looked into the problem of foreign espionage and directly resulted in the formation of a counter-espionage section in what was then M.O.5, so that he can claim to have been a founder of the Security Intelligence Service. In the same year he sat on another sub-committee to judge the merits of the rival parties in the dispute between Admiral Sir John Fisher, First Sea Lord, and Admiral Lord Charles Beresford, then commanding the Channel Fleet. Allegations of incompetence and professional misconduct flew in all directions, but the outcome was a vindication of Fisher in all respects but one: Haldane had a large hand in the committee's conclusion that Fisher's refusal to create a naval General Staff on the lines of that established at the War Office was an oversight which must at once be remedied. It was probably this experience which prompted Haldane to make the extremely far-sighted suggestion that a Minister of Defence be created to oversee both services, though two world wars would be necessary before that lesson was driven home.

By 1909 the strain of Haldane's demanding life was beginning to tell. He was having trouble with his sight, which severely restricted his work at the War Office, and it was discovered that he had developed diabetes, which necessitated a strict diet—something of a penance for a man of Haldane's interests, but one which he bore with fortitude. In his last two years at the War Office focus sharpened on the likelihood of war alongside France and against Germany, and at the celebrated meeting of the CID on 23 August 1911 when Sir Henry Wilson revealed the army's plans to transport as many divisions of the expeditionary force as possible to the French left wing in the event of war, Haldane followed his professional advisers in rejecting the navy's unconvincing plans for a close blockade of the German North Sea coast and major combined operations against Heligoland. He was also under increasing pressure from Sir Henry Wilson to support an alliance with France in the specific case of German aggression, pressure which he resisted because it would mean introducing conscription and might drive Turkey into the arms of the Triple Alliance.[48]

In 1911 Haldane had been given a peerage so that he could support the government in the Lords while the Marquess of Crewe was in India. In July of the following year the sudden illness of Lord Loreburn offered him the place he had originally sought: he was swiftly created Lord Chancellor and replaced at the War Office by Colonel Jack Seely. In the first days of August 1914 he returned briefly to his old post to relieve Asquith—who had temporarily taken over in the aftermath of the Curragh affair—of some of his burdens, and after only a few days made one of the most unfortunate suggestions of his career in urging that Kitchener go to the War Office in his stead. Already, however, Haldane's well known liking for Germany was affecting his public position. In September 1914 he offered his resignation. It was refused, and the following January Asquith briefly put his former colleague on the War Council, but public pressure proved too strong and on 26 May 1915 Haldane was jettisoned by Asquith, with some reluctance. He at once filled his time with legal work in the appeal courts and also chaired a Royal Commission on the University of Wales, but his domestic circumstances were distressing: he had constantly to be shadowed by detectives, threats were made on his life, and on at least one occasion his pro-German record resulted in his being physically assaulted in the street. The war's end saw a recurrence of his diabetes and a growing disenchantment with the wreckage of the Liberal Party, which he left to serve as Lord Chancellor in the first Labour government of 1924. He continued his work in education to the last, and died on 19 August 1928.

Haldane's military reputation rests chiefly on the twin pillars of the expeditionary force and the Territorial army. He effected his reforms with little in the way of active political support from either of the two Prime Ministers he served, which perhaps made his task easier than that of his immediate predecessors, who had had to cope with Balfour's widely recognised expertise in defence questions; Campbell-Bannerman never discussed Haldane's reforms with him, but did advise him to give whatever credit was going to the soldiers and never to be seen to be making capital for himself, 'In short, to be as unlike his two predecessors as he can.' [49] He was undoubtedly fortunate in having the services of a group of highly able subordinates at the War Office: Grierson, Ewart, Haig and Ellison all played important roles in his success, and formed part of an imaginative and fertile caucus over which Haldane presided with urbanity and wisdom. When war came in 1914, one part of his 'National Army'—the British Expeditionary Force—proved capable of meeting conditions no one had foreseen with accuracy. That more use was not made of its partner, the

Territorial Army, was Kitchener's fault. His epitaph was provided by the undergraduates of Bristol University who pulled his cab through the streets of the city in 1920. 'Who saved England?' they cried. 'Haldane!'

Notes

Material from the Royal Archives appears by gracious permission of HM the Queen.

1   Eric Ashby and Mary Anderson, *Portrait of Haldane*, Macmillan, London, 1974, pp. 53–7, 60–8.
2   John Gooch, *The Plans of War: the General Staff and British Military Strategy* c. *1900–1916*, Routledge & Kegan Paul, London, 1974, pp. 32–61.
3   E. Haldane (ed.), *Richard Burdon Haldane: an Autobiography*, Hodder & Stoughton, London, 1929, p. 183.
4   British Library [hereafter BL], Haldane to Campbell Bannerman, 8 December 1905, Add MSS 41218. Haldane's own version was that he was not offered the War Ministry until 17 December: *An Autobiography*, pp. 173–81. But see also *Journals and Letters of Reginald, Viscount Esher*, Nicholson & Watson, London, 1934–38, II, p. 126; and National Library of Scotland [hereafter NLS], Esher to Haldane, 9 December 1905, MS 5906.
5   Ewart diary, 13 December 1905. See also A. C. Pedley, *Notes on the Days that are Passed, 1877–1927*, pp. 113–15, War Office Library, A.011.1; and N. G. Lyttelton, *Eighty Years: Soldiering, Politics, Games*, Hodder & Stoughton, London, 1927, p. 276.
6   *Journals and Letters*, II, p. 126.
7   *Lancashire Lad: Journal of the Loyal Regiment*, LV, p. 8. See also L. S. Amery, *My Political Life*, Hutchinson, London, 1953, I, p. 212.
8   Esher papers, Esher to Haldane, 19 December 1905, 'War Office Reconstitution Committee, 1903–5'.
9   NLS, Haldane to Rosebery, 19 December 1905, MS 5906.
10   'Draft report on the possibilities of serious invasion: Home Defence', 11 November 1903, Cab. 3/1/18A.
11   Robertson papers, 'Memorandum upon Military Forces required for Over-Sea Warfare', 4 January 1906, Liddell Hart Centre for Military Archives, King's College, London, I/2/6.
12   NLS, Grey to Haldane, 8 January 1906, MS 5907. Haldane to Grey, 17 January 1906, FO 800/102. Sanderson to Grierson, 15 January 1906, *British Documents on the Origins of the War*, III, No. 214.
13   Notes on conferences held at 2 Whitehall Gardens on 19 December, 6, 12 and 19 January 1906. Cab. 18/24.
14   R. B. Haldane, first Viscount Haldane of Cloan, *Before the War*, Cassell, London, 1920, pp. 29–33, 151; *An Autobiography*, p. 187.
15   Edward M. Spiers, *Haldane: an army Reformer*, Edinburgh University Press, 1980, p. 73.
16   Minute, Grierson to Lyttelton, 30 July 1904, WO 32/526/79/186.
17   Minute, Grierson to Stopford, 16 March 1905, WO 32/527/79/396.
18   Ewart diary, 28 February and 9 May 1906.
19   Minute, Douglas to Lyttelton, 16 March 1906, WO 32/1043/79/1000.
20   Minute, Nicholson to Lyttelton, 22 March 1906, *ibid*.
21   Army Council Précis No. 278: Proposed divisional Organization of Troops at Home, June 1906, p. 58, WO 163/11.
22   'Notes on the organization and administration of the military forces of the United Kingdom', 18 June 1906, p. 2, Cab. 3/1/38A.

23   A. J. A. Morris, 'Haldane's army reforms, 1906–8: the deception of the Radicals', *History*, LVI, 1971, p. 18.

24   H. Gordon, *The War Office*, Putnam, London, 1935, pp. 87–90.

25   *Journals and Letters*, II, pp. 167–8.

26   'Wastage in War', 26 April 1906, WO 32/8813. Cited in D. W. French, 'Some aspects of social and economic planning for war in Great Britain *c.* 1905–1915', unpublished PhD thesis, London University, 1978, p. 29.

27   Esher papers, Esher to Campbell Bannerman, 1 March 1906, 'Letters and Memoranda, vol. I, 1895–1906'.

28   Royal Archives, Esher to Knollys, 9 June and 30 September 1906, W 40/31, 58. Kitchener papers, Esher to Kitchener, 16 August 1906, PRO 30/57/33.

29   Wilson diary, 12 March, 1906.

30   BL, Campbell-Bannerman to Edward VII, 7 July 1906, Add. MSS 52512. Wilson diary, 19 June 1906.

31   Royal Archives, Memorandum, 2 September 1906, W 49/100.

32   Esher papers, Lucas to Esher, 16 October 1906, 'Army Letters, Vol. IV'.

33   Esher papers, Haldane to Esher, 18 October 1906, *ibid.*

34   Esher to Haldane, 19 October 1906, *Journals and Letters*, II, p. 196.

35   Esher papers, Lucas to Esher, 22 October 1906, 'Army Letters, vol. IV'.

36   Esher papers, Esher to Repington, 6 October 1906, 'Letters and Memoranda, vol. I, 1895–1906'.

37   Ewart diary, 10 December 1906. BL, Haldane to Campbell Bannerman, 9 January 1907, Add. MSS 41218.

38   'Report of a Sub-committee appointed by the Prime Minister to consider the scheme of military organization proposed by the Secretary of State for War', 14 December 1906, p. 7, Cab. 3/2/4/55A.

39   BL, Clarke to Balfour, 1 March 1907, Add. MSS 49702.

40   Hansard, fourth series, CLXX, 4 March 1907, c. 506.

41   Roberts papers, Esher to Roberts, 28 August 1907, box X, 20930/R.29.15.

42   'Invasion: Report of a Sub-committee . . . to reconsider the question of oversea attack', 22 October 1908, Cab. 3/2/44A.

43   'Our position as regards the Low Countries', 8 April 1907, Cab. 18/24. Ewart diary, 26 October 1907.

44   'Report of the Sub-committee . . . on the Military Needs of the Empire', 24 July 1909, Cab. 4/3/1/109B.

45   NLS Haig diary, 18 February 1909, H.2.I.

46   C. aC. Repington, *Vestigia*, Constable, London, 1919, p. 259. Robbins displays considerable confusion in asserting that Haldane 'continued to develop his army council into a General Staff': K. G. Robbins, *Sir Edward Grey: a Biography of Lord Grey of Falloden*, Cassell, London, 1971, p. 178. The two had quite separate existences, linked only by the fact that the Chief of the General Staff was one of the seven members of the Army Council.

47   Milner to Amery, 11 February 1907; quoted in A. M. Gollin, *Proconsul in Politics*, Blond, London, 1964, p. 133. See also J. E. Kendle, *The Colonial and Imperial Conferences, 1887–1911: a Study in Imperial Organization*, Longmans, London, 1967, p. 158.

48   Wilson diary, 6 and 9 May 1912.

49   BL, Campbell-Bannerman to Haliburton, 27 February 1906, Add. MSS 41218.

5

KITCHENER AND THE EXPANSION OF THE ARMY

PETER SIMKINS

When, on 4 August 1914, Britain became directly involved in a general European conflict for the first time in nearly a hundred years, the higher direction of the War Office was subject to a curious form of divided responsibility. Since the resignation of J. E. B. Seely at the end of March that year, over his mishandling of the Curragh incident, Asquith had deferred the appointment of a new Secretary of State for War, combining the office with that of Prime Minister. As war approached, however, it was clear that the overall burdens of government would leave him with little opportunity to attend to the War Office. 'It was quite impossible for me to go on, now that war is actually in being,' he told Venetia Stanley, on 5

August; 'it requires the undivided time and thought of any man to do the job properly, and as you know I hate scamped work.'[1]

His first instinct was to entrust to Haldane, then Lord Chancellor, the task of supervising the military machinery which the latter had largely constructed and best understood. 'I am finishing my judicial work tomorrow,' Haldane informed his sister on 3 August, 'and then take over the war office—remaining chancellor and Asquith remaining war minister and delegating the work to me.'[2] In the event this makeshift solution was stillborn. Haldane's return to the War Office provoked an immediate, if unjustified, outburst in the press, the *Daily Express* declaring on 5 August, 'This is no time for elderly doctrinaire lawyers with German sympathies to play at soldiers.'[3] As Grey later observed, it was suggested that Haldane's known interest in German philosophy must make him pro-German, while his earlier work at the War Office, though admired by his Cabinet colleagues and soldiers alike, 'was not in the knowledge of, or at any rate not present to, the public mind'.[4]

The outcry against Haldane was accompanied by a rising chorus of demands for the appointment to the War Office of Field Marshal Earl Kitchener of Khartoum, who was in England on leave and whose name, by 1914, stood as a symbol of victory and achievement. Born near Listowel in County Kerry on 24 June 1850, Horatio Herbert Kitchener had passed out of the Royal Military Academy at Woolwich in December 1870, having qualified creditably, but without distinction, for a commission in the Royal Engineers. After several years of survey duties in Palestine and Cyprus he joined the Egyptian Army in 1883, attracting wider notice for his reconnaissance and intelligence work during the Gordon relief expedition of 1884–85. Then, following two years as Governor General of the Eastern Sudan, he became first Adjutant General of the Egyptian Army, and then in 1892, Sirdar. Kitchener transformed the Egyptian Army into an effective fighting force, and his period of command culminated in the reconquest of the Sudan and the victory of Omdurman in 1898. His next appointment, as Governor General of the Sudan, lasted less than a year, as in December 1899 he was sent to South Africa as Chief of Staff to Lord Roberts, succeeding him as Commander-in-Chief in South Africa in November 1900. If, as in the Sudan, his successes stemmed more from careful planning and an ability to solve problems of transport and supply than from any real tactical flair, his policy of attrition eventually wore down Boer resistance and he played a conciliatory role in the subsequent peace settlement.

As Commander-in-Chief in India from 1902 to 1909 he became embroiled in a protracted quarrel with the Viceroy, Lord Curzon, over the system of dual control by which the Military Member of the Viceroy's

Council had come to assume an authority which challenged that of the Commander-in-Chief. In forcing Curzon's resignation on this issue Kitchener not only re-established the supremacy of the Commander-in-Chief but confirmed his own power and influence into the bargain. Nevertheless he also introduced a series of overdue reforms in India, including the organisation and grouping of standardised divisions to meet the threat of external aggression rather than that of internal rebellion. In addition, he modernised training, improved the mobilisation machinery and stimulated military education by setting up a staff college. On leaving India he embarked on a tour of the Far East, Australasia and the United States, during which he advised the governments of Australia and New Zealand on their respective defence organisations. He accepted the post of British Agent in Egypt in 1911, devoting his term of office there to social reforms and the development of the Egyptian and Sudanese economies.

Impressive as his record was, Kitchener had shortcomings which grew more pronounced as his career flourished. His intolerance of opposition and interference, his seemingly infinite capacity for work and his inherent inability to delegate responsibility all caused him to disregard normal procedures and to act as his own Chief of Staff and military secretary. Rawlinson noted after the battle of the Atbara in 1898, 'He is an absolute autocrat, does exactly what he pleases, and won't pay any attention to red-tape regulations, or to the keeping of records of telegrams and letters.' [5] This tendency to over-centralise was nurtured by years of independent command on the frontiers of the empire and Kitchener had always avoided entering the War Office, preferring appointments in which his personal authority could be more freely exercised. Having spent most of his life abroad, he was ignorant of conditions at home. 'I don't know Europe; I don't know England, and I don't know the British Army,' he once confessed to Sir Edward Carson.[6] However, while his autocratic leanings mattered relatively little in the context of a limited and independent field command, they created considerable difficulties when he was called upon to serve within the framework of a highly organised administration.

Despite these weaknesses Kitchener could offer the government a priceless asset in August 1914. As one of his biographers has commented, he inspired the British people 'with a confidence which the strenuous attempts of three administrations to effect a root-and-branch reform of the Army failed to impart between 1902 and 1914'.[7] On 3 August, as Kitchener was preparing to return to Egypt, the military correspondent of the *Times* spoke for many when he urged the nomination of a Secretary of State for War whose time was not fully occupied with other affairs, pointing out that 'Lord Kitchener is at home, and his selection for this onerous and important post would meet with warm public approval'.[8] J. A.

Spender of the *Westminster Gazette* felt obliged to convey to 'the proper
quarter' the warning that, should Kitchener be allowed to depart, 'there
would tomorrow be such an uproar against the Government as had not
been known in our time'.[9]

At this stage Asquith still favoured Haldane for the War Office and in
recalling Kitchener from Dover merely explained to him that 'with matters
in their present critical position, I was anxious that you should not get
beyond the reach of personal consultation and advice'.[10] The prospect of
Kitchener at the War Office was, indeed, viewed with misgivings on both
sides. On 4 August Kitchener asked Asquith 'if there is any objection now
to my making arrangements to leave for Egypt on the P. & O. next
Friday',[11] while Haldane told Sir Ian Hamilton that he had taken over the
War Office himself rather than let Kitchener have it.[12] Even so, by 5
August Asquith and Haldane were convinced that Kitchener's appointment
would guarantee public support for the Cabinet and that as a soldier he
would give the government a non-party element at a time when national
unity was vital. Walter Runciman, the President of the Board of Trade,
observed that Asquith no doubt foresaw 'the political convenience of
having the unattackable K. at the War Office and at his board'.[13]
Accordingly, on 5 August, Kitchener was persuaded to accept the post.
Asquith recorded that 'K. was, to do him justice, not at all anxious to come
in, but when it was presented to him as a duty he agreed', adding, 'It is a
hazardous experiment, but the best in the circumstances, I think.'[14]
Kitchener's feelings were reflected in his remark to Sir Percy Girouard:
'May God preserve me from the politicians.'[15] In contrast, most people
greeted the news with relief. Asquith's daughter later wrote that 'The
psychological effect of his appointment, the tonic to public confidence,
were instantaneous and overwhelming.'[16]

Initially Kitchener dominated a Cabinet which was prepared to hand
over to him almost total responsibility for the conduct of the war. He at
once assumed a place in the Cabinet hierarchy second only to the Prime
Minister, his position being underlined by the fact that he sat next to
Asquith at Cabinet meetings.[17] In the words of Lloyd George, who, as
Chancellor of the Exchequer, had himself been Asquith's principal
lieutenant up to the outbreak of war;

> In 1914 he was practically military dictator and his decisions upon
> any questions affecting the war were final. The Members of the
> Cabinet were frankly intimidated by his presence because of his repute
> and his enormous influence amongst all classes of the people outside.
> A word from him was decisive and no one dared to challenge it at a
> Cabinet meeting.[18]

With Asquith and Churchill, the First Lord of the Admiralty, Kitchener formed part of a triumvirate which few in the Cabinet felt disposed to question. Kitchener and Asquith enjoyed a special relationship, for Kitchener needed the Prime Minister's guidance in political matters and Asquith relied heavily on Kitchener's military judgement. As Balfour wrote to Bonar Law on 26 September 1914, 'I doubt whether he [Asquith] possesses any influence with either K. or Churchill in military matters, or whether, if he does possess such influence, he would care to exert it.'[19]

Unfortunately, Kitchener was fundamentally ill suited to the Cabinet system of government. Accustomed to making his own decisions, he was not attuned to the concept of collective responsibility. Lloyd George wrote that 'His main idea at the Council table was to tell the politicians as little as possible of what was going on and get back to his desk at the War Office as quickly as he could decently escape'.[20] Kitchener's in-built distrust of politicians was increased by the suspicion, not without foundation, that his colleagues could not keep secrets. 'I cannot tell them everything,' he told Sir Maurice Hankey in September 1915, 'because they are so leaky . . . If they will only all divorce their wives I will tell them everything!'[21] As a result Kitchener tended to evade or block questions in Cabinet. Charles Hobhouse, the Postmaster General until May 1915, described him as 'quite remarkably astute and untruthful, in all matters big and small',[22] and Alfred Emmott, the First Commissioner of Works, wrote in his diary, 'He is never frank and tells lies if he does not want to tell at all.'[23]

Signs of disenchantment began to show themselves in the Cabinet only a few weeks after he took office. On 28 September 1914 Lloyd George clashed with him on the question of sending Nonconformist chaplains to the front, and a month later the two men had 'a royal row' over the formation and status of the proposed Welsh Army Corps, a project dear to the heart of Lloyd George.[24] The latter felt it necessary to remind Kitchener he was not a dictator and that 'he was only one among 19, and must stand criticism in the same way as any other member of the Cabinet'.[25] Asquith had fewer reservations, and his faith in Kitchener remained firm at this time. 'My own opinion of K.'s capacity increases daily,' he wrote on 3 November. 'I think he is a really fine soldier, and he keeps his head and temper, and above all his equability wonderfully, considering how all three are tried.'[26] Asquith's talents as a mediator and Kitchener's willingness to concede minor points papered over the cracks of discord for a while, even causing Lloyd George to admit that Kitchener was 'a big man'.[27] On the other hand, Kitchener revealed growing impatience when he remarked to Sir Edward Grey, 'I am afraid I cannot go on if the army that has to fight is to be run as a political machine.'[28]

His consistent hostility to any form of extra-departmental interference lay at the root of the struggle he waged with Lloyd George over the question of munitions production. At the outbreak of war responsibility for the supply of munitions to the army rested with the Master General of the Ordnance, one of the four military members of the Army Council. Kitchener himself had quickly recognised the need for a substantial increase in munitions output but seemed unable to comprehend that, in an age of mass armies, any large-scale expansion involved factors, such as the mobilisation of manufacturing resources and the distribution of labour, which transcended the bounds of War Office authority. His reluctance to accept alternative administrative machinery for the direction and supervision of munitions production hampered efforts to find an early solution to these broader problems and limited the ability of industry to respond in full to the demands of modern war. In refusing to take his political colleagues into his confidence on this key issue Kitchener weakened his own position in the Cabinet and helped undermine the credibility of the government when the extent of the shell shortage became more widely known in the spring of 1915.

The grip which Kitchener maintained on the national imagination was reflected in the indignant public reaction to the attacks made on him during the 'Shells Scandal' campaign in the Northcliffe press, and enabled him to survive the formation of a coalition government, and the creation of a separate Ministry of Munitions under Lloyd George, in May 1915. However, the removal from the War Office of control over munitions production showed how far Kitchener had slipped from the lofty pinnacle he had occupied in the Cabinet in the opening months of the war. The new Cabinet was a cumbersome and divided body, depicted by L. S. Amery as 'little more than a debating society in which everybody differed, and in which nothing was ever definitely decided until events forced some sort of decision'.[29] Lacking experience in the cut and thrust of debate, Kitchener was ill at ease in such a setting. Herbert Samuel portrayed the clashes between Lloyd George and Kitchener, for example, as being 'like a fight between the nimble swordfish and the massive whale'.[30] Kitchener could no longer command unquestioning support for his decisions and was now increasingly liable to judgement and criticism simply as a member of a team.

The failure of offensive operations in the Dardanelles and on the western front in the summer and autumn of 1915 reduced his credit with the Cabinet even further. On 17 October 1915 Asquith warned Kitchener of a plot by Curzon, Lloyd George and others to drive a wedge between them and oust Kitchener from office. 'So long as you and I stand together,' he wrote, 'we carry the whole country with us. Otherwise, the Deluge!'[31] Matters were brought to a head by Lloyd George, who, on 31 October, sent a long letter to Asquith, criticising Kitchener for not taking adequate steps to meet the Austro-German invasion of Serbia, and attributing the setbacks in France to Kitchener's mismanagement of the munitions problem. He threatened to raise these issues in the Cabinet and predicted that 'the moment these facts are told in the House of Commons I have very little doubt what will be thought and said by all sections'.[32] A crisis was averted by despatching Kitchener to the Dardanelles to report on the situation there, with Asquith taking charge of the War Office while he was gone. 'We avoid by this method of procedure the immediate superession of K. as War Minister, while attaining the same result,' Asquith explained to Lloyd George on 3 November.[33]

Even at this point no one in the Cabinet was willing to grasp the nettle of public disapproval by openly demanding Kitchener's removal. Sir George Riddell, the newspaper proprietor, noted in his diary on 30 November, 'If K. resigns the Government will be much weakened in the country. The people implicity believe in K. and distrust the politicians.'[34] All the same, advantage was taken of Kitchener's absence to knock away most of the remaining props of his power. Having already taken over the four Royal Ordnance Factories in August, Lloyd George now secured the transfer of the Ordnance Board and its entire research and development establishment to the Ministry of Munitions, thus leaving the War Office with few duties in this sphere save those of fixing army requirements in munitions and overseeing their distribution. During November the ground was also prepared for the subsequent appointment of Sir William Robertson as Chief of the Imperial General Staff and the one authoritative channel through which the government received all advice on military operations. Not for the first time, Kitchener was persuaded to stay in office by an appeal to his sense of duty, but while he continued to provide the government with a facade of unity until his death in June 1916 his real authority was now confined solely to War Offiice administration, recruiting and supply. Kitchener's considerable reputation had prompted the Cabinet in 1914 to allow him to bear an almost crushing weight of responsibility. Apart from assuming the routine burdens of his department, he also undertook to raise, equip and train the biggest army Britain had ever put into the field; to direct the expansion of munitions production; and to supervise the conduct of British military operations in all theatres. These extended powers rested on shaky foundations, as they were delegated to Kitchener personally and informally by the Cabinet and were largely undefined. Since the new authority of the Secretary of State for War was uniquely dependent upon Kitchener's individual prestige, the lessening of his influence in the Cabinet meant that, by the end of 1915, the office itself had declined to a status not unlike that of the old Secretary at War.

In many respects the load placed on Kitchener's shoulders in 1914 disclosed the unpreparedness of the government for the type of conflict it now faced. In November 1914 a special Cabinet committee was set up to review the strategic situation as a whole. This body, known as the War Council, comprised the Prime Minister, the Chancellor of the Exchequer, the Secretaries of State for War, India and Foreign Affairs, and the First Lord of the Admiralty. Balfour, a member of the opposition, was brought in because of his long service on the Commitee of Imperial Defence, and the CIGS and First Sea Lord also attended regularly. Within four months its membership had grown to thirteen and the previous disadvantages of having too large a directing body therefore recurred. After the formation of the coalition government the War Council gave way, in June 1915, to the Dardanelles Committee, which included five ministers from the earlier Cabinet as well as five Conservatives and the professional heads of the services. The Dardanelles Committee, initially intended to deal with operations in that theatre, was gradually drawn into considering broader stategic issues. By October 1915 this body, like its predecessor, was too big and it was replaced the following month by a five-man War Committee, though the latter once again subsequently increased in size. In each case the trend towards self-enlargement defeated the original purpose of such committees, while the retention of ultimate authority by the full Cabinet robbed them of executive power.

The problems surrounding the central direction of the war effort were compounded by the fact that Kitchener was the senior field-marshal in employment. His military rank confused his relations with his professional advisers and the commanders in the field and made it harder for him to provide that link of mutual interpretation between the Cabinet and the army which normally came from having a politician as Secretary of State for War. Some of these problems might have been eased had Kitchener made more use of the machinery at his disposal, but he made little effort to adapt his style of administration to his new circumstances. He entered the War Office both ignorant of, and prejudiced against, its organisation. Lord Midleton, himself a former Secretary of State for War, found in 1914 that 'Kitchener condemned the system adopted in 1904 . . . and ignored the new Board'.[35] Haldane too remarked to Sir Almeric Fitzroy on 9 August 1914 that Kitchener had 'some difficulty in recognising that he has not to begin the organisation of the army *de novo*, but merely takes over a highly perfected system, which he is asked to make the best of'[36] At the same time his long-standing indifference to established procedures caused severe administrative headaches, and Asquith noted with concern on 12 August 1914 that 'Lord K. has rather demoralised the War Office with his bull in the china shop manners and methods'.[37] An interesting sketch of his administrative weaknesses has been left by Orlo Williams, who worked at the War office as a civilian for seven months in 1914 and 1915:

> He [Kitchener] *was* the War Office, and all the vital decisions emanated from the Secretary of State's own room, often in the form of autograph telegrams written in pencil on pieces of notepaper. Also, when one of these autograph telegrams was sent, its circulation within the War Office was extremely limited, with the result that important executive branches were often in the dark as to the policy in which they were involved'[38]

In view of Kitchener's tendency to concentrate authority in his own hands it was perhaps not surprising that the Army Council and General Staff were permitted to drift into abeyance. He rarely saw his principal advisers as a body and it therefore became virtually impossible for them to present him with a firm collective opinion. By neglecting such help as the General Staff could offer, Kitchener only fostered the growth of a system in which political considerations and the suggestions of amateur strategists outweighed professional counsel. This state of affairs was made worse by the departure to France of most of the leading members of the General Staff at the outbreak of war, thus robbing the War Office of many of its abler figures. Sir Charles Douglas, who remained as CIGS, was described by Lord Esher as a conscientious but unimaginative soldier, although Esher himself hardly inspired resistance to the Secretary of State's methods when he reminded Douglas and others that Kitchener 'has been given by the Government absolute authority, and there is really nothing more to be said'.[39] Douglas died of overwork in October 1914 and was succeeded by Sir James Wolfe Murray, an officer whose unsuitability for the post was illustrated by his own admission that he sometimes left meetings of the War Council 'with a very indistinct idea of any decision having been arrived at all'.[40] Asked by the Commission of Inquiry into the Dardanelles in 1917 whether he had ever assembled sufficient information to form a judgement on that venture, he replied:

> I had not, I could have got it no doubt; but Lord Kitchener was a man who had a very overwhelming personality, we will say, and was a man of very great experience, and it did not appear to me that he, having, so to speak, taken the whole thing and working on it almost entirely himself, to be necessary or desirable that I should interfere.[41]

The Dardanelles Commissioners observed that, at meetings of the War Council, the military experts did not consider it their duty to express an opinion unless asked to do so, or to intimate dissent if they disagreed with the views set forth by their minister.[42] This lack of strong professional advice was reflected all too clearly in the irresolute handling of the Dardanelles campaign, which led, in turn, to a reassessment of the position and functions of the General Staff during the latter half of 1915. On 22

September 1915, at a meeting from which Kitchener was absent, the Cabinet decided that the General Staff at home must be reinforced. Asquith wrote to Kitchener to convey the unanimous feeling of his political colleagues that 'it has become essential that both you yourself, and the Government, should have the best intelligence that the Army can supply for our common purpose'.[43] Sir Archibald Murray became CIGS on 25 September and at once gave the General Staff a stronger voice, presaging the strategy adopted in 1916 with his arguments that the western front was the decisive theatre of war. His brief tenure of the post was, however, overshadowed by the failure of the Loos offensive and the deteriorating situation in the Dardanelles. Sir William Robertson's appointment as CIGS in December 1915 confirmed the revival of the General Staff, for as a condition of taking office he insisted that the CIGS should henceforth become the Cabinet's only source of advice on military operations. Although Kitchener retained constitutional authority for the army, he was shorn of responsibility as to how and where it should be employed. Contrary to expectations, Robertson and Kitchener worked together in comparative harmony during the last six months of the Secretary of State's life. Having at last accepted the need for sound professional advice, Kitchener not only avoided interfering in strategy but gave Robertson his full backing in the Cabinet and War Committee.

As Secretary of State for War Kitchener did not directly instigate any basic shift in Britain's strategic orientation. When he entered the War Office the British Expeditionary Force was already committed to serving in France, and the war on the western front rapidly took on a form which was to endure until 1918 and which Kitchener himself could do little to influence. From the outset he maintained that Britain must stand firm alongside France. Where Kitchener differed from most of his political and military colleagues was in his estimate that the war would last at least three years and that British military strength could not be fully deployed until 1917. Although, in the meantime, he was determined to hold the Entente together and avoid defeat, he was opposed to the launching of great offensives in the west before the British armies in France and Flanders were capable of striking a decisive blow. Certainly he could not be said to have played a leading part in initiating alternative strategic ventures. As a recent study has underlined, when confronted by strong poltical demands for the Dardanelles scheme Kitchener 'was prepared to accept it and then try to justify it afterwards'.[44] In fact the irresolution which he exhibited over the entire campaign only emphasised the narrowness of his strategic ability and experience.

It was in convincing the British government and people that they must prepare for a long struggle, and in providing the necessary impetus for the mobilisation of national resources, that Kitchener made his most profound contribution to the war effort. He was almost alone among Britain's principal soldiers and statesmen in predicting that the war would be a prolonged and costly affair. This was no sudden 'flash of instinct', as Grey has implied,[45] for in the autumn of 1911 Kitchener had told Esher that a general conflict would only be ended and victory achieved by 'the last million' of men that Britain could throw into the scales.[46] The strength of the army on mobilisation, including the Regular Reserve, the Special Reserve and the Territorial Force, barely reached a total of 700,000 men. Kitchener rightly viewed the existing military organisation as wholly inadequate for anything other than a war of limited liability, and on becoming Secretary of State he took immediate steps to expand the army. On 7 August 1914, some twenty-four hours after he had installed himself at the War Office, parliamentary approval was given for an initial increase of 500,000 men and, the same day, Kitchener outlined his proposals to the Cabinet. Declaring that the war could not be won solely by the exercise of sea power, he insisted that Britain must be ready to place armies of millions in the field and to sustain them there for several years.[47] As Kitchener later admitted, the plan for the expansion of the army was, at this point, 'rough-hewn' in his mind, but he aimed to create:

> ... such a force as would enable us continuously to reinforce our troops in the field by fresh divisions, and thus assist our Allies at the time when they were beginning to feel the strain of the war with its attendant casualties. By this means we planned to work on the up-grade while our Allies' forces decreased, so that at the conclusive period of the war we should have the maximum trained fighting army this country could produce.[48]

Basing his calculations on a war lasting three years, Kitchener intended to build a series of new armies, complete in all their branches. He announced in the House of Lords on 25 August that 'The scale of the Field Army which we are now calling into being is large and may rise in the course of the next six or seven months to a total of thirty divisions continually maintained in the field'.[49] This meant, as he explained on 17 September, four new armies in addition to the original expeditionary force.[50] By the summer of 1915 the pressure of events had caused the gradual upward revision of this target to a total of seventy divisions.

Bowing to Asquith's judgement that the introduction of conscription would have a divisive effect upon the nation, Kitchener resolved to raise his new formations by voluntary enlistment, expanding the regular army through the Adjutant General's department of the War Office rather than through the County Associations which recruited and administered the Territorial Force. It was more than symbolic that the First New Army was

originally termed the 'New Expeditionary Force'.[51] Kitchener's decision to
by-pass the Territorial organisation was undoubtedly dictated partly by
prejudice against non-professional soldiers. Grey reported that he called it
a 'Town Clerk's Army'.[52] 'I prefer men who know nothing to those who
have been taught a smattering of the wrong thing,' Kitchener once told
Violet Asquith,[53] and on his first morning as Secretary of State he informed
Sir Charles Harris, the Assistant Financial Secretary at the War Office,
that he 'could take no account of anything but Regular soldiers'.[54]

There were, however, more solid grounds for his reluctance to use the
framework offered by the County Associations. The Territorial force had
been created mainly for home defence, and although Haldane had
envisaged its potential as a basis for expansion and as a reserve for the field
if the need arose, there was no statutory obligation for its members to fight
overseas. The actual strength of the force on mobilisation was some 62,000
below establishment,[55] and its degree of training fell far short of the ideal. In
1913, for instance, only 76 per cent of its officers and 66 per cent of its
other ranks had attended annual camp for the full period of a fortnight.[56]
The force had to recruit up to establishment and train the new men before it
could properly perform its primary role in home defence, let alone supply
reinforcements for the BEF. In the early weeks of the war, therefore, it was
by no means clear how much Kitchener could rely on the Territorials. If
they were swamped by masses of raw recruits it was reasonable to assume
that they might be rendered temporarily incapable of carrying out any
function at all. The military correspondent of the *Times* pointed out the
dangers on 11 August 1914, when he forecast that it would take months
for Kitchener's new units to become efficient. 'It will not be advisable,' he
said, 'in any way to diminish the value of our Reserve or Territorial
formations for the benefit of a force which will take so long to create.'[57]

Kitchener's serious reservations about the Territorial Force, appear to
have been short-lived. As early as 13 August Esher recorded that 'He
realises that he will be forced to make use of the Territorials for foreign
service, while his new armies are in course of formation; of course, he
knows nothing of the organisation of our home armies, but he is learning'.[58]
On 9 August the military members of the Army Council registered
Kitchener's decision that if any Territorial units volunteered *en bloc* for
service abroad their offer would be accepted.[59] By 25 August Kitchener
was able to state that over seventy battalions had so volunteered.[60] Two
weeks later it was proposed to duplicate all Territorial battalions in which
60 per cent of the strength had undertaken to serve overseas, and on 21
September the County Associations were authorised to form second-line
Territorial units for every battalion accepted for foreign service. In
November instructions were issued that when a unit proceeded abroad and

was replaced at home by a second-line unit, a third-line formation should be raised, thus releasing even second-line battalions for the front. By the end of 1914 twenty-three Territorial battalions had gone to the western front, while three divisions left for India and one for Egypt to replace regular units on garrison duty. In all, 318 Territorial battalions saw front-line or garrison service abroad during the war, as against 404 of the battalions raised for Kitchener's own new armies.[61] The statistical evidence alone gives the lie to criticisms that Kitchener neglected the Territorial force. His policy allowed it not only to retain its place in the home defence structure but also to reinforce the BEF at a critical juncture in 1914–15; by the same token, it also had the less desirable result of permitting two organisations to exist side by side, with all the waste and dispersal of effort that this implied.

On 7 August 1914 the newspapers carried Kitchener's first appeal for 'an addition of 100,000 men to His Majesty's Regular Army, in view of the present grave National Emergency'.[62] The men who answered the call were to enlist for three years or the duration of the war. The appeal was followed on 11 August by details of the proposed organisation of the First New Army. The six regional commands in Britain were each to provide a complete infantry division by raising at least one battalion for grafting on to every line regiment.[63] The new 'Service' battalions, as they were called, were numbered consecutively after existing units of the parent regiment. By the time the Third New Army came into existence in the second week of September, however, the territorial basis for the new divisions was being abandoned. The great reserves of manpower were in the northern and Midland cities and in London, not in Ireland or the rural areas. Ultimately the four counties of the industrial north supplied nearly one-third of all service battalions to be raised.

The wave of national support which had swept Kitchener into the War Office revealed itself again in the enormous numbers of volunteers who flocked into the recruiting stations in the autumn of 1914. By the beginning of September 1914 some 30,000 men were daily being attested,[64] a figure which represented the average *yearly* intake before the war, and the rapidly swelling ranks of the new armies soon began to pay the price for Kitchener's failure to impose some sort of ceiling on enlistments until the recruiting machinery and the resources of the regimental depots were able to cope with the flood of volunteers. Indiscriminate recruiting had serious long-term effects on industry, for the many skilled men who joined the army in 1914 could not easily be replaced later in the war. In the short term the new armies themselves suffered from acute shortages of accommodation, clothing and weapons.

Kitchener began to lose control of the situation at an early stage. In the first days of September 1914 he agreed to a scheme of deferred enlistment under which recruits, once attested, would remain at work and would receive 6*d* a day until the army was ready to take them. Unfortunately, no attempt seems to have been made to announce this change in the press, and many who had given up their jobs to enlist found themselves unemployed and with only a meagre subsistence allowance. Parliamentary pressure compelled Asquith to raise this allowance to 3*s* a day on 10 September,[65] whereupon recruits streamed in almost as fast as ever in some areas. At first Kitchener had hesitated to intervene, telling Sir Stanley von Donop, the Master General of the Ordnance, 'I have held up my finger, and the men are flocking to me in thousands; how can I hold up my hand, and tell them to go back?'[66] On 11 September, however, the War Office tried to stem the flood by raising the height standard for recruits to 5 ft 6 in. The measure gave the impression that the government felt free to pick and choose men and might not need so many recruits as it had originally suggested. Despite the subsequent reduction of the height standard to 5 ft 3 in., the recruiting figures never again approached the high-water mark of early September 1914.

The extent to which Kitchener was forced to call upon civilian help in the raising of the new armies was another indication of War Office impotence in the face of the recruiting flood. He was only too pleased to accept offers of assistance from members of Parliament, local authorities and leading citizens who, throughout the country, and acting in his name, lent or hired halls to house bigger recruiting offices, assembled doctors and clerks to handle the thousands of volunteers, and arranged to accommodate and feed the men while the regimental depots were over-strained. The most remarkable manifestation of this surge of civilian effort lay in the formation of the 'Pals' battalions, largely raised by the mayors and corporations of large cities and towns or by self appointed committees of local dignitaries and industrialists. Lord Derby, who raised some of the first 'Pals' battalions in Liverpool towards the end of August 1914, is generally credited with the idea of their formation, but in fact the concept appears to have originated in the War Office. On 12 August, twelve days before Derby approached Kitchener with his scheme, Sir Henry Rawlinson, then Director of Recruiting, proposed the formation in London of a Service battalion of the Royal Fusiliers from among 'City employees who would be willing to enlist if they were assured that they would serve with their friends.'[67] Recruiting began on 21 August, and six days later the Stockbrokers' Battalion, as it was popularly known, was 1,600 strong. The 'Pals' idea struck a responsive chord in all levels of British society, and 145 such battalions had been raised by October 1915. If one includes Territorial battalions recruited under the County Associations, as many as

643 of the 993 infantry battalions formed during Kitchener's term of office were raised outside the direct War Office recruiting channels.[68]

Men joining 'Pals' units were often much better off during the difficult period of adjustment to army life than those who enlisted in the first three new armies, as they were permitted to live at home and report daily while their training camps were being prepared. The local raisers were also given considerable latitude in other matters, such as the selection of officers.[69] The local committees similarly bore the responsibility for housing, feeding and clothing their recruits until the War Office could take them over. The expenses incurred were later refunded, mostly in the summer of 1915, but at least one raising committee in Durham declined the War Office allowance of over £10,000.[70] In this sense many 'Pals' battalions were virtually private citizen armies for several months.

The housing of the new armies was one of the biggest problems which the War Office had to solve. At the beginning of the war there was only sufficient accommodation in barracks for 174,800 men.[71] Large numbers of troops were placed for a time under canvas or in schools and hired buildings. Kitchener was not always sympathetic towards the overcrowded recruits, and on one occasion complained to Asquith that 'the damned fools of doctors were always insisting on ridiculous allowances of cubic space'.[72] The War Office drew up a programme for the construction of hutted camps to house 850,000, but bad weather and labour troubles delayed its completion until well into 1915. When the weather deteriorated in the late autumn of 1914 conditions in the tented camps became intolerable, causing at least 800,000 men to be billeted on the civilian population for the winter.[73] Here too the raisers of 'Pals' units enjoyed certain advantages, for they could make use of local government machinery to get camps built near by. Unlike the War Office, they knew local conditions and contractors and could more closely regulate the work involved.[74]

Nowhere was the inadequacy of pre-war calculations more apparent than in the sphere of munitions. In August 1914 the output of the Royal Ordnance Factories, and of the few private firms which handled government contracts, was tailored to the concept of a short war. Scant provision had been made to meet demands other than those arising from the need to sustain the BEF in a campaign expected to last a few months at most. The armaments industry was unable to produce more than 6,000 rifles a month, and when the army had been supplied on mobilisation there remained a reserve of only 150,000 to meet both the wastage of the BEF and the requirements of the new formations. The artillery situation was equally grave. In August there were enough guns for eight divisions, with a small reserve for wastage, while the production of shells for the four main types of gun then in use barely exceeded 30,000 rounds a month.[75] On 17 September Kitchener informed the House of Lords that the chief difficulty facing the new armies was already 'one of *matériel* rather than *personnel*'.[76] In the opening week of the war contracts had been placed for arms and equipment for the first six Kitchener divisions, but the War Office, geared to the administration of a small army, was not yet capable of grappling with this problem in detail. On 12 October the Cabinet Committee on Munitions was formed, and by the end of the month it had sanctioned huge expenditure to subsidise the expansion of munitions firms and had begun to check the unrestricted enlistment of skilled workmen. These measures laid the foundation for an adequate future organisation, yet they inevitably took some months to show any appreciable results.

If the moment was ripe in May 1915 for industrial mobilisation on the lines advocated by Lloyd George, it is doubtful whether this could have been successfully implemented in the previous autumn. The policy of expanding production through the existing armaments firms had much to commend it in the first weeks of the war, because these firms alone had experience of munitions manufacture. Ordinary engineering firms could not take up such work overnight, and it was to a major extent the knowledge of shell-making which they picked up as sub-contractors that later helped them to organise their own resources on a wider and more independent basis under the Ministry of Munitions. The shortages of ammunition in the spring of 1915 were brought about by arrears of deliveries rather than lack of orders. The real achievement of the War Office was the creation of capacity to meet the thirty division standard laid down in 1914, and the results of its labours are more fairly measured by the supply position in December 1915 than in May that year. Between December 1914 and December 1915 the output of small-arms ammunition increased tenfold, and the production of shells rose from 871,700 to 23,663,186. Even in May 1915 the War Office was obtaining in three days the amount of ammunition normally produced in one year in time of peace.[77] These increases would almost certainly have been greater if Kitchener had not fought for so long to keep munitions production under War Office control, yet, given the problems he had inherited, the figures were not unimpressive.

As the country entered the second year of the conflict the mobilisation of manpower again became a dominant issue. In June 1915 enlistments in the army dropped to under 100,000 a month for the first time since the beginning of the war, and the enormous losses on the fighting fronts led to a revival of the arguments in favour of conscription. In general, the army and Conservatives advocated conscription while the Liberals and organised labour opposed it, although a few Liberals, including Lloyd George and Churchill, favoured compulsory military service and some Conservatives resisted its introduction. Asquith, whose main concern was to maintain the unity of the Cabinet and the country, was loath to back conscription until he was satisfied that there was a universal demand for the replacement of the voluntary system. In this situation the conscriptionists regarded Kitchener's support as vital, believing that if he promoted the idea of compulsory service the nation would accept it. During the summer of 1915 he refrained from providing a clear lead. He was not against conscription in principle but felt that it was still too early to institute such a policy. Apart from his loyalty to Asquith, he was also convinced that a vast influx of conscripts in 1916 would use up all the reserves of men before the underlying problems of trench warfare had been solved, and he wished to keep enough men in hand for Britain to deliver the decisive blow at the right time.

Asquith temporarily removed the sting from the controversy by forming a War Policy Committee under Lord Crewe to investigate the need for compulsory military service, and Kitchener was asked to give evidence on 22 August 1915 concerning the army's manpower requirements. He objected to oral interrogation and told Asquith that he would be obliged to resign if this method were enforced.[78] Asquith persuaded him to change his mind, and Kitchener met the committee on 24 August. He conceded that he could not expand the army to the new seventy division standard by voluntary means alone and indicated that he would demand a conscription Bill by the end of the year but wished to see the figures produced by the National Register before deciding. He regretted the raising of the question at this juncture, as he had intended to wait for the moment when a conscription Bill could be presented to Parliament on a non-party basis.[79]

The National Register had been taken on 15 August with the object of affording the government a more precise picture of Britain's resources of manpower, and subsequently showed that 2,179,231 single men of military age were still not in the forces.[80] The Conservatives felt sufficiently emboldened by this, and by Kitchener's attitude, to press the matter. On 15 September Lord Selborne made a fresh attempt to enlist Kitchener's support, giving a thinly veiled hint that his credibility with both the officers and the rank and file of the army depended on his coming out strongly in favour of conscription and cautioning him that 'if they think that you delay too long to ask for it, there will be a serious revulsion in their feelings towards you'.[81] Kitchener stuck to his position, replying, 'I daresay notwithstanding the delay the army will trust me to do my best for them whatever that is worth.'[82]

The number of casualties incurred at Loos caused him to shift his posture over the next two weeks. On 8 October Kitchener presented the Cabinet with a memorandum which began with the admission that voluntary recruiting was breaking down. He noted that even to keep existing units at strength would require some 35,000 recruits a week, a figure now far above the actual weekly average. He proposed a scheme combining voluntary and compulsory service, by which the War Office would allot to each district a quota of men to be recruited by a certain date; should voluntary enlistments fall short of this quota, the balance would be raised by a ballot of the remaining eligible men of military age.[83]

Both sides rejected Kitchener's proposals as unwieldy and impracticable and, with the unity of the Cabinet dissolving, Asquith prevailed upon him to make one last effort to save the voluntary principle by calling in Lord Derby as Director General of Recruiting to administer a scheme under which all men between eighteen and forty-one were asked to attest their willingness to serve when summoned. The attested men would be divided into two groups, married and single, each subdivided into twenty-three classes according to age. Classes were to be called up in order, the youngest single men before the older, and bachelors before married men. Those working in key or 'starred' industries would be exempt from military service. The choice of Lord Derby demonstrated Asquith's political adroitness, for Derby himself was a supporter of conscription and if the scheme failed to produce the necessary recruits Asquith could justly claim that the voluntary system had been found wanting. Initially the Derby scheme seemed to be a success, as the opportunity it provided for men to volunteer without an immediate obligation for service led 2,829,263 to attest by 15 December. However, when the returns were analysed its defects became more evident. Anticipating that they would be called up last of all, the married men attested in larger numbers than the bachelors, and, of some 1,489,000 single men not in 'starred' occupations, over 650,000 had apparently failed to register.[84]

Meanwhile other events had conspired to push the country further along the road to compulsory service. On 6 December the Inter-Allied Military Conference at Chantilly recommended that in 1916 the Austro-German armies should be attacked with maximum forces in the main theatres of war and that, pending such attacks, powers such as Britain which still possessed reserves of manpower should embark on vigorous action to wear down the enemy. In the same month the government finally agreed to evacuate the forces from Gallipoli, while the appointment of Robertson as CIGS swung British strategic counsels resolutely towards concentration on the western front. The opponents of conscription in the Cabinet were driven to alter their tactics and now contended that the size of the field army should be fixed at fifty-seven divisions in order to avoid placing an undue strain on vital industries and the country's financial resources. These arguments were curtly refuted by Kitchener, who exclaimed to Haig,

'When one looks at the streets full of loafers, and sees the extravagance going on in all Departments of Government, their statements are given the lie.'[85]

The first Military Service Bill, which established the principle of conscription, was placed before Parliament on 5 January 1916, cleared both Houses by large majorities and became law on 27 January. It compelled the attestation of all unmarried men and childless widowers between eighteen and forty-one, exempting those engaged on important war work, sole supports of dependants, the unfit and approved conscientious objectors. Liberal anti-conscriptionists were partly appeased by the formation of a Cabinet committee to examine the competing military and economic factors surrounding compulsory service. This committee reported early in February that the army should have a target of sixty-two divisions in the field by the end of June, with three months' reserve, and that the needs of home defence should be met by five divisions without reserves. It was felt that this could be achieved without industrial disaster, 'though not without grave dislocation of industry, and even some risk'.[86] These recommendations were basically in accord with the views of the War Office,[87] and subsequently received Cabinet approval.

Nevertheless, recruiting returns were still insufficient to maintain the army at the newly agreed size or to furnish replacements for the casualties expected in the summer offensive. Exemptions were being granted too liberally by the local tribunals set up under the Act: between 1 March 1916 and 31 March 1917 779,936 men were exempted, whereas only 371,500 were compulsorily enlisted.[88] In March 1916 the War Office had to call up the younger married groups who had attested under the Derby scheme, provoking protests in the press that such men should not be sent to the front when the nation's resources in single men had not been fully exploited. The call was now for total conscription and equality of sacrifice, and as a new Cabinet crisis loomed the War Office again came to occupy a central position in the debate.

Robertson backed the demand for universal conscription but Kitchener, for a time, held to his own belief that the unattested married men should be kept back until 1917. He shrewdly remarked to Esher that 'if Robertson and Haig feel unduly strong they may embark upon enterprises that will eat up all our available reserves, and ... next year when the French are exhausted we shall find ourselves in a similar dilemma'.[89] To his credit, Robertson refused to allow the conscriptionists to use these differences of opinion to force Kitchener from office, although he continued to air his personal views. On 21 March he reminded the Cabinet of the critical manpower situation, noting that the current recruiting figures were barely capable of meeting normal wastage on the western front and offered no reserve capacity for major operations or for other theatres. 'We cannot expect to secure a favourable peace without hard fighting,' he proclaimed, 'and that means heavy losses which we must be prepared to suffer and replace.'[90] Kitchener was by now aware that his influence in the country and with the army would completely disappear if he withheld his support any longer and agreed to a proposal that the Army Council should prepare a paper confirming the arguments of the CIGS. In this paper, circulated to the Cabinet on 6 April, the Army Council warned of potential disaster unless every able-bodied man who was not required for industry could be made available to the army.[91] For different reasons, Kitchener and Robertson at last presented a united front on the question of universal compulsory service, and Asquith could do nothing to water down their demands. A new Military Service Act, extending liability for service to all men between the ages of eighteen and forty-one, received the royal assent on 25 May. Britain had finally recognised that her long tradition of voluntary enlistment was no answer to the challenges of modern war.

A fortnight later Kitchener himself was dead. Having accepted an invitation to head a mission to Russia to investigate questions of military and financial co-operation, he sailed from Scapa Flow in the cruiser HMS *Hampshire* at 4.45 p.m. on 5 June. Shortly before 8 p.m. the *Hampshire* struck a mine off the Orkneys and sank within fifteen minutes. Kitchener was not among the handful of survivors. His death came less than a month before the ranks of his new armies were decimated in the slaughter of the first day of the Somme. It was appropriate that these new armies popularly bore Kitchener's name, for it was his foresight and energy in the first weeks of the war that had planted the seed from which they grew. His conviction that the war would last at least three years had caused the British government and people to revise most of their earlier ideas about the scale on which the national resources should be mobilised to meet the situation. Moreover the shortages of military manpower in 1918 appear, in retrospect, to underline the wisdom of his belief that these resources, once mobilised, should be husbanded until the decisive blow could be administered.

However, if Kitchener had visualised the end, he did not always prove so successful in organising the means. Lloyd George compared him with 'one of those revolving lighthouses which radiate momentary gleams of revealing light far out into the surrounding gloom and then suddenly relapse into complete darkness'.[92] Leo Amery aptly described him as 'a great improviser, but also a great disorganiser'.[93] The problems involved in expanding the munitions industry were undoubtedly exacerbated by his reluctance to relinquish War Office control, while his delay in backing universal conscription only added to the difficulties of planning ahead and establishing the necessary machinery for the systematic marshalling of manpower reserves. For all his faults, the inspiration he gave in 1914 at least enabled the British people to create a vastly expanded army despite the previous deficiencies in experience and preparation, but, in the final analysis, it was essentially a *national* effort. Without the overwhelming support and enthusiasm of the majority of the population no administration could have raised nearly two and a half million men for the army by purely voluntary methods in less than seventeen months from the outbreak of war.

Notes

1   Asquith to Venetia Stanley, 5 August 1914, Montagu papers.
2   Haldane to his sister, 3 August 1914, R. B. Haldane papers, NLS MS 6012.
3   *Daily Express*, 5 August 1914.
4   Viscount Grey of Fallodon, *Twenty-five Years, 1892–1916*, Hodder & Stoughton, London, 1925, II, p. 68.
5   Major General Sir Frederick Maurice, *The Life of General Lord Rawlinson of Trent*, Cassell, London, 1928, p. 34.
6   Ian Colvin, *The Life of Lord Carson*, Gollancz, London, 1936, III, p. 79.
7   Sir Philip Magnus, *Kitchener: Portrait of an Imperialist*, Murray, London, 1958, p. 175.
8   *The Times*, 3 August 1914.
9   J. A. Spender, *Life, Journalism and Politics*, Cassell, London, 1927, II, p. 63.
10   Asquith to Kitchener, 3 August 1914, Kitchener papers, PRO 30/57/76.
11   Kitchener to Asquith, 4 August 1914, Kitchener papers, PRO 30/57/76.
12   Ian B. M. Hamilton, *The Happy Warrior: a Life of General Sir Ian Hamilton*, Cassell, London, 1966, p. 266.
13   Runciman to Sir Robert Chalmers, 7 February 1915, Runciman papers.
14   H. H. Asquith, *Memories and Reflections, 1852–1927*, Cassell, London, 1928, II, p. 24.
15   Girouard to Austen Chamberlain, 9 December 1929, Chamberlain papers, AC 14/2/6.
16   Violet Bonham Carter, *Winston Churchill as I Knew Him*, Eyre & Spottiswoode and Collins, London, 1965, p. 316.
17   Edward David (ed.), *Inside Asquith's Cabinet: from the Diaries of Charles Hobhouse*, Murray, London, 1977, p. 229.
18   David Lloyd George, *War Memoirs*, Nicholson & Watson, London, 1933–36, I, p. 499.
19   Balfour to Bonar Law, 26 September 1914, Balfour papers, BL Add. MSS 49693.
20   Lloyd George, *War Memoirs*, I, p. 76.
21   Lord Hankey, *The Supreme Command, 1914–1918*, Allen & Unwin, London, 1961, I, p. 221.
22   David (ed.), *Inside Asquith's Cabinet*, p. 231.
23   Emmott diary, 13 June 1915, Emmott papers.
24   Asquith, *Memories and Reflections*, II, p. 47.
25   A. J. P. Taylor (ed.), *Lloyd George: a Diary by Frances Stevenson*, Hutchinson, London, 1971, p. 7.
26   Asquith to Venetia Stanley, 3 November 1914, Montagu papers.
27   Asquith, *Memories and Reflections*, II, p. 48.
28   Kitchener to Grey, 28 October 1914, Grey papers, PRO FO 800/12.

29   L. S. Amery, *My Political Life*, Hutchinson, London, 1953, II, p. 67.

30   Viscount Samuel, *Memoirs*, Cresset, London, 1945, p. 118.

31   Asquith to Kitchener, 17 October 1915, Kitchener papers, PRO 30/57/76.

32   Lloyd George, *War Memoirs*, pp. 514–18.

33   Asquith to Lloyd George, 3 November 1915, Lloyd George papers, Beav. Lib. B.L.Ll.G. D/18/2/12.

34   Lord Riddell, *War Diary*, Nicholson & Watson, London, 1933, p. 140.

35   The Earl of Midleton, *Records and Reactions, 1856–1939*, Murray, London, 1939, p. 156.

36   Sir Almeric Fitzroy, *Memoirs*, Hutchinson, London, 1927, II, p. 564.

37   Asquith to Venetia Stanley, 12 August 1914, Montagu papers.

38   Orlo Williams, 'The War Office from the inside', *National Review*, July 1919, pp. 735–6.

39   M. V. Brett and Viscount Esher (ed.), *Journals and Letters of Reginald Viscount Esher*, Nicholson & Watson, London 1934–38, III, p. 178.

40   Dardanelles Commission, Minutes of Evidence, q. 2648, Cab. 19/33.

41   *Ibid.*, q. 2605, Cab. 19/33.

42   Dardanelles Commission, *First Report*, HMSO, London, 1917, Cd 8490, p. 10.

43   Asquith to Kitchener, 23 September 1915, Kitchener papers, PRO 30/57/76.

44   John Gooch, *The Plans of War: the General Staff and British Military Strategy* c. *1900–1916*, Routledge & Kegan Paul, London, 1974, p. 312.

45   Grey, *Twenty-five Years*, II, p. 69.

46   Viscount Esher, 'Lord K.', *National Review*, July 1916, p. 686.

47   Winston S. Churchill, *The World Crisis, 1911–1914*, Thornton Butterworth, London, 1923, p. 235.

48   Speech to members of Parliament, 2 June 1916. The whole text is given in Sir George Arthur, *Life of Lord Kitchener*, Macmillan, London, 1920, III, pp. 326–42.

49   *Debates on Army Affairs, House of Lords, Session 1914*, HMSO, London, 1915, c. 453.

50   *Ibid.*, c. 488.

51   Minutes of Meetings of the Military Members of the Army Council, 9 August 1914, WO 163/44.

52   Grey, *Twenty-five Years*, II, p. 68.

53   Violet Bonham Carter, *Churchill as I Knew Him*, p. 319.

54   Sir Charles Harris, letter to *The Times*, 28 August 1928.

55   *General Annual Reports on the British Army: 1 October 1913 to 30 September 1919*, PP 1921, Cd 1193, XX, p. 473.

56   *The Annual Return of the Territorial Force for the Year 1913*, PP 1914, Cd 7254, LII, p. 412.

57   *The Times*, 11 August 1914.

58   Brett and Esher (ed.), *Journals and Letters*, III, pp. 177–8.

59   Minutes of Meetings of the Military Members of the Army Council, 9 August 1914, WO 163/44.

60   *Army Debates, House of Lords, Session 1914*, c. 452.

61   These figures have been compiled from the details given in Major A. F.Becke, *History of the Great War: Order of Battle of Divisions*, Parts *1 to 4*, HMSO, London, 1935–45; and Brigadier E. A. James, *British Regiments, 1914–1918*, Samson, London, 1978.

62   *The Times*, 7 August 1914.

63   Minutes of Proceedings of the Army Council, 1914: 11 August 1914, WO 163/21.

64   This figure is taken from the daily recruiting returns submitted to the Adjutant General for the period 4 August to 27 December 1914: Adjutant

General's papers, WO 162/3.

65 *Parliamentary Debates, House of Commons, 1914*, LXVI, c. 668.

66 Speech by Sir Stanley von Donop to the Kitchener Scholars' Association, 5 December 1930, Von Donop papers, IWM 69/74/1.

67 H. C. O'Neill, *The Royal Fusiliers in the Great War*, Heinemann, London, 1922, pp. 9–10.

68 Becke, *Order of Battle of Divisions, Parts 1 to 4*; James, *British Regiments*, pp. 42–118.

69 Sir Montagu Barlow (ed.), *The Lancashire Fusiliers: the Roll of Honour of the Salford Brigade*, Sherratt & Hughes, London, 1919, p. 27.

70 Lieutenant Colonel W. D. Lowe, *War History of the 18th (S.) Battalion Durham Light Infantry*, Oxford University Press, London, 1920, p. 13.

71 'Supply Services During the War (August, 1914, to March, 1919)': note by the Quartermaster General to the Forces, *Statistics of the Military Effort of the British Empire during the Great War, 1914–1920*, HMSO, London, 1922, p. 833.

72 Asquith, *Memories and Reflections*, II, p. 32.

73 *Statistics of the Military Effort of the British Empire*, p. 833.

74 Barlow (ed.), *The Roll of Honour of the Salford Brigade*, p. 27.

75 Brigadier General Sir James E. Edmonds, *Military Operations: France and Belgium, 1914*, Macmillan, London, 1925, II, pp. 11–17.

76 *Army Debates, House of Lords*, 1914, c. 489.

77 *Statistics of the Military Effort of the British Empire*, p. 477; *History of the Ministry of Munitions, Volume I, Part I*, HMSO, London, 1922, appendices III and IV, pp. 146–50.

78 Kitchener to Asquith, 22 August 1915, Kitchener papers, PRO 30/57/76.

79 Kitchener's evidence to the War Policy Committee, 24 August 1915, Cabinet papers, Cab. 37/133/10.

80 Figure given in the *Report on Recruiting by the Earl of Derby, Director-General of Recruiting*, PP 1916, Cd 8149, XXXIX, p. 519.

81 Selborne to Kitchener, 15 September 1915, Selborne papers, 80.

82 Kitchener to Selborne, 17 September 1915, *ibid.*

83 Memorandum on 'Recruiting for the Army', 8 October 1915, WO 159/4.

84 Lord Derby, *Report on Recruiting*, PP 1916, Cd 8149, XXXIX, p. 519.

85 Kitchener to Haig, 14 January 1916, Kitchener papers, PRO 30/57/53.

86 Report of the Cabinet Committee on the Co-ordination of Military and Financial Effort, 4 February 1916, Cabinet papers, Cab. 37/142/11.

87 Note by Kitchener on the report of the Cabinet Committee, 7 February 1916, Cabinet papers, Cab. 37/142/17.

88 *Statistics of the Military Effort of the British Empire*, p. 367.

89 Brett and Esher (ed.), *Journals and Letters*, IV, p. 17.

90 Memorandum by Robertson, 21 March 1916, Robertson papers, KCL 1/11.

91 Army Council memorandum, 6 April 1916, Chamberlain papers, AC 19/1/36.

92 Lloyd George, *War Memoirs*, II, p. 751.

93 Amery, *My Political Life*, II, p. 23.

6

LESLIE HORE-BELISHA AT THE WAR OFFICE

BRIAN BOND

When Neville Chamberlain succeeded Stanley Baldwin as Prime Minister in May 1937 he rather surprisingly promoted Duff Cooper to the Admiralty and replaced him with the successful Minister of Transport, Leslie Hore-Belisha. Chamberlain clearly expected the latter, who was energetic, ambitious and only forty-three years old, to shake the War Office out of its notorious inertia and conservatism, but there is also evidence to suggest that he expected Hore-Belisha would be a more suitable instrument than the rebellious Duff Cooper to implement the government's 'limited liability' role for the army.[1]

The army had suffered even more than the other two services from the 'locust years' following the first world war, and it received the lowest priority when a cautious programme of rearmament began in the mid-1930s. When Hore-Belisha entered the War Office the army's fortunes were at their nadir: its role was uncertain, its equipment mostly obsolete, and its production base almost non-existent. Perhaps worst of all was the atmosphere of pessimism and despondency which was beginning to affect even the more progressive-minded officers and would-be reformers. Consequently, despite the handicaps of being a Jew and having a military record lacking in social distinction (Hore-Belisha had attained the rank of major in the Royal Army Service Corps in the first world war), the advent of this dynamic personality to the War Office on 28 May was widely welcomed. For example, General Ironside, newly appointed to Eastern Command, noted in his diary on 29 May, 'We are at our lowest ebb in the Army and the Jew may resuscitate us. I hope that he hasn't been ordered to cut us down, and yet surely we can be cut down in our overhead expenses ...' And the next day Ironside added, 'I lay awake in the morning and thought of Hore-Belisha. He will probably be our saving. He is ambitious and will not be lazy like some of the others were. He starts in when things are at their worst and will have to show results.'[2]

'Flamboyant' is the first adjective that springs to mind in describing Hore-Belisha. He was an outstanding orator and had been the first post-war president of the Oxford Union. He had an almost oriental love of splendour in his personal surroundings and was utterly unpractical in simple matters such as shaving, packing and driving. He was fertile in imagination; eager for new ideas; and zealous in pushing through reforms—as he had proved in his successful campaign to reduce traffic accidents. In personal relations he was a man of contradictions: though demanding and sometimes inconsiderate, he was capable of inspiring affection and devotion among those who worked closely with him. On the other hand he could be irritating and even infuriating to people not in sympathy with him. He was habitually unpunctual and could be rude and overbearing. He could display intolerance towards generals and civil servants with minds slower than his own, and he had the reprehensible habit of asking soldiers and junior officers what they thought of their seniors. He was sensitive about his Jewish race and middle-class background, and—perhaps by way of compensation—had great faith in the importance of publicity and self-advertisement. Though sensitive to criticism, particularly in the press, he sometimes tended to be naively complacent regarding the loyalty and friendship of fellow politicians and generals.[3] Lastly, since serving as a Financial Secretary to the Treasury from 1932 to 1934, he had become very much a 'Chamberlain man': this allegiance stood him in good stead on taking office, but as a National

Liberal in a government and Parliament dominated by Conservatives it meant that his political position was extremely vulnerable.

Initially Hore-Belisha knew very little about the army and its problems but, as his great Liberal predecessor at the War Office R. B. Haldane had proved, this need not necessarily be a disadvantage. Unlike Haldane, however, Hore-Belisha characteristically chose to look outside the War Office and the General Staff for an independent view of the whole field of necessary military reforms. For his chief, though always unofficial, mentor he selected Captain B. H. Liddell Hart, the brilliant and influential defence correspondent of the *Times*, to whom he had been introduced by Duff Cooper. Since Liddell Hart has devoted virtually the whole of the second volume of his *Memoirs*[4] to what both men came to regard as their 'partnership', it is only necessary to mention here that the War Minister relied on this prolific, progressive and unorthodox source of advice to an astonishing extent during his first nine months or so in office. Liddell Hart was extremely well informed; he probably entertained a more comprehensive and radical programme for reform than any inhabitant of the War Office; and his strategic thinking on the role of the army was at that time in close accord with the government's. Inevitably, however, there was much professional prejudice against him from the outset, and not exclusively, one must record, on the part of conservative generals. For the more reactionary it was sufficient to note that Liddell Hart was a journalist who had only attained the rank of captain in the first world war. Others naturally resented his powerful advocacy of the doctrine of 'limited liability' for the army, and his pressure in the newspapers for the promotion of mechanised warfare experts such as Hobart and Pile. But the fundamental reason for hostility to him was the General Staff's understandable resentment at a rival source of advice without responsibility so close to the War Minister. In justice to Liddell Hart it should be stressed that he would have welcomed the legitimising of his position as a member of a formally constituted research group, but it seems that Hore-Belisha did not insist on this innovation and it was successfully resisted by Liddell Hart's own apointee as Deputy Chief of the Imperial General Staff, Sir Ronald Adam.[5]

Within a few weeks of taking office Hore-Belisha encountered the same tight financial constraints on military expenditure which had greatly exasperated his predecessor. In February 1937 the government had approved a defence budget of £1,500 million to be spent by all three services over the next five years. A Treasury Inter-Service Committee carefully scrutinised the separate programmes and frequently referred proposals, no matter how urgent, if they involved an outlay in excess of the ration allotted. As Hore-Belisha sadly recorded in his diary on 13 July

1937:

> My proposal for the provision of war equipment, war reserves and
> maintenance for four Territorial divisions [£43 million] was turned
> down today ... I argued with Simon [Chancellor of the Exchequer],
> but he was quite firm that at present there should be no increase in the
> cost of the Army's programme. I pointed out that the Army's
> programme was behind that of the Navy and Air Force ... It was a
> disheartening business for the War Office.[6]

By the late summer of 1937, in close collaboration with Liddell Hart, he
had worked out a far-reaching programme for army reorganisation the
keynote of which was the reduction of infantry units, particularly in the
garrison of India, in order to save funds for increased mechanisation. But
these initial proposals met with so much obstruction and outright
opposition that Hore-Belisha became convinced that a wholesale
replacement of the senior generals at the War Office must precede more
constructive reforms. By August 1937 he had discovered that General Sir
Harry Knox, the Adjutant General, was 'his chief obstacle and the main
reason why Duff Cooper failed'. The CIGS, General Sir Cyril Deverell,
possessed some fine soldierly attributes but was reduced to blustering
incoherence by Liddell Hart's radical proposals as purveyed to him by
Hore-Belisha. He refused to consider reducing the garrison of India, simply
declaring, 'I've been there twelve years and I tell you that you cannot
reduce it.' When Hore-Belisha asked the CIGS what changes he would
advise if it were decided that there should be no expeditionary force,
Deverell answered that he 'would not alter the present arrangements one
iota'. By mid-November, therefore, Hore-Belisha had decided that he
would like to remove Deverell and replace him with a much younger man,
the recently appointed Military Secretary, Lord Gort.[7]

Before making sweeping changes in the Army Council and military
commands Hore-Belisha took care to enlist the support of the Prime
Minister, particularly as he had already decided to remove one member of
the Army Council, Sir Hugh Elles, the Master General of Ordnance, and
replace him with a Director General of Munitions Production. In this move
he had the backing of Gort. Among the objectives which Hore-Belisha
listed in a letter to the Prime Minister on 1 November were:

1. The elimination of the 1914–18 mentality, which persists in
    regarding the whole role for which the Army is being prepared as
    a repetition of its task in the last war.
2. The elimination of the attitude towards any new development,
    such as Mechanization and Anti-Aircraft defence, as taking away
    money needed for the new '1914–1918' Army.
3. The elimination of the India obsession, which refuses to allow
    objective examination of the proper disposition and organisation

of our Imperial Forces . . .
4. The elimination of the sentimentality which regards appointments
    and promotions as governed by the comradely principle of
    'Buggins's Turn'.[8]

Even after he had received the Prime Minister's consent to the dismissal
of Deverell and Knox, the War Minister remained extremely nervous,
stressing to Liddell Hart that he was risking his career. After the 'purge'
had been carried out on 1 December without much adverse comment
Hore-Belisha was exultant. He told Liddell Hart that the latter had given
him the courage to do it and they were 'a great combination'.[9]

Lord Gort, a fighting general *par excellence*, somewhat reluctantly
became CIGS, with Sir Ronald Adam as his deputy, Hore-Belisha's idea
being that the former would supply the drive and the latter the brains.
Major General Clive Liddell (no relation to Liddell Hart) succeeded Knox,
and Archibald Wavell, whose taciturnity had deprived him of a good
chance of becoming CIGS, was transferred from Palestine to Southern
Command. This looked like a promising team to rejuvenate the War Office
and reform the army.[10] Within a few weeks, however, Liddell Hart received
disturbing reports that Gort was 'soft-pedalling on radical proposals' and
displaying resentment at the journalist's close relationship with the War
Minister. Even Adam showed distinct signs of coolness towards him.
Worse still, there were rumours that Hore-Belisha was hated in the
Cabinet. His advertising and obvious ambition were resented; his recruiting
figures were suspect, and it was feared that he would leave his colleagues in
a mess.[11]

Meanwhile the vexed question of the role of the army, which had been
allowed to drag on unresolved since 1934, was coming to a head in the
autumn of 1937. The army's order of priorities as between home defence,
imperial garrisons, defended bases and providing an expeditionary force for
employment in the empire or in Europe determined its financial allocation
and consequently affected every aspect of reform. Moreover, if the
Continental commitment was renounced or placed last, the army was likely
to suffer in competition with the other services for scarce production
facilities and skilled labour.

Hore-Belisha entered office with no pronounced strategic views and with
a much keener interest in improving the terms of service and living
conditions of the other ranks. He was therefore a willing convert to Liddell
Hart's ideas on 'limited liability', particularly as the latter stressed that
streamlining of obsolescent arms would secure economies that would
permit the creation of two mechanised divisions.[12] In October, at the Prime
Minister's urging, Hore-Belisha read the chapter on the role of the army in
Liddell Hart's latest book, *Europe in Arms*, which argued that if Britain

was obliged to make a military contribution to a Continental ally (i.e.
France) it should take the form of a small, high-quality mechanised force.
This reading probably only served to reinforce the impressions which the
War Minister had derived from his recent attendance at the French autumn
manoeuvres. He was enormously impressed by the Maginot Line, which,
he was informed, required only 100,000 men to garrison, leaving a large
reserve for the field army. 'When the French realise that we cannot commit
ourselves to send an Expeditionary Force,' he noted on his return, 'they
should be all the more induced to accelerate the extension of the Maginot
Line to the sea.' He told Liddell Hart that the French agreed with the
latter's arguments in articles in the *Times* that two mechanised divisions
would be far more valuable as a British reinforcement than four infantry
divisions.[13] Both men evaded the real issue, which was that without a
definite *political* commitment there would be neither mechanised nor
infantry divisions ready to send in an emergency.

Hore-Belisha's memorandum on the role of the army, which was
presented to the Cabinet early in December 1937, was entirely Liddell
Hart's draft, even to the phrasing. The War Minister, though grateful, was
understandably becoming sensitive to the accusation that he was a mere
mouthpiece for an *éminence grise*.[14] When, on 22 December 1937, the
Cabinet considered Sir Thomas Inskip's proposals for the defence
programme as a whole, there was no serious challenge to a definitive
statement which placed a possible Continental commitment last in order of
the army's priorities. If an expeditionary force had to be sent overseas in a
crisis its most likely destination henceforth was deemed to be an 'Eastern'
theatre, i.e. the defence of Egypt against an Italian attack from Libya.
What chiefly pleased ministers about Inskip's proposals for the army, given
their profound emotional aversion to a Continental commitment, was the
prospect of considerable savings on stores and equipment. There would be,
for example, a saving of some £14 million in capital cost on the field force.
Operations against a second-class opponent outside Europe would require
a lower scale of reserves, particularly in the provision of tanks and heavy
guns. Hore-Belisha concurred in these reductions because he accepted that
the overriding priority was the development of anti-aircraft defences at
home. Like other ministers, he did not at this time give sufficient weight to
Inskip's warning that:

> If France were again to be in danger of being overrun by land armies,
> a situation might arise when, as in the last war, we had to improve an
> army to assist her. Should this happen, the Government of the day
> would most certainly be criticised for having neglected to provide
> against so obvious a contingency.[15]

In the early weeks of 1938 Hore-Belisha drove an unwilling General

Staff to draw up a new organisation for the army in the light of its revised priorities. The General Staff, and in particular the CIGS, Lord Gort, and his new director of Military Operations and Intelligence, Major General Henry Pownalln were less than enthusiastic about this task because they believed the 'limited liability' policy to be both illusory and dangerous: war with Germany on the Continent was becoming ever more likely and an expeditionary force must be prepared in advance; it would be criminal to send out troops ill trained and under-equipped; and in practice—whatever politicians might say in peacetime—it would be impossible to limit Britain's liability to a hard-pressed ally in war. On 28 February, only a month after taking office, Pownall was moved to record one of many diatribes against the War Minister in his diary:

> He has an amazing conceit, thinking himself in the direct line of descent with Cardwell and Haldane in matters of Army organisation. He knows nothing about it—even in his service in the R.A.S.C. he seems to have acquired no military knowledge at all—and he doesn't seem to listen and he will not read what is put before him. Impossible to educate, thinking he knows when he doesn't know, impatient, subject to a lot of improper outside influence, ambitious, an advertiser and self-seeker—what can we do with him? And to think that he classes himself with Haldane as a reformer!! It would be funny if it were not so lamentable and dangerous.

Senior War Office officials also resented being harangued by Hore-Belisha to accelerate the rearmament programme when in fact, as a consequence of the army's revised priorities, they had been ordered by the Treasury to cut expenditure by £82 million over the next two years. Pownall recorded sourly that Hore-Belisha 'has no idea of how to get people to work for him. Ginger is sometimes needed by everyone, but we shall get no further if he limits himself to cracking the whip.'[16]

Unfortunately this metaphorical 'cracking of the whip' was becoming, in the spring of 1938, a substitute for practical reforms as the War Minister's energy appeared to diminish after the early burst of activity.

Several explanations may be suggested for this change of tempo. First, Hore-Belisha remained acutely conscious of the risks he had taken in 'purging' the high command and had literally worked and worried himself into a state of exhaustion. Secondly, the army's low priority in rearmament and the virtual abandonment of a Continental commitment afforded the minister very little political leverage in the Cabinet—where the War Office's difficulties seldom elicited much sympathy anyway. Thirdly, as the Liddell Hart *Memoirs* make abundantly clear, the new military team at the War Office—even those like Gort and Adam whom Liddell Hart regarded as friends and allies—were bitterly opposed to Hore-Belisha's association with an outsider. They became obstructive towards new proposals, suspecting, often correctly, that they derived from Liddell Hart. For his part, Hore-Belisha was increasingly disappointed at the lack of reforming zeal shown by his new team, particularly Gort, but knew that another purge was impossible. After all the press publicity about dynamic 'new brooms' he was clearly stuck with them. This surely explains why he gradually allowed the partnership with Liddell Hart to dissolve in 1938, though, unfortunately for both men, the generals remained convinced that the minister was still 'in a journalist's pocket'.

Though Hore-Belisha's difficulties at the War Office were increasing, his public reputation remained high. He was adept at gaining press coverage for the army and himself, and in a rather drab period his flamboyant figure was a gift to the cartoonists. His first Army Estimates speech, on 10 March 1938, was a personal triumph. His cautious exposition of the army's revised priorities was almost universally applauded, since very few politicians—or soldiers—relished involvement in another European war. Even Hitler's absorption of Austria (the *Anschluss*) on the very day of Hore-Belisha's speech failed to ring warning bells regarding Britain's military unpreparedness.

But Hore-Belisha's popularity derived mainly—and deservedly—from his passionate endeavours to make the army a more humane, honourable and respected profession. The army, as he neatly put it, should be 'a part of the nation, not apart from the nation'. In his first year in office he could justly boast of improvements in recruiting, the removal of numerous petty restrictions on the soldier's liberty and better terms of service. There would, for example, be progressive increases in pay, special proficiency pay, and increased family allowances. He displayed great concern for the soldiers' health and diet, and secured maximum publicity from the appointment of Sir Isadore Salmon, MP, managing director of J. Lyons & Co., as honorary catering adviser to the army.[17] These measures, and Hore-Belisha's obvious relish in visiting military establishments, where he chatted and drank beer with ordinary soldiers, won him a national reputation as 'the soldier's friend'. His habit of by-passing formalities inevitably created some enemies among officers who felt snubbed, while his critics unfairly alleged that he was only out for cheap personal publicity. For the moment, however, he was riding high.

In the late summer of 1938, however, Hore-Belisha's handling of the Sandys affair, or 'Sandys storm', cast doubt on his political judgement. Duncan Sandys, a young Conservative MP and son-in-law of Sir Winston Churchill, was a second lieutenant in a Territorial anti-aircraft unit. He obtained from the adjutant disturbing information about the inadequacy of the air defences, including full details of the emergency plan for the defence of London, which were highly secret. Towards the end of June he informed

Hore-Belisha that he intended to raise the matter in a parliamentary question unless the War Minister could contradict the information, which of course he knew to be impossible. Instead of talking to Sandys himself, Hore-Belisha consulted the Prime Minister and accepted his advice that Sandys should be interviewed by the Attorney General. The latter unwisely threatened the MP with the Official Secrets Act. Within a few days the affair had got out of hand, the House of Commons setting up both a select committee and a committee of privileges while Hore-Belisha was establishing a military court of inquiry. Gort was furious with Hore-Belisha for exposing him unnecessarily to the hostile questioning of the three Labour members of the select committee, one of their first questions being 'I suppose you dislike politicians?' Gort's veracity was also queried, and it was wrongly assumed that he favoured severe punishment for Sandys and his informant. The select committee eventually reported on 28 September, during a more momentous crisis: it criticised Sandys for the provocative way he had raised the issue, the Attorney General for his inept handling of Sandys, and Hore-Belisha for failing to postpone the court of inquiry once parliamentary proceedings had begun. [18]

Liddell Hart warned Hore-Belisha as early in the Sandys affair as 3 July that he had made a bad mistake in alienating Churchill, and had also, in effect, delivered himself into the hands of the General Staff. In the autumn he was disturbed to find that the War Minister appeared complacent about the effects of the Sandys case and also naively assumed that Gort was loyal to him. Pownall's running commentary on the affair in his diary shows that Liddell Hart's anxiety was well founded. Pownall was probably correct in concluding that Hore-Belisha and Sandys could easily have avoided a showdown had they not been intent on achieving one.[19]

Though its importance was somewhat obscured at the time by the Sandys case, the late summer of 1938 witnessed the culmination of one of Hore-Belisha's most significant and lasting reforms, namely the radical restructuring of the system of officer appointments, promotions and tenure of posts. The officer career structure had been badly affected by the rapid demobilisation of the mass armies after 1918, and by the protective attitudes and military 'trade unionism' caused by subsequent reductions. In short, the officer corps became top-heavy as senior officers of first world war vintage stayed on to earn a maximum pension; key appointments were filled on the principle of Buggins's turn; promotion in the middle ranks was distressingly slow; and discontent was exacerbated by the deplorable practice of placing officers on half pay between appointments. Prompted by Liddell Hart—and this must be noted as one of *his* greatest achievements as an indirect reformer—Hore-Belisha introduced the following measures:

1. Reduction of the retiring age of generals and lieutenant-generals from sixty-seven to sixty, and of major-generals from sixty-two to fifty-seven.
2. Reduction of command and staff appointments from a four- to a three-year tenure.
3. Abolition of the system of half pay.
4. Introduction of time-promotion, so that officers should be promoted captain after eight years' service and major after seventeen.

On 5 August the *London Gazette* contained the names of nearly 2,500 officers in twenty closely printed pages. It was the largest single list of promotions in British military history.[20]

Although the Munich crisis did not cause Hore-Belisha to rebel against Chamberlain's policy to the point of resignation, as it did Duff Cooper to his eternal credit, it did alert him to the dreadful fact of the army's impotence and first caused him to question the feasibility of the 'limited liability' policy. His contemporary diary entries make clear his unease at Chamberlain's personal diplomacy, which had the effect of 'bereaving Czechoslovakia of its power to exist'. He realised too that Britain was powerless to implement her guarantee to the rump of Czechoslovakia, and feared that the proposed solution 'might only be a postponement of the evil day'. While he accepted that pressure on Czechoslovakia to yield territory in order to prevent war was unavoidable, given the state of British defences, he drew the moral that Britain must now rearm vigorously.[21]

The Munich crisis also caused Hore-Belisha's reputation to plummet in that the mobilisation of the anti-aircraft defences revealed to a wider public what was already common knowledge in official circles, namely the capital's virtual defencelessness against air attack. The War Minister was only to a small extent culpable, but he had given hostages to fortune by exaggerating the number of anti-aircraft guns available. Hore-Belisha responded to criticism by demanding 600 more 3.7 in. guns and 1,000 two-pounders in defiance of General Staff advice. In November Sir Edward Spears, MP, circulated a brochure of complaints about the anti-aircraft deployment to a number of fellow members which Pownall took to be an effort to shake Hore-Belisha out of office.[22]

Political discontent with Hore-Belisha's performance at the War Office culminated in a widely publicised 'Junior Ministers' Revolt' in mid-December whose ringleader was R. S. Hudson, Secretary of the Department of Overseas Trade. Hore-Belisha was particularly distressed to find his trusted Parliamentary Under Secretary, Lord Strathcona, among the malcontents. Rather like a medieval peasant rising, the revolt was ill organised and lacking in clear objectives. Chamberlain quashed it by dismissing Strathcona and reassuring Hore-Belisha that he had done extremely well; indeed, that he considered him the best Secretary of State for War since Haldane. Hore-Belisha told Liddell Hart a few months later that his fate had trembled in the balance. Chamberlain had spoken smooth words but was not to be relied upon. Hore-Belisha had 'pulled a gun on him' by making it clear that if he fell the Prime Minister would also be involved, especially over his rejection of Hore-Belisha's proposal to set up a Ministry of Supply, which had been one of the charges of the War Minister's critics. Hore-Belisha realised by early 1939 that Churchill, whom he admired, was the rising leader, and was now sorry that he had antagonised him.[23]

Early in December 1938 the role of the army again came under review and the General Staff impressed on the War Minister that if war broke out in western Europe the expeditionary force would certainly be dispatched, despite its unpreparedness, and there would be a first-class scandal. Gort pointed out that the army's share of the £2,000 million defence allocation was only £277 million and of this only £78 million was intended for the field force. Hore-Belisha, already depressed by his failure to secure a Ministry of Supply or any real increase of tempo in rearmament, skilfully presented the army's viewpoint to his generally unsympathetic Cabinet colleagues, omitting the strategic arguments for a Continental commitment which they hated to hear. By early January 1939, however, Hore-Belisha had abandoned his pretence that he was not challenging government policy on the army's priorities, and now argued openly that the concept of limited liability must be abandoned.

On 2 February the War Minister recorded a major success: the Committee of Imperial Defence approved the provision of complete equipment and reserves for the four regular divisions of the field force and also for the first four of the twelve Territorial divisions. Even at this stage the Cabinet insisted on some petty economies by postponing planned dates of embarkation (hence reducing the standard of stores and reserves), and by slightly lowering the state of readiness of the Territorial divisions. Hore-Belisha's valiant fight was, however, rewarded by an additional £55 million for the regular field force. Shortly after the Cabinet had finally approved the preparation of a small field force for European war in mid-February, Pownall visited Aldershot, where he was much comforted to see a demonstration of new weapons at last beginning to appear in bulk. 'The Army,' he recorded proudly, 'is coming to life again, no longer a "depressed class".'[24] For this improvement, though belated and still on a modest scale, Hore-Belisha deserved much of the credit.

In presenting his second Army Estimates, on 8 March 1939, Hore-Belisha found himself defending a role for the field force virtually identical to that so courageously but vainly advocated by his predecessor, Duff Cooper. The War Minister now admitted that the position regarding a Continental commitment had changed drastically since the previous March. Although, he stressed, there was no binding commitment to France, if Britain *did* become involved in war her effort would not be half-hearted or based upon any concept of limited liability. In describing what was in truth still only a *potential* field force, Hore-Belisha indulged in characteristic hyperbole. Whereas, he said, the BEF created by Haldane before 1914 had comprised only six regular infantry divisions and one cavalry division, the force which he was organising would consist of four regular infantry and two armoured divisions supported by thirteen Territorial divisions, making a grand total of *nineteen* divisions. The War Minister gained considerable political capital and kudos from his impressive reference to nineteen divisions, but the General Staff was well aware that several of them scarcely existed except on paper.

Hore-Belisha was on firmer ground in announcing further reforms designed to make the army better fed, better housed, better educated, better paid and, not least important, better trained, with trade qualifications for civil employment after leaving the service. The practical success of his social reforms was manifest in the increased flow of recruits both for the ranks and for commissions.[25]

In the moment of triumph, with the press on the whole applauding his Estimates speech, Hore-Belisha wrote to express his gratitude to Liddell Hart for inspiring so many of his reforms. He ended with a light-hearted word of advice. 'Stick to your last and don't become that most confused personality, known as a politician.'[26] He was shortly, however, to embark on a campaign to lay the basis for a greatly expanded army which would dismay his former mentor. In March and April 1939 Hore-Belisha was primarily responsible for introducing two measures which, in stark contrast to previous assumptions of a small but mechanised army, envisaged a national force approaching the scale of the first world war and consisting largely of poorly equipped infantry divisions.

The first of these dramatic decisions was announced to both Houses of Parliament on 29 March. On the previous day Halifax impressed on Hore-Belisha that it was imperative to give some clear sign of Britain's determination to resist aggression. The War Minister now favoured some form of compulsory service, but the Prime Minister had recently repeated his pledge that conscription would not be introduced in peacetime. On the spur of the moment, and without consulting the Army Coucil, Hore-Belisha suggested doubling the Territorial Army so as to take full advantage of the recent upsurge in volunteering. Chamberlain jumped at the proposal and agreed that it should be announced immediately. The plan was to increase the peace establishment of the TA from 130,000 to its war strength of 170,000 and then double it to set a target of 340,000. This would be achieved by allowing all units to over-recruit beyond their establishment to provide the cadres for duplicate units. This was a spectacular piece of window-dressing but its practical implications were staggering. The existing drill halls were nowhere near adequate in number or capacity; there was a great shortage of equipment, uniforms and weapons; and perhaps worst of all, the force could not be trained without drawing the bulk of the instructors from already hard-pressed regular units. The service chiefs accepted this *fait accompli* philosophically, but they were not amused.[27]

In April 1939 two very different pressures forced Chamberlain to accept the necessity for some form of conscription. French pressure for such a manoeuvre as a touchstone of British determination to resist Germany had grown steadily since December 1938. The other source of pressure was domestic, namely the government's obsessive fear of a devastating attack from the air and its wish to guard against this threat by manning at least a portion of the anti-aircraft defences round the clock. Chamberlain suggested that the Territorials might keep their normal daily jobs and man their guns and searchlights at night for periods of three to six months, but the General Staff advised that this was absolutely impracticable and Hore-Belisha agreed. He decided that conscription was the only solution to the anti-aircraft manpower problem, bearing in mind that the War Office was simultaneously trying to reinforce the overseas garrisons and build up the field force. He became exasperated to the brink of resignation by Chamberlain's prevarication and certainly risked his political career by forcing the issue. At the end of April the government introduced the Military Training Bill and rapidly forced it through Parliament despite fierce opposition from the Labour Party. Its main provision was that 200,000 conscripts (politely termed 'militiamen') would be embodied for six months. After three months' initial training, batches of 20,000 would take over the air defence duties for three-month periods. The remainder not required for air defence would be trained, where possible, with regular army units. Conscripts would be employed only on home defence duties in peacetime. Despite immense difficulties in finding uniforms and tents the first batch of 30,000 militiamen reported for duty on 15 July.[28]

In the short term the introduction of conscription served only to exacerbate rather than solve the War Office's problems of raising divisions for war, since it set impossible targets for all kinds of equipment, uniforms, weapons and accommodation. In political terms the gesture doubtless helped to cement the belated Anglo-French entente, but there is no evidence whatever that it deterred Hitler: on the contrary it may even have encouraged him to attack Poland while his western opponents were still disorganised. It is, however, arguable—and Pownall penned this opinion—that some form of compulsion was unavoidable and it was preferable to get the worst of the chaos over before the outbreak of war.[29] From this viewpoint, and it is a plausible one, Hore-Belisha performed one of his greatest services as War Minister by pushing through the measure when he did against the bitter opposition of the Prime Minister and some of his Cabinet colleagues. It is noteworthy that even Sir John Simon, who had resigned as Home Secretary in 1916 in opposition to conscription, became convinced in April 1939 that Hore-Belisha's case was unanswerable.[30]

By the summer of 1939 the atmosphere at the War Office had become extremely strained as frantic preparations were made to organise and equip a field force for the Continent while simultaneously laying the foundation for a national army of first world war magnitude. In these conditions harmonious relations between the War Minister and his principal professional advisers were essential, but, with a few notable exceptions such as General Adam, they deteriorated rapidly as war approached. Gort and Pownall especially resented Hore-Belisha's making high level appointments without consulting them, particularly his recall of General Ironside from Gibraltar to become Inspector General of Overseas Forces and—it was widely assumed—commander-in-chief designate of the field force. Pownall suspected, probably wrongly, that Hore-Belisha was looking for an opportunity to give Gort an overseas command in order to get him out of the War Office, while Gort was now so hostile towards his political master that he shunned him as much as possible, employing Adam as his deputy. On his part Hore-Belisha now realised too late that Gort was simply not intelligent enough to be CIGS, but there was little if any personal animosity on his side. Hore-Belisha's military assistant at this time, Major General J. C. Haydon, believed that the War Minister and his CIGS were so different in outlook that a genuine partnership was impossible:

> On the one hand, Gort was very conservative, inclined to be rather rigid and austere, reserved and completely *English* in his attitude. He was absorbed by his soldiering and—apart from the sea—I do not know that he had many other serious interests or enthusiasms in life. I do not think he ever really understood politicians . . .
> In contrast, Hore-Belisha was 'continental' in outlook; a fluent French speaker, inclined to be flamboyant; at times rather ebullient. Essentially a warm character, ready to expand and be at his entertaining best when in the company of those he knew to be friends. He possessed an acute sense of the value of publicity which he enjoyed while Gort abhorred it.

Against Pownall's jaundiced view, however, Haydon did not believe that

Hore-Belisha sought publicity purely for himself. Haydon perceived the tragic aspect in the unhappy relationship between two fervent patriots who were temperamentally incompatible.[31]

One unfortunate consequence of this disharmony at the highest levels of the War Office was that the appointment of the commander-in-chief of the field force and his senior staff officers was deferred until the day on which war was declared. Ironside had such good reason to expect the appointment that he went to Aldershot and began to assemble his personal staff. General Sir John Dill, however, also had strong claims to the post. In the event Hore-Belisha by-passed both and selected Gort: a decision congenial to both men but, in Haydon's view, one determined by merit rather than personal considerations. The War Minister had long admired Ironside's dynamism and outspokenness and, despite his reputation for intrigue and indiscretion, pressed for his appointment as CIGS. There was some opposition to Ironside's appointment in the newly constituted War Cabinet, but with Churchill's support he was approved. In retrospect these choices were soon to appear ill judged. Gort was an adequate commander in some respects but Ironside would probably have been better. Gort took Pownall with him as his chief of staff and so deprived the War Office of the two men familiar with the plans for the field force. Ironside struggled manfully to do his duty as CIGS, but, incredibly, he had never before served in the War Office and by his own admission was not suited to the task. He too began to record contemptuous opinions of Hore-Belisha in his diary. Dill, who was widely regarded in the army as the obvious and almost ideal choice for CIGS, had to be satisfied for the time being with a corps command in France.[32]

Though he became a member of the War Cabinet, Hore-Belisha's reputation was not enhanced during the opening weeks of hostilities. This was partly due to the fact that there was now less scope—or opportunity for publicity—in improving the soldiers' comfort and welfare, which had been his real burning interest. His grasp of such matters as military organisation and strategy had never been his strong point and he had relied heavily upon Liddell Hart's guidance in these areas. It was also unfortunate for him that the army—in contrast to the Royal Navy, now once again under Churchill's dynamic leadership—seemed to be doing very little. The anticipated Luftwaffe assault on London had not occurred, while, from the public's viewpoint, the Allies appeared to be deplorably passive on the western front while Poland was being overrun.

The episode which provided the pretext for Hore-Belisha's enemies to close in for the kill, namely the notorious 'pill-box affair', seems doubly ironic in retrospect. First, it is clear from the detailed accounts of two senior officers who accompanied him on his tour of the field force, Francis de Guingand and John Kennedy, that Hore-Belisha was genuinely trying to help Gort.[33] Secondly, at the very time that the frontier defences became a fatal bone of contention between the War Minister and the generals, Gamelin was persuading the Supreme War Council that in event of a German attack in the west the Allied left wing, including the field force, would abandon its lines and advance into Belgium.

On 18 and 19 November Hore-Belisha was taken on a conducted tour of the British front. He was favourably impressed by the troops' good spirits but correctly perceived that the Allied defences were weak, as indeed General Dill, commanding 1st Corps, confirmed. Gort treated Hore-Belisha to his peculiar brand of schoolboy humour, making him climb a muddy bank and keeping him shivering in a howling gale while he explained in exhaustive detail first world war actions fought in that area. When they at last got inside a château Gort flung open a window, and when they emerged into the rain he shouted jovially, 'Isn't it a grand day!' The fastidious politician was given bully-beef sandwiches and ribbed so unmercifully about them by Gort that even Pownall was embarrassed. Hore-Belisha bore all this stoically and without complaint, but he did come away with the impression that the defences were being constructed too slowly and in the wrong way. As he confided to Brigadier Kennedy:

> There ought to be hundreds of pill-boxes, every hundred yards if necessary. Pakenham-Walsh [the Chief Engineer of the field force] had an enormous file with six designs in it, and no pill-boxes have been built except two, although they have been in that position a month or more.

On his return the War Minister informed the Army Council of his disquiet about the scarcity of pill-boxes and the slow rate of progress; and at a second meeting on 24 November he mentioned that some Dominion representatives who had been to France had criticised the inadequacy of the defences to the Prime Minister. As de Guingand's contemporary note reveals, Hore-Belisha became somewhat obsessed by the pill-box issue, 'but his whole attitude was one of endeavouring to help rather than one of criticism'.[34] In handling the affair Hore-Belisha made some inept and tactless moves which might have irritated a more benevolently disposed commander-in-chief than Gort. But, given Hore-Belisha's prompt gesture of repentance, the matter could easily have been amicably resolved had he not been dealing with such hypersensitive and bitter opponents as Gort, Pownall and Pakenham-Walsh. These officers resented any criticism at all, since they believed they were doing their best in adverse conditions which the War Minister had totally failed to grasp. But his particular 'crimes' (in Pownall's term) were that he had inaccurately presented the facts to the Army Council, discussed the matter in Cabinet after Ironside had left, sent a *verbal* reprimand to Gort through a subordinate officer (Pakenham-Walsh), and dispatched the CIGS to inspect the defences on the authority of the War Cabinet. Perhaps most galling of all to GHQ was Hore-Belisha's mistaken impression that the French were setting an example in the construction of pill-boxes and could serve as a model for the British.[35]

At the end of November Ironside visited the field force to assess the justice of Hore-Belisha's criticisms. Initially he probably had some sympathy with them, but he found GHQ and the front-line commanders seething with rage at the War Minister's charges and returned wholly converted to Gort's viewpoint to report adversely on Hore-Belisha to the King and the Prime Minister. Earlier, at Hore-Belisha's first mention of the subject, the CIGS had ominously warned him to be careful how he dealt with his C-in-C. 'He was put in by the King and must not be monkeyed about.'[36] On 2 December Hore-Belisha wrote to Gort in emollient terms assuring him that no criticism had been intended and that the incident was now closed. This olive branch was ignored.[37]

Whether or not Gort actively encouraged him or merely acquiesced, it is now clear that his chief of staff, Henry Pownall, acted as the 'hatchet man' who was determined to cut Hore-Belisha down. In late November Pownall visited London and poured his poisonous views of Hore-Belisha into the receptive ears of Lord Hardinge, the King's private secretary, P. J. Grigg, the new PUS at the War Office, Sir Horace Wilson, head of the civil service, and Sir Maurice Hankey, formerly Secretary of the CID and the Cabinet and now a member of the War Cabinet. After Ironside's visit Pownall wrote to Grigg to ensure that the CIGS would have to report to the Prime Minister, and persuaded Lord Munster (Gort's ADC and no friend of Hore-Belisha's) to ensure that the King became involved. Some idea of the venom of Pownall's sustained diatribe against the War Minister in his diary can be gathered from the following extract:

> Tiny [Ironside] talks of 'not kicking a man when he's down', it's no good being Old School Tie with H-B, you have to fight him with his own weapons. One crushes a snake even if it does happen to be on the ground.

Pownall then dispatched a list of Hore-Belisha's 'Major Crimes' to Grigg and to one of the King's ADCs. Early in November the King visited GHQ and, according to Pownall, said he realised that Hore-Belisha must go. At dinner the King actually asked Pownall who should replace Hore-Belisha at the War Office, and his suggestion of Malcolm MacDonald seemed to meet with royal approval. Finally, in mid-December, the Prime Minister visited GHQ and Pownall impressed on him that the generals lacked confidence in the War Minister. 'I have no doubt,' wrote Pownall on Chamberlain's departure, 'that the Prime Minister will have H-B out of the

War Office at the earliest opportunity. Let us hope that that will come soon.'[38]

On 14 December, just before leaving for France to visit GHQ, Chamberlain saw Hore-Belisha and asked him if he had confidence in Gort and Ironside. According to Hore-Belisha's diary note Chamberlain said, 'I had only to tell him if I wanted to make a change.' Hore-Belisha altruistically answered that he had faith in both generals. After his visit to France the Prime Minister summoned Hore-Belisha to another interview on 20 December, told him that feeling against him was still strong at GHQ, and advised him to be careful because some people were out to make trouble for him. Hore-Belisha pressed vainly for details and rather naively concluded that he had made a good impression, noting, 'The Prime Minister was extremely nice and ended by saying that he had complete confidence in me, adding, "You have great courage and do not mind being criticised".'[39]

It seems, however, that Chamberlain was perturbed by Hore-Belisha's air of complacency and failure to take the hint of his unpopularity, and subsequently decided, towards the end of December, that it would be advisable to transfer him to another office in order to appease the generals. Chamberlain wished to mitigate the blow to Hore-Belisha's pride by offering him the Ministry of Information, a particularly important assignment just then and a move which would not necessarily appear as a demotion. On 1 January Lord Halifax told his private secretary, Sir Alexander Cadogan, of the proposed change and the latter noted, 'This blinding—and exquisitely funny. I hadn't time to get my breath, but on thinking it over, came to the conclusion that Jew control of our propaganda would be a major disaster.' On 3 January Cadogan described the plan as 'catastrophic', and the next day he advised Halifax to suggest to the Prime Minister that H-B be got rid of altogether. 'He will get the worst of both worlds if he merely shifts him.' Halifax accepted Cadogan's advice and told Chamberlain shortly before he was due to see Hore-Belisha on 4 January that the Foreign Office objected to having the latter at the MOI. It would have a bad effect both because Hore-Belisha was a Jew and because his methods would detract from British prestige. Chamberlain was placed in an awkward position, because he had already offered the War Office to Oliver Stanley. An hour before his appointment with Hore-Belisha he accepted Halifax's advice and decided to offer him the Board of Trade—a definite step down from the War Office.[40]

A painful interview took place in which the Prime Minister was unable to give the astonished Hore-Belisha a clear explanation for his apparent *volte face*. Churchill had flown to France that morning, and Hore-Belisha, regarding him as a friend, telephoned him for advice. He was shattered to learn that Chamberlain had revealed his proposed changes to Churchill that morning. Hore-Belisha consequently rejected Churchill's advice to take the Board of Trade and composed a dignified letter of resignation dated 5 January.[41]

According to Cadogan's diary Chamberlain was worried about the resultant press and parliamentary 'pother over Horeb', and blamed Halifax, saying he would not have set things in motion had he realised at the start that he couldn't offer Hore-Belisha the MOI. But according to Iain Macleod's biography Chamberlain was relieved when Hore-Belisha refused the Board of Trade. Ironside, though not, it seems, directly implicated in Hore-Belisha's fall and surprised at the news, recorded a reaction that was common among the generals:

> Changing horses in mid-stream is always a bad thing, but I must say that I had a feeling of intense relief on the whole. The man had utterly failed in war to run his show and we should have had a disaster. He is much better out of it.[42]

Hore-Belisha decided to make a dignified rather than a combative resignation speech in the interests of national unity. For a few weeks the newspapers buzzed with speculation about the causes of his sudden fall until the controversy was eclipsed by far more important events in Scandinavia and France. He was puzzled at the way he had been ousted from office, so soon after receiving emphatic assurances of the Prime Minister's confidence in him, but was mercifully unaware of the range and bitterness of the opposition. He correctly suspected that Gort and his influence at the Palace, rather than Ironside, had been responsible for his fall; and, when he told Liddell Hart that he thought Pakenham-Walsh was also hostile, Liddell Hart pointed out that Pakenham-Walsh was a friend of Churchill, whom he had advised in preparing his *Marlborough* volumes.[43] This was just one instance of Hore-Belisha's unhappy knack of making enemies in influential positions.[44]

An impartial judge must surely conclude from the cool perspective permitted by the passage of forty years that although Hore-Belisha had made mistakes and revealed limitations he was much 'more sinned against than sinning'. His removal as an immediate result of the tragi-comic pill-box affair now seems all the more unjust when we know that it virtually ended his political career, for apart from a brief tenure of the Ministry of National Insurance in 1945 he was never again to hold high political office. He died suddenly in France in February 1957 with his great political ambitions largely unfulfilled.

Hore-Belisha was both lucky and unlucky in the timing of his tenure of the War Office. Lucky because he was appointed at just about the time when the likelihood of war began to arouse the public to the army's utter unpreparedness and so provided an impetus to challenge the generals' inertia and the Treasury's stranglehold. On the other hand, nearly twenty years of neglect could not be remedied overnight, and the War Minister was inevitably—though unjustly—blamed when shocking weaknesses were exposed, as in the anti-aircraft defences in the scares of September 1938 and April 1939.

Secondly, as this chapter has stressed, Hore-Belisha's political base was extremely weak. As an unorthodox, flamboyant National Liberal he cut a strange figure in Chamberlain's largely Conservative government and was essentially dependent on the Prime Minister's personal support. There were always political cliques opposed to him, as the 'Junior Ministers' Revolt' revealed, and he added to his enemies while at the War Office by his personality, methods and measures. His use of Liddell Hart as an unofficial adviser was, on balance, a definite benefit for the army, but it was probably more responsible than any other factor for the bitter antagonism which he stirred up on the part of many senior officers. In the end he was left pathetically exposed to enemies in the army, the civil service and the Foreign Office. Considerable royal influence was also brought to bear on behalf of Lord Gort by the latter's friend, Lord Hardinge. It is hard to avoid the conclusion that even had the pill-box incident not occurred, or been smoothed over, Hore-Belisha could not have survived much longer at the War Office.

In retrospect it is clear that Hore-Belisha staked his reputation as a military reformer on the new team of senior officers which he appointed to replace the 'old guard' in the winter of 1937. Some of his (and Liddell Hart's) best selections could not be fitted in; others became tired and ill or lacked drive; and others became antagonistic. Yet it would be quite wrong to leave the impression that he was incapable of working amicably with all senior soldiers. Quite the contrary; as the recollections of Generals Adam, de Guingand, Haydon and Kennedy all show, he could inspire loyalty and devotion in those who worked very closely with him. As Sir John Kennedy wrote:

> I had never seen the side of his character that caused him to be disliked by so many soldiers . . .
> He was extremely kind to me; for all his fads and affectations, I never found him anything but easy to deal with. And I am in no doubt that the Army was deep in his debt.[45]

Hore-Belisha's outstanding achievement lay in improving the conditions of service for officers and other ranks and in bringing the army and the nation closer together. Disgruntled generals accused him of trying to 'democratise the army', but as he interpreted it that was surely a charge to be proud of. So long as Hore-Belisha held office the army was seldom out of the news, and after his downfall he was long remembered with affection by thousands of ordinary soldiers and their families. For these accomplishments, and for creating the foundations of the national citizen army of 1939–45, his name is deservedly linked with Haldane's as an outstandingly successful War Minister.

Notes

1   Brian Bond, *Liddell Hart: a Study of his Military Thought*, Cassell, London, 1977, p. 108.

2   R. Macleod and D. Kelly (eds.), *The Ironside Diaries, 1937–1940*, Constable, London, 1962, p. 24.

3   J. R. Colville, *Man of Valour: Field Marshal Lord Gort, V.C.*, Collins, London, 1972, p. 74, and F. de Guingand, *Operation Victory*, Hodder & Stoughton, London, 1947, pp. 19–23. For revealing comments on Hore-Belisha's character and tastes see Robert Rhodes James (ed.), *Chips: the Diaries of Sir Henry Channon*, Penguin Books, London, 1970, pp. 34, 152, 193, 224, 279–83, 289.

4   B. H. Liddell Hart, *Memoirs*, II, Cassell, London, 1965. All references are to this volume.

5   Liddell Hart papers, Centre for Military Archives, King's College, London, 11/H-B 1937/59 and 11/H-B 1938/91.

6   R. J. Minney, *The Private Papers of Hore-Belisha*, Collins, London, 1960, p. 35, and see also N. H. Gibbs, *Grand Strategy*, I, HMSO, London, 1976, p. 65.

7   Liddell Hart papers, 11/H-B 1937/14, Talk with Hore-Belisha, 21 August 1937. Liddell Hart, *Memoirs*, pp. 11, 43, 55.

8   Minney, p. 66.

9   Liddell Hart papers, 11/H-B 1937/114, 115, 118, 120, 127.

10 Colville, p. 81.

11 Liddell Hart, *Memoirs*, p. 82.

12 See Bond, *Liddell Hart*, chapter 4.

13 Minney, pp. 56–9; Liddell Hart, *Memoirs*, p. 30.

14 Liddell Hart, *Memoirs*, p. 75.

15 Gibbs, *Grand Strategy*, pp. 467–71.

16 Brian Bond (ed.), *Chief of Staff: the Diaries of Lieutenant General Sir Henry Pownall, Vol. I, 1933–1940*, Leo Cooper, London, 1972, p. 136, and diary entry, 28 March 1938. All published quotations are from vol. I. The original diaries may be consulted in the Centre for Military Archives, King's College, London.

17 Minney, pp. 93–6; Colville, p. 91.

18 Minney, pp. 122–8; Colville, pp. 97–9.

19 Liddell Hart papers, 11/H-B 1938/146, 147, 152. Bond (ed.), *Chief of Staff*, pp. 151–4, 165, and Pownall diary entries, 20 June–18 July 1938, *passim*.

20 Liddell Hart, *The Defence of Britain*, Faber, London, 1939, pp. 326–33. Minney, pp. 131–2.

21 Minney, pp. 138–46.

22 Bond (ed.), *Chief of Staff*, pp. 147–8, 165–6. Diary entry, 7 November 1938.

23 Minney, pp. 161–4. Liddell Hart papers, 11/H-B 1939/3. See also Iain Macleod, *Neville Chamberlain*, Muller, London, 1961, p. 284.

24 Gibbs, pp. 508–13. Minney, pp. 170–2. Colville, pp. 119–21. Bond (ed.), *Chief of Staff*, pp. 172–5, 186–90.

25   Minney, pp. 173–82. Liddell Hart, *Memoirs*, pp. 223–4.

26   Minney, p. 184.

27   *Ibid.*, pp. 187–8. P. Dennis, *Decision by Default*, Routledge & Kegan Paul, London, 1972, pp. 197–200. Lord Ismay, *Memoirs*, Heinemann, London, 1960, p. 93. Bond (ed.), *Chief of Staff*, pp. 200–2.

28   P. Dennis, pp. 193–5, 211–25. Minney, pp. 191–8, 204–7.

29   Bond (ed.), *Chief of Staff*, p. 202.

30   Minney, p. 197.

31   Liddell Hart papers, 11/H-B 1939/11. Papers of Major General J. C. Haydon, Imperial War Museum 77/190/2c, Haydon to J. R. Colville, 29 January 1970. Colville, pp. 137–8. Bond (ed.), *Chief of Staff*, pp. 209–10.

32   Minney, pp. 229–31. Colville, p. 134. *Ironside Diaries*, pp. 93–4. Haydon papers, Haydon to Colville, 29 January 1970.

33   Liddell Hart papers, 11/H-B M/34, Note by F. de Guingand, and F. de Guingand, *Operation Victory*, pp. 38–42. Sir John Kennedy, *The Business of War*, Hutchinson, London, 1957, pp. 33–9.

34   Liddell Hart papers, 11/H-B M/34.

35   Minney, pp. 257–64. Colville, pp. 157–65.

36   *Ironside Diaries*, pp. 164–7.

37   Liddell Hart papers, 11/H-B M/34—a copy of Hore-Belisha's letter to Gort dated 2 December 1939 is appended to de Guingand's note.

38   Bond (ed.), *Chief of Staff*, pp. 256–68.

39   Minney, pp. 266–9.

40   I. Macleod, *Chamberlain*, pp. 285–6. D. Dilks (ed.), *The Diaries of Sir Alexander Cadogan*, Cassell, London, 1971, pp. 241–4.

41   Minney, pp. 269–73.

42   *Cadogan Diaries*, pp. 243–4. Macleod, *Chamberlain*, p. 287. Colville, pp. 163–5. *Ironside Diaries*, p. 194.

43   Liddell Hart papers, 11/H-B 1939/2, 8, 9.

44   Colville, p. 77, describes how Hore-Belisha antagonised the British military attaché in Paris, Colonel F. G. Beaumont Nesbitt, first by receiving the French War Minister, Daladier, while in his bath, and second by asking Beaumont Nesbitt's opinion of senior officers. In November 1939 the military attaché told Brigadier John Kennedy that it was good for his soul to meet Hore-Belisha occasionally; he disliked him so much that it was a very good exercise in self-control. See Kennedy, *The Business of War*, pp. 33–4.

45   Kennedy, *The Business of War*, pp. 149–51.

DUNCAN SANDYS
AND THE INDEPENDENT
NUCLEAR DETERRENT

COLIN GORDON

Duncan Edwin Duncan-Sandys, invariably known simply as Duncan Sandys, was born in 1908 and after Eton and Oxford joined the Foreign Service in 1930, resigning five years later on his election to the House of Commons as Conservative MP for the Norwood division of Lambeth. The same year he underlined his commitment to politics by marrying into one of the great English political families; his bride was Diana Churchill, daughter of a father who at that time was widely regarded in the Commons as a politician with a past but no future. Commissioned in an artillery regiment of the Territorial Army in 1938, he was one of the founders of the Air Raid Protection Institute. This earned him some notoriety when he criticised the government for its scanty attention to anti-aircraft defence in the period between Munich and the declaration of war. Mobilised on its outbreak, he saw active service in the brief Norwegian campaign of 1940 before he was disabled and invalided out of the army the following year. Returning to the House of Commons, he spent the remainder of the war first as Financial Secretary at the War Office, later as Parliamentary Secretary to the Minister of Supply, finally acting as chairman to a Cabinet committee for defence against flying bombs and rockets. The war in Europe over, he acted as Minister of Works in the caretaker government which preceded the electoral victory of the Labour Party in the 1945 general election and the Allied victory over Japan.

The return of Labour saw Sandys not only out of office but out of Parliament; he flung himself into politics of a different sort, becoming a leading protagonist of a united Europe, an aim which had widespread if somewhat shallow support as European society sought to restructure itself politically and economically after the upheavals of the war years. One of the founders of the European Movement, Sandys was chairman of its international executive until 1950; returned in that year to the Commons as MP for the Streatham division of Wandsworth, he represented that constituency for the succeeding quarter of a century, until his elevation to the House of Lords in 1974. On returning to active politics he became chairman of the parliamentary council of the European Movement and a member of the consultative assembly of the Council of Europe. In this latter capacity he was chairman of the working party established to follow up Churchill's sonorous call in 1950 for the formation of a European army. The working party reported in a matter of weeks, by which time some of the members of the assembly were beginning to have second thoughts. A few months later the French Prime Minister, René Pleven, produced his own plan for the formation of such an army, and autumn 1951 saw Churchill, now the British Premier, being urged from the assembly to join Britain to the proposed European Defence Community and accept the office of European minister of defence. It was not an offer which could be accepted, and Sandys, who had done a great deal behind the scenes to keep Churchill when out of office in the European limelight, was content that it should be so. In any case, his own attentions had now a different focus, for on the formation of the Conservative government in October 1951 he had been appointed Minister of Supply.

Created in 1939 to supervise the purchase, manufacture and sale of articles for the public service, the Ministry of Supply was transformed by the demands of war. As well as being the supply department to the War Office it controlled many aspects of war production and became involved in the activity of all government departments. After the war it absorbed the

Ministry of Aircraft Production; when Sandys took it over he assumed responsibility for the supply of strategic raw materials, military aircraft, munitions, including atomic weapons, and guided missiles. Whilst not a member of the Cabinet, the Minister of Supply attended meetings of its defence committee, and Sandys bore a heavy burden during the first part of his father-in-law's tenure of office. This was the period when the Korean rearmament programme inherited from Labour was being 'stretched' to respond to the view of the Chancellor of the Exchequer, R. A. Butler, that Attlee's proposal to double defence expenditure within three years could not be achieved without overstraining the economy.

Following Churchill's illness in 1953, several members of his Cabinet hoped that he would resign the following summer; to the chagrin of Eden and the dismay of Macmillan, however, he contented himself with reorganising the government. Macmillan exchanged the Ministry of Housing and Local Government for the Ministry of Defence and Sandys, who replaced him, thus entered the Cabinet. Now in confident middle age, he enjoyed the reputation of being a minister with a mind of his own, temperamentally disinclined to accommodate himself readily to his civil service advisers. When Sir Anthony Eden finally succeeded to the premiership in April 1955 he was confirmed in office and directed to tackle the explosive problem of the various rent control Acts. The result was the Rent Bill, which cut a swathe through restrictive legislation to the accompaniment of much adverse criticism both inside and outside the Commons. During this period and illustrative of his independence of mind was Sandy's refusal to listen to departmental advice and have nothing to do with the formation of the Civic Trust, a highly successful innovation which had the minister's enthusiastic support and with which he has since continued his association. He also demonstrated a preference for proposals in writing, if necessary for written draft succeeding written draft, a characteristic ruefully recalled by his staff when he was summoned by Harold Macmillan to become Minister of Defence following the Suez débâcle and Eden's breakdown in health at the end of 1956.

Macmillan wanted Sandys at the Ministry of Defence because he had decided as Chancellor of the Exchequer that defence should be obtained more cheaply and had been unable so to persuade Antony Head, Secretary for War since October 1951, who had been passed the defence portfolio just before the Anglo-French invasion of Suez. Macmillan wanted 'in the light of present strategic needs, a defence policy which will secure a substantial reduction in expenditure and manpower'. Head would not deliver, and he was supported by the service ministers and the chiefs of staff. Accordingly Macmillan got rid of Head and put in a minister who he knew would not flinch in the face of opposition from the services.

In the circumstances Duncan Sandys could accept the offer both as a compliment and as a challenge, for up to that time the Ministry of Defence did not rate highly in political estimation. It was younger in creation to the Ministry of Supply, for, while some parts of the job went back to the appointment of Sir Thomas Inskip as Minister for the Co-ordination of Defence in 1936, the title of Minister of Defence was created by Churchill for himself in 1940 and the ministry itself was not formally established until 1946. Inskip's title described his functions; he was to co-ordinate the work of the civil and military sub-committees of the Committee of Imperial Defence. This committee was suspended during the war, its functions being undertaken by the War Cabinet, and disappeared in 1946, being replaced by the only Cabinet committee of which Parliament and the public were officially informed, the defence committee. The Act establishing the ministry inelegantly declared the minister to be 'in charge of the formulation and general application of a unified policy relating to the armed forces of the Crown as a whole and their requirements', but in practice he reverted to being a co-ordinator:

> The Ministry of Defence . . . was seen not as a higher echelon of command imposed on the armed forces but as an extension of the normal structure of government, by intergovernmental committees ultimately responsible through such channels as the chiefs of staff committee to the defence committee of the Cabinet. It was a system of government . . . rather than a system of command.[1]

Macmillan had been Minister of Defence during the last six months of Churchill's premiership and found the ministry 'a queer kind of affair'. No clear frontiers had been drawn between the powers of the minister and the heads of the service departments, who claimed that with their separate accounting officers responsible to Parliament and their duties laid down by statute they had full independence. Ambiguity extended to the Cabinet's defence committee. Without fixed membership or functions but with the service ministers normally attending accompanied by their chiefs of staff

> in the normal course of discussion, the Prime Minister as chairman naturally turned to the service ministers or to the admirals, generals and air-marshals concerned for comment or advice. Thus while authority nominally resided in the Minister of Defence, unless this post was combined with the premiership, effective power still remained with the service ministers and their professional advisers.[2]

Eden's memoirs make it clear that even when Churchill handed over the ministry to Lord Alexander he 'never accepted in his heart the position of a minister of defence divorced from his own authority. In impatient moments he would sometimes murmur that the post did not exist.'[3] Eden himself appointed Sir Walter Monckton to the post when the latter asked to be transferred somewhere less exacting than the Ministry of Labour. Despite his concern to remedy the inherent weaknesses of the system, Macmillan as Prime Minister ran up against strong opposition and it was not until the end of his term of office that he was able to bring about a reorganisation of the whole structure.

At the beginning of his premiership, however, he had appreciated that one way to overcome the services' gambit of appealing to their expertise was to drive an expert wedge between them. In an earlier attempt to reduce the annual wrangle between the service ministers and the Treasury as to the allocation of the defence budget Eden had had created the post of chairman to the Chiefs of Staff committee. His function was to present the collective view of the chiefs of staff; the minister himself was empowered to ensure that the composition of each of the services and the balance between them gave effect to the strategic policy laid down by the defence committee. Macmillan designated the chairman of the Chiefs of Staff committee 'chief of staff to the Minister'; henceforth, in the event of disagreement between the chiefs, he was to present his own view. More important, in the ordinary run of things he could be used as the agent of the minister in dealings with the service chiefs themselves. That the ordinary run of things was unlikely to be placid was indicated by the powers given to the new minister in Macmillan's statement to the Commons in January 1957. In addition to responsibility for 'formulating, in the light of present strategic needs, a defence policy which will secure a substantial reduction in expenditure and manpower' he was also to undertake 'reshaping and reorganising the armed forces . . . all matters affecting the armed forces . . . any matter of service administration or appointments which . . . are of special importance.[4]

Sandys's tenure of office indeed proved tempestuous, and he had every need of tenacity to carry out the Premier's directives. In the event, his authority received formal confirmation in a White Paper on the central organisation of defence which appeared in July 1958. The minister was expressly authorised to decide all matters of defence policy, the service ministers being allocated responsibility for the administration of the three services. Further, the minister was made responsible for the execution of military operations approved by the Cabinet or the defence committee, and for this purpose—in effect the issuing of operational orders—he was provided with a Chief of Defence Staff, the existing combined posts of chairman of the Chiefs of Staff committee and chief of staff to the minister being abolished. The joint planning staff of the services was made directly responsible to the new Chief of Defence Staff in his capacity as chairman of the Chiefs of Staff committee and he was empowered to call for assistance in the performance of his duties on the naval, general and air staffs. In Michael Howard's happy description 'the relations of the chief of defence staff with the chiefs of staff committee were ... delineated with the circumspect precision of a man making his way over the thinnest of ice'.[5] To assist the minister himself a new creation, the Defence Board, was established, comprising the three service ministers, the Minister of Supply, the Chief of Defence Staff, the three chiefs of staff, the Chief Scientist and the permanent secretary to the ministry. Here all major issues of policy and inter-service problems could be discussed, it being specifically stated that the minister could transfer to his own ministry any function common to two or more services. And, at the higher level, membership of the Cabinet's defence committee was defined with the significant proviso that, while all members would receive all relevant papers, actual attendance on particular occasions would be determined by the Prime Minister. The chiefs of staff were to be in attendance and in addition might be invited to attend meetings of the full Cabinet.

This definitely shifted the distribution of power and authority from the service ministers and their professional advisers to the Minister of Defence; it provoked unkind references in the Commons to Hitler's *Oberkommando der Wehrmacht* and to the perils of separating the formulation of policy from its execution. However, even at the time of the publication of the White Paper it was being questioned whether it went far enough. Its logical extension was reached five years later when Peter Thorneycroft announced in the spring 1963 defence debate that he as minister intended to centralise the operational requirements of the separate services under the Ministry of Defence, which in future would comprise the 'essential cores' of the Admiralty, the War Office and the Air Ministry. Later, in July 1963, there appeared a further White Paper on the central organisation of defence which confirmed that the heads of the service ministries would henceforth be ministers responsible to the head of the Ministry of Defence but which altered the latter's title to that of Secretary of State for Defence. Thorneycroft was not to remain in office long enough to do more than oversee the organisational changes involved, but he handed over a ministry well suited to the character of the first of the defence supremos, Denis Healey. And that which linked Sandys to Healey, extending through the tenure of the ministry by Harold Watkinson and Peter Thorneycroft, was what one commentator described as 'the great weight of reactionary, but none less sincere, opposition to reform which is to be found in every great public service'.[6]

Not that structural reform was the initial bone of contention between Duncan Sandys and the service chiefs; rather, he challenged them in one area where they had hitherto regarded themselves as authoritative, the definition of doctrine. The chiefs of staff themselves had not found it easy to agree on doctrine, notably when Field Marshal Montgomery was one of their number ten years previously. Montgomery had favoured a Continental strategy in the event of a Soviet attack on Western Europe, the committal of British ground forces to the physical defence of every acre. His peers favoured an air strategy while insisting that the whole argument was artificial until the intentions of the United States were known. The issue went to the defence committee of the Cabinet and was settled in Montgomery's favour; when the North Atlantic treaty committed the United States to the defence of Western Europe, Montgomery, who was at the head of the military planning structures created under the earlier Brussels treaty, agreed that the earlier estimates of the number of divisions needed to hold the Soviets could be revised downward now that American support could be relied upon. The new figure of ninety-six divisions indicated a belief that even in the atomic era God remained on the side of the big battalions and that a European war would be lengthy and demand the employment of reserve forces. Even before the signing of the North Atlantic treaty, the 1948 National Service Act committed British conscripts not only to full-time colour service but also to part-time service with the Territorial Army. After Korea colour service was extended, swelling the army-in-being, and 250,000 reservists were called up for refresher training, which tested the mobilisation procedures. By 1952, at the Lisbon council meeting of the Atlantic allies, it was agreed that now that the American Strategic Air Command was locked into the West European system of defence there was a need for some fifty divisions 'in appropriate combat readiness'. Divided among the allies, this entailed Britain providing nine or ten regular and reserve divisions in 1952 and being in a position within a couple more years to furnish nine regular divisions at once and nine additional reserve divisions by D-Day + 30.

However, even as the Lisbon council was in session the British defence programme inherited by Churchill from Attlee was being stretched. A few weeks later the new Conservative government's economic survey declared that the balance of payments was critical, that even with reduced expenditure 10 per cent gross national product was being absorbed by 900,000 servicemen, and that by the end of the following year the civilian labour force employed in defence work would be 2 million. Churchill, once again Minister of Defence, had returned from Washington at the beginning of 1952 profoundly impressed by the role that the American joint chiefs of staff allocated to their Strategic Air Command. His British chiefs of staff knew that the best they could provide in the way of ground forces was eleven regular and twelve reserve divisions at the cost of heavily burdening the economy. The Lisbon force goals demanded the commitment to Europe of all but a couple of their regular divisions. The better to resolve their quandary, they took themselves off to a country retreat to try to relate defence means to ends. The outcome was Global Strategy Paper 1952.

GSP 1952 advocated that, for the future, much greater reliance should be placed upon the forthcoming British atomic weapon than upon conventional forces. The deployment of British air-strike forces equipped with atomic weapons would enhance the overall deterrent posture of the Atlantic alliance and facilitate the defence of peculiarly British interests if deterrence failed. They also looked to the acquisition of tactical nuclear weapons as a means of achieving the fire-power envisaged at Lisbon without the disagreeable necessity of achieving the Lisbon force goals. Outside Europe they looked to the possibility of reducing British forces in view of the fact that at least some of the current overseas deployment was conditional upon an obsolete second world war strategy.

The doctrine outlined by the British chiefs of staff challenged established NATO orthodoxy, which had not envisaged a leading atomic role for Britain and emphasised the value of reserve forces. Thus General Eisenhower in April 1952:

> the number of divisions pledged does not fully represent the magnitude of the effort required ... each nation must produce a variety of combat and service support elements ... these requirements raise manpower and equipment totals to twice or three times those represented within the combat divisions.[7]

Not only did the British chiefs of staff's views fail to harmonise with those of the NATO planners and the Americans; they failed to conform to their own conduct. Sir Roderick McGrigor secured for the Royal Navy an affirmation of the need to keep the sea lanes open in time of war, a maritime strategy which harked back to the second and indeed to the first world war. This implied acceptance of the possibility of 'broken-backed' war, conceded by Sir John Slessor for the RAF and by Sir William Slim for the army as a short-term rationale which would be reduced in appeal with the deployment of the atomic and outmoded with the advent of the thermonuclear weapon. Paradoxically enough, when General Eisenhower became the American president and when perceptions of a Soviet threat declined with the death of Stalin, the US joint chiefs looked with a more indulgent eye upon the prescriptions of their British opposite numbers, and 'massive retaliation' entered the vocabulary of strategy.

The British and American chiefs of staff shared a basic uncertainty about the duration of a future war between the Atlantic allies and the Soviet Union which amounted to a general admission that it was not necessarily going to be short and sharp. This accorded with the opinion of Churchill. In assuring the House of Commons that war was neither inevitable nor imminent, he declared with oratorical relish that this was because war would mean the overrunning and communisation of Western Europe while 'at the same time Soviet cities, airfields, oilfields and railway junctions would be annihilated with, possibly, the complete disruption of Kremlin control over the enormous populations which are ruled from Moscow'.[8] The 1954 defence White Paper envisaged a European conflict in less rhetorical but more chilling style:

> it seems likely that such a war would begin with a period of intense atomic attacks lasting a relatively short time but inflicting great destruction and damage. If no decisive results were reached in this opening phase, hostilities would decline in intensity, though perhaps less so at sea than elsewhere, and a period of 'broken backed' warfare follow, during which the opposing sides would seek to recover their strength, carrying on the struggle in the meantime as best they could.[9]

Three years or so later, Field Marshal Montgomery envisaged the possibility of broken-backed warfare continuing for as long as two years after the initial nuclear exchange had been won by the West.[10]

The chiefs of staff had to consider not only all-out war in Europe but also limited war outside Europe, and particularly in the Middle East, together with intervention in other parts of the world where political and economic stability might be perceived as a British interest. This provided the Royal Navy with a rationale for the aircraft carrier as a mobile base for the projection of military power, a case which could be supported by the experience of war in Korea. The army could appeal to the need for limited war and police capabilities outside Europe while at the same time claiming a role in a total European war by insisting that the enemy would have to be held long enough for the air force to pound him into submission. They also refrained from drawing attention to the difference between themselves and their American counterparts because they had, in fact, faced up to the realisation that in the 1950s Palmerston's celebrated dictum—that Britain had no permanent allies, only permanent interests—needed reconsideration. NATO doctrine continued to emphasise the value of ground forces and of reserves; speaking in June 1954, six months after the 'massive retaliation' speech of Secretary of State Dulles, General Gruenther, Supreme Allied Commander Europe, declared that

> if war should take place three years from now we would use atomic weapons. We are working on a philosophy to have a force in being that is the smallest possible and to depend on reserve forces. We feel that it will not hold that long unless we have atomic power to support it. In our thinking we visualise the use of atomic bombs in support of our ground troops. We also visualise the use of atomic bombs in enemy territory.[11]

Uncertain, then, as was the rationale for broken-backed war, a similar uncertainty on the part of the SHAPE avoided schism.

Meanwhile the British chiefs could rub along reasonably well with the politicians at home. Churchill found their views to his taste; always solicitous for the Royal Navy, he was ready to support both Slessor and Slim. Thus in speaking to the Commons in July 1952 he insisted upon the need to develop the latest weapons against the outbreak of world war and then went on that in the event of

> the continuation of armed peace or cold war ... the technical developments ... will not help us much in that. It is by more conventional armaments, mainly in fact by the infantry soldier, serving in so many parts of the world, that we have to make our contribution towards security against communist encroachment.[12]

During Eden's premiership there seemed to be a happy concordance between the views of the British chiefs of staff, the American joint chiefs and the Prime Minister's anxiety to reduce the forces he had committed to NATO when he was Foreign Secretary. In July 1956 Admiral Radford, chairman of the US joint chiefs of staff, suggested a general lowering of American force levels and in particular a reduction in the five divisions then stationed in Germany to token forces equipped with nuclear weapons. This coincided with Eden's opinion that while the political reasons for the stationing of British and American troops on the ground in Europe under NATO command still remained

> it is on the thermonuclear bomb and atomic weapons that we now rely, not only to deter aggression, but to deal with aggression if it should be launched. A 'shield' of conventional forces is still required; but it is no longer our principal military projection. Need it be capable of fighting a major land battle?[13]

But Eden's concern to get costs as well as forces in Germany down had led him to direct Selwyn Lloyd when Minister of Defence to initiate a series of studies which resulted in some cuts affecting all three services; the process not being an easy one, Eden sought to strengthen the Ministry of Defence to make it less difficult in the future. A small and select Cabinet working party in the early summer of 1956 continued the examination of defence policy, but an indirect testimonial to the continued resilience of the service ministries was indicated in October 1956 when Eden replaced Selwyn Lloyd's successor Monckton by Anthony Head. Secretary for War since Churchill's premiership, Head had declined earlier suggestions that he might improve his career prospects by taking over a civil department. When Eden asked him whether he wanted further powers on promotion to the Cabinet as Minister of Defence he replied that he was satisfied with things as they stood. Macmillan, then Chancellor of the Exchequer, grasped the implication and on becoming Prime Minister not only replaced

Head; he also replaced the Air Minister and the First Lord of the Admiralty, and got them and the Secretary for War to accept the brief that he had prepared for his chosen minister for defence before he confirmed their appointments.

The power that Sandys wielded, then, was power put into his hand by the Prime Minister. Sandys repaid the confidence that had been reposed in him and in the event had his powers confirmed in summer 1958 when the White Paper on the central organisation of defence appeared. There were new features, however; apart from the designation of the post of Chief of Defence Staff, the most important innovation was the creation of the Defence Board to act as a baffle between the service ministers and the defence committee of the Cabinet. It would seem that Sandy's original intention had been to confine the service ministers to the board and to exclude them from the defence committee. This the Cabinet overruled, leaving their attendance subject to the discretion of the Prime Minister.

If, then, Sandys was no major innovator as far as organisation was concerned, what of his achievements as far as policy was concerned? The 1957 defence White Paper was presented by the new minister as an outline of future policy 'involving the biggest change of military policy ever made in normal times'. This was an exaggeration, as some were quick to point out at the time:

> it [the White Paper] introduces no basic revolution in policy, but merely rationalises and (probably for the first time) explains in admirably intelligible form tendencies which have long been obvious and policies most of which successive British governments have accepted and urged upon their allies for some years.[14]

But if Sandys was protesting too much, what was it that caused his name to become so closely associated with the British nuclear deterrent?

The first part of the answer relates to his relations with the service chiefs. After a flying visit to Washington upon appointment he embarked upon a series of acrimonious meetings with the chiefs of staff while paying scant attention to the service ministries. Relying for advice on his own staff, his first statement on defence went through a dozen drafts before it was finally published so late that it only just preceded the budget. Its content offended all the service chiefs, even the Chief of the Air Staff, Sir Dermot Boyle, who had more cause than his colleagues to welcome it. Later the ill will spread to the service ministers, who resented the attempt to confine them to the Defence Board, and it was sustained by a creeping barrage of criticism of the minister by both service officers and civil servants which culminated in a celebrated critique by Lieutenant General Sir John Cowley. This, delivered at the Royal United Services Institute some three weeks after Sandys had left the ministry, and previously cleared by the Secretary of

State for War, reverberated for weeks in the serious press, aroused the anger of Macmillan and provoked the enunciation of new rules on clearance to ensure that so public a statement of dissent could not occur in the future.

Sandys also became so closely identified with the British deterrent because of the gusto with which he defined policy and the zest with which he brought the public to face some unpalatable truths. Speaking in the Commons while his White Paper was still in draft, he spoke of the US Strategic Air Command being equipped with bombs hundreds of times more powerful than those dropped on Hiroshima and insisted upon the wisdom of assuming that the same was true of the Soviets. Given the likelihood of Britain being soon exposed to rocket attack, he concluded that 'the present superiority of the means of attack over defence, coupled with the catastrophic consequences of thermo-nuclear war, virtually determines the course we must follow'.[15] The White Paper itself called for frank recognition of the fact that 'there is at present no means of providing adequate protection for the people of this country against the consequences of an attack with nuclear weapons'. In February 1958, in a White Paper which was more expansive, he emphasised that the West was prepared to respond to a major Soviet conventional attack by initiating nuclear war, and insisted that 'these stark facts should be stated plainly, since the one thing which might conceivably tempt the Soviet Union into military adventure would be the erroneous belief that the West, if attacked, would flinch from using its nuclear power'.[16] But in fact there were those in the West who did flinch: that same month saw the re-emergence of the 'Victory for Socialism' group of left-wing Labour MPs and trade union leaders and the founding of the much more significant and heterogeneous Campaign for Nuclear Disarmament.

The first year of Sandys's term of office coincided with a brilliant diplomatic offensive by Marshal Bulganin on the testing of nuclear weapons; *Sputnik* went up in October 1957. The following year some Western commentators spoke of a 'missile gap' in favour of the Soviet Union and Khrushchev exploited the situation by reopening the Berlin crisis. On Christmas Day 1958 the message from Moscow was not one of peace and good will; Foreign Minister Gromyko described the Soviet proposals on Berlin as designed to prevent that city from becoming 'a second Sarajevo'. Small wonder that in such an environment of domestic nervousness and international tension the emphasis that Sandys placed on nuclear weaponry ensured him celebrity, even in a government led by such a consummate political performer as Harold Macmillan. And, once engaged, that which kept attention on Sandys was his insistence not only that should Britain maintain a deterrent but that it should be independent.

It had been taken as axiomatic after the war that, given that atomic weapons existed, Britain would want to acquire them; when Sir Henry Tizard, chairman of the defence research policy committee, argued after the Soviet test explosion of an atomic bomb in the late summer of 1949 that Britain should leave the production and development of such weapons to the United States and concentrate on strengthening its Continental land forces he was overruled by Attlee. Churchill confirmed the development of the thermonuclear weapon. But the general assumption was that the British weapon formed part of an alliance deterrent, to be employed if deterrence failed against targets which might otherwise be neglected by Strategic Air Command:

> unless we make a contribution of our own ... we cannot be sure that in an emergency the resources of other powers would be planned as exactly as we would wish, or that targets which would threaten us most would be given what we consider the necessary or deserved priority in the first few hours.[17]

When the British and French governments found their military action in Suez condemned not only by the Soviet Union but also by the United States a reappraisal was clearly in order. Called by Macmillan to reformulate defence policy 'in the light of present strategic needs', Sandys addressed the issue carefully. In his first statement to the Commons as Minister of Defence he announced that National Service would be ended as soon as possible, and that Britain's allies had been advised to expect reductions in her forces on the Continent. Both were welcomed statements, the first having a particular appeal as far as the general public were concerned. He proceeded with the assertion that, because of Britain's vulnerability to nuclear attack, military effort had to be concentrated on the prevention of war rather than on defence should it break out, but he shied away from answering the question he himself raised as to whether the provision of deterrent forces should be left to the United States. He did, however, spell out the implication for British conventional forces in Europe of a deterrent strategy: their role was to co-operate with other Allied forces to forestall a quick *coup de main* and to hold the line until nuclear retaliation could be undertaken. He concluded that, having settled the contribution Britain should make to the deterrent,

> we have to ask ourselves whether we should, in addition, provide other forces which do not directly contribute to the deterrent but which would be desirable for waging war should the deterrent fail. We must as far as possible resist the temptation to dissipate our limited resources on forces which in themselves have no deterrent value ...[18]

Settling the British contribution to the deterrent and deciding what forces should be provided in the event of deterrence failing were matters in which the chiefs of staff were not accustomed to having their judgement disregarded. On this occasion they found their views brushed aside by a new minister who preferred to listen to his own senior departmental staff and to the Chief Scientist, and who briskly dismissed the current shape of the forces as the outmoded outcome of the Korean rearmament programme. When the White Paper finally appeared weeks later than was normally the case, his prescriptions were sweeping: defence against major aggression in Europe was to be ensured by the V-bomber force carrying atomic and, later, nuclear weapons and protected by a reduced Fighter Command, to be supplemented later by medium-range ballistic missiles; ground forces in Europe were to be reduced; apart from carriers the number of naval vessels was to be cut; National Service was to be phased out by 1960, and by the end of 1962 the total number of regular servicemen stabilised at 375,000, a reduction of 77,000. While the possibility of broken-backed war was specifically allowed for in relation to the navy, all three services were said to have a part to play in 'bringing power rapidly to bear in peacetime emergencies or limited hostilities', and to this end RAF Transport Command was to expand in order to be able to move the central reserve swiftly around the globe. During the ensuing debate Sandys revealed that Britain's deterrent was not to be viewed simply as a contribution to an overall Western capability but as a self-contained national deterrent:

> so long as large American forces remain in Europe and American bombers are based in Britain it might conceivably be thought safe . . . to leave to the U.S.A. the sole responsibility for providing the nuclear deterrent. But when they have developed the 5000 mile intercontinental ballistic rocket, can we really be sure that every American administration will go on looking at things in quite the same way? We think it is just as well to make certain that an appreciable element of nuclear power shall in all circumstances remain on this side of the Atlantic so that no one shall be tempted to think that a major attack could be made against Western Europe without the risk of nuclear retaliation . . . I am quite sure that our European neighbours feel the same and are glad to know that Britain intends to remain a nuclear power.[19]

Robust as was this assertion, it did not square easily with the statement early on in the White Paper that 'the growth in the power of weapons of mass destruction has emphasised the fact that no country can any longer protect itself in isolation', and there were other instances of failure either to think things through or to express arguments and conclusions clearly and succinctly. The very breadth of the policy opened whole avenues of speculation; thus the day after the White Paper was published the *Times* declared it to be

courageous and clear-thinking; it admits that Britain cannot be
defended against nuclear attack and draws the logical conclusion that
a distinction must be made between preparations for deterring and
preparations for waging global war ... global war is not the
Clausewitzean 'continuation of policy by other means' but the
negation of all policy. It is inconceivable, therefore, that it could arise
except by accident, from a local conflict which got out of hand. The
deterrent against the local conflict is therefore the root of all
deterrence.[20]

But just as the minister emphasised deterrence, so the nature of deterrence
merited a central place in any serious critique, a point not consistently
appreciated at the time in the parliamentary debate. It commended itself
naturally enough to one of the authors of GSP 1952, Sir John Slessor, who
qualified his welcome of the White Paper as a clear statement of established
policy 'in one respect, one on which the white paper is least clear and is
even ambiguous, namely the nature of the total war envisaged if the
deterrent fails to deter'. In a nutshell, his conclusions were that if Sandys
envisaged broken-backed war the economies he had announced would
make such a strategy more difficult of execution; if he envisaged a short,
violent and predominantly nuclear exchange, then any notional savings
should go 'not to reduce the overall allocation of our resources to the
fighting services, but to apportion them more in accordance with the real
requirements of modern strategy, particularly by the avoidance of such
dangerous reductions in the strength of the Army'. Without coming down
in favour of either a long or short global war he wanted sufficiently large
forces on the ground in Europe to deal with a range of enemy action from a
frontier probe to a full-scale attack: in the latter event, forces sufficiently
large to demonstrate to the enemy that he was embarking on war to the
death—literally.

The observations of the *Times* were provocative, those of Slessor
persuasive; both would have benefited had they been expressed in the
context of an analysis of the theory of deterrence. Instead they and
Sandys's statements of British defence policy fell into a sequence of
pragmatic responses to the introduction of the atomic weapon into the
panoply of war only twelve years previously. The dramatic ending of the
war with Japan brought no immediate realisation that atomic weapons
were truly strategic, capable of obtaining the end of strategy, the imposition
of the will of the state upon an adversary. As the weapons themselves and
the means of their delivery were developed further, however, and as the
Soviet Union began to deploy them, not only were they more and more
generally described as *the* strategic weapon; they increasingly came to be
described as *the* deterrent. But this was rendering to the part the attributes
of the whole, for all configurations of military power have a deterrent

effect. And, while some forms of military power have more of a deterrent effect than others, the context in which the power is deployed affects its credibility as a deterrent because the essence of deterrence—any deterrence—lies in readiness to turn power into force, to transform threat into reality.

Viewed in these lights, Sandys's enunciation of defence policy lays itself open to criticism on several grounds, the most important being that he attributed too much importance to the deterrent value of nuclear weapons because he did not pay sufficient attention to the context in which they were deployed. This was at the root of Slessor's worry that

> the armies of the alliance will absorb a quite unjustifiable proportion of their resources in material and manpower by equipping themselves with weapons that they may never be able to use, either in Europe or localised war elsewhere.[21]

For the fact was that British conventional forces were not called simply to contribute to deterrence in Europe; they had 'to defend British colonies and protected territories against local attack and undertake limited operations in overseas emergencies'. Not only did the provision for defence outlined by Sandys throw too much weight on the deterrent effect of nuclear weapons; they rendered the other components of the British defence forces as ill suited to limited war and police operations outside Europe as to broken-backed or short war within.

However, the immediate assessment of Sandys's policy was made in the House of Commons, wherein, as one percipient and witty observer put it,

> every defence debate . . . includes some far-ranging estimate of the chances of mankind's survival in the second half of the twentieth century, a highly technical dissertation on aircraft or missiles, and also an impassioned plea that Highland regiments should be allowed to retain their kilts.[22]

Confident in the support of the Prime Minister, he easily outstrode the criticism. Emmanuel Shinwell, who might have been expected to speak with some authority, having been Secretary for War and Minister of Defence, founded his speech neither on theory nor on practice but on emotion and admitted that he could conceive of 'a situation where in a conventional war it might be more endurable to suffer defeat, even humiliation, even if it means survival on a limited scale than to use the nuclear weapon and be destroyed'.[23] John Strachey, who had succeeded Shinwell as Secretary for War, addressed the right issue when he spoke of the danger of over-emphasising the nuclear deterrent and underestimating conventional forces and 'the tragic dilemma that, faced by a frontier incident, . . . we must accept a small but perhaps fatal *fait accompli* or blow up the world',[24] but he failed to challenge Sandys sufficiently on theory. Outside the Commons, the chiefs of staff fumed at the practical steps outlined by the Minister of Defence. While accepting that Sandys was following the spirit of GSP 1952, the RAF was aggrieved that its planned supersonic bomber had been axed and its fighter aircraft disparaged in favour of missiles; the navy objected to the reduction in all but its carrier force, while the army gagged on the acceptance by Sandys of an actuarial estimate that the maximum size of a regular army would be 165,000 when the Hull Committee had previously concluded that it needed at least 200,000 men to carry out its appointed tasks.

Sandys himself implicitly recognised the force of assertions that the services were not well structured for an extra-European role by blurring the distinction between the Middle East and Europe. Thus, according to the White Paper, 'apart from its own importance, the Middle East guards the right flank of N.A.T.O.' and in the event of an emergency involving the Baghdad pact 'British forces in the Middle East would be made available ... these would include bomber squadrons based in Cyprus capable of delivering nuclear weapons'. Any credibility in the implied extension of the nuclear deterrent to the Middle East had already been undermined by the military operations undertaken the previous year at Suez. Indeed, the tenuous nature of British interests in the Middle East was indicated by the notice given in the White Paper that the number of troops maintained in Libya would be reduced and that 'as a result of the termination of the treaty with Jordan, Britain has been relieved from the responsibility for defending that country'. Ultimately the rationale for the credibility of nuclear deterrence in Europe was survival; in the late 1950s no such rationale applied to the Middle East. And even in Europe there was an added dimension to the issue of credibility. The creation of a nuclear deterrent capability required a highly developed scientific and technological foundation; its maintenance in an era of rapid technological change would require an even more sophisticated and therefore costly base in the future. The continuance of the independent British deterrent depended upon the healthy expansion of the British economy.

Neither Macmillan nor Sandys was unaware of this; but rather than seeing such provision as a charge on the economy they regarded it as a fillip. For there was another rationale for the provision of an independent British deterrent which could not be spelled out in the White Paper or articulated in the Commons. It was intended to affect the behaviour not only of adversaries but also of allies; indeed, it was hoped that it would restore the confidence of the British electorate. The Suez débâcle had bewildered a largely uninformed public whose attitude to Egypt had been infused with the good-humoured contempt with which successive drafts of conscripts had viewed that country. In such circumstances the independent nuclear deterrent was seen as a domestic ju-ju whose properties restored pride and confidence even if it was not fully understood. Externally it was to assume the aspect of a totem, to enforce recognition of British standing within an Atlantic alliance still obsessed with military defence; its possession would restore credibility to the Conservative concept which saw Britain at the centre of three concentric circles encompassing the Commonwealth, Western Europe and North America. Sandys's candour in reflecting upon the consequences of the development of the 5,000 mile intercontinental ballistic missile was disingenuous and for the domestic audience; there was no intention or possibility of Britain 'going it alone'. Selwyn Lloyd had sketched the rough outline of an Atlantic community linking the United States and Canada with Britain and Europe at the North Atlantic Council meeting of December 1956; it failed to survive the chilly reserve of Dulles; but for the duration of his premiership Macmillan hankered after what he half jokingly and half seriously called his 'Grand Design' for primacy in the Atlantic alliance to be shared by Britain, France and the United States.

Ambitious as this aspiration would have been for any government, it stood some chance of success when the government was led by Macmillan, who had occupied all the great offices of state and who was prepared to exploit his wartime friendship with Eisenhower. In the aftermath of the first British thermonuclear test he obtained a pledge from the president for the amendment of the legislation which had hitherto throttled the flow of nuclear information and associated technology between the United States and Britain. As Chancellor of the Exchequer he had served notice on the Atlantic allies that some assistance would have to be forthcoming across the exchanges for the British Army of the Rhine. After the 1957 defence White Paper announced that BAOR would be cut back, four months of haggling produced a compromise by which although the Germans were to pay £12 million per annum for three years BAOR was to remain at 55,000 strength only until the end of the year; after that it would be reduced to 45,000 and retained at that level until April 1961. Meanwhile Sandys had not only had the chairman of the US joint chiefs of staff endorse one part of his programme by advocating a reduction of American troop numbers in Europe; at the December 1957 meeting of the North Atlantic Council the British emphasis on nuclear deterrence seemed corroborated by the announcement that the United States was now ready to provide tactical nuclear weapons and intermediate-range ballistic missiles to her allies.

Notwithstanding the rows with the service chiefs and strained relations with the service ministries, then, Sandys seemed to be fulfilling admirably the charge laid upon him by the Prime Minister, and his confidence in himself was reflected in the firm, almost magisterial tone of his second White Paper, which appeared at the normal time in February 1958. There was one feature, however, which illustrated political adroitness rather than intellectual consistency, a manipulation of doctrine to support the assertion that *Sputnik* did not indicate a shift in the balance of power in favour of the Soviets. Medium-range ballistic missiles were said to dominate every target of value in the Soviet Union, and it was affirmed that corresponding capability on the part of the Soviets in respect of Western Europe would afford them no advantage in the absence of additional capability to strike at strategic air bases within the United States itself; by the time the Soviet Union deployed intercontinental missiles the United States would also have them. But this was implicitly to invoke the reliability of the United States nuclear deterrent in respect of her allies, which had been explicitly declared less than reliable by Sandys himself the previous year. What commanded attention, however, was his chilling assertion that the Western alliance was ready to initiate nuclear war in the event of a major conventional attack upon Europe and his announcement that RAF Fighter Command would be still further reduced. The reliability of the American guarantee was, of course, a matter of political faith, incapable of proof or disproof this side of Armageddon; what could more profitably be questioned was the efficacy of the British deterrent force. The magisterial aura of the Minister of Defence was accordingly badly damaged when in spring 1958 the Director of Plans RAF mounted briefing sessions for air force personnel and newspaper correspondents which differed markedly from the White Paper in their arguments for a second generation of both bomber and fighter aircraft and for an airborne as opposed to a fixed-site missile. Living up to its nickname, the 'silent service' seeded the more prestigious newspapers with carefully shaped propaganda which gradually moved from calling for a carrier-borne contribution to the deterrent to the advocacy of a fully sea-based missile force. In addition, criticism, Whitehall gossip and leaks to the press on the part of civil servants drove Sandys to have his authority confirmed in the White Paper on the central organisation of defence in July 1958. Clipping the wings of the defence chiefs, however, and the creation of the Defence Board as an anvil on which to strike his advisers still did not quell challenges to his policy, as witnessed by the furore occasioned by Lieutenant General Sir John Cowley's address to the Royal United Services Institute in which he criticised reliance on the nuclear deterrent on both moral and practical grounds and deplored neglect of the conventional forces.

During Sandys's last year there were strong indications that he was beginning to temper his own *élan*. The defence White Paper for 1959 hinted at technological problems concerning Blue Streak, the missile so confidently anticipated in 1957; the TSR2 was to be procured for the RAF for both ground support and tactical operation, while the Royal Navy was to receive new frigates to counter the increasing deployment of Soviet submarines. Only in regard to BAOR were the confident measures of 1957 being implemented. The onset of the Berlin crisis in November 1957 had enhanced perceptions of a Soviet threat and accordingly affected British readiness to maintain force levels in Germany and German readiness to make the concessions on support costs to keep them at 55,000 strength. The White Paper confirmed that their fire-power was to be augmented by the supply of Corporal guided missiles. But even here reality was less portentous than the minister's presentation, because the Corporal's warhead was American and the use of the missile thus a matter for Anglo-American decision. This served to underline the decline in Sandys's confidence; two years previously he had struck out for an independent British nuclear deterrent, but in the defence debate of 1959 he declared that

> the United States has given categorical assurances that she still regards an attack upon any N.A.T.O. country as an attack upon herself and will come to its aid with all necessary force. Her Majesty's Government places complete reliance upon these solemn undertakings.[25]

The reason for playing down the independent nature of the British deterrent and expressing such confidence in the United States was that the bills were beginning to come in. The defence Estimates were back over £1,500 million, an increase of £48 million, and the sophisticated equipment to maintain the British deterrent in the '60s still remained to be provided. In order to get it, the British government would have to milk the Anglo-American relationship; in effect, within two years the notion that an independent British deterrent would establish British standing in the Atlantic alliance and breathe new life into the Anglo-American relationship was beginning to look over-optimistic; rather, the Anglo-American relationship had to be cultivated in order to maintain the British deterrent and thus elevate Britain within the alliance. The slide was on towards the cancellation of the fixed-base guided missile Blue Streak, the quest for the Anglo-American air-launched Skybolt missile and the final acquisition in December 1962 of the wholly American seaborne missile Polaris.

Fortunately for Sandys it was not he who had to do the sliding, for in October 1959 Macmillan decided in the aftermath of his electoral victory to sweep away the Ministry of Supply and divide the Ministry of Transport and Civil Aviation into new Ministries of Transport and Aviation. The first was to take over from the Admiralty naval shipbuilding and ship repairing; the second was to embrace not only civil aviation but also research, development and production of both civil and military aircraft, and guided and atomic weapons, radar and electronics. As Minister of Aviation Macmillan wanted Sandys,'a man of determination and courage' as he described him in his memoirs; not without difficulty he managed to persuade him to leave Defence. One of the reasons for Sandys's reluctance to move was his commitment to the principle of a fixed-site missile and refusal to accept the steadily hardening unanimity of the chiefs of staff that such a weapon would be outmoded if ever its increasing development costs led to its deployment. From his new ministry, however, he continued to resist the pressure from the military to fill the gap between fixed-base and mobile land or sea-based missiles with Skybolt. His successor, Harold Watkinson, yielded, and the Cabinet's defence committee finally overruled Sandys. There was, then, some rough justice in his being spared the fury of the Commons, which was vented on his hapless successor when he announced the cancellation of Blue Streak in April 1960. Writing of it years later in his memoirs, Macmillan acknowledged that he was still uncertain whether the decision had been a wise one, an admission which could be regarded as a tribute to the advocacy as well as the tenacity of Sandys.

What was certain was that he had made his mark on post-war defence policy, a mark associated with his championing of the British deterrent at the expense of conventional forces. His predecessor, Antony Head, was in no doubt about his impact; speaking in the Commons when Blue Streak was cancelled he called for a re-examination of defence policy based on high technology:

> I am frightened that if we embark upon this expensive field, the expenditure may push out what is required to make our conventional forces effective and that through our example conventional forces throughout the whole Western alliance may become less and less.[26]

It is, when one considers it, a compliment to Sandys that two decades later one of his old opponents, Sir John Cowley, should be making the same point, declaring his astonishment

> that our official government policy still is to maintain and up-date at great expense an 'independent nuclear deterrent' ... would it not be more sensible to spend the enormous sum of money required to up-date the deterrent on providing our Navy, Army and Air Force with more and better conventional arms and equipment?[27]

According to Sir Harold Wilson a week is a long time in politics. That his policy has endured for twenty years and still arouses hostility is the measure of Duncan Sandys's achievement.

Notes

1   Michael Howard, 'Organisation for defence in U.K. and U.S.A., 1945–1958', *Brassey's Annual*, 1959, pp. 69–77.
2   Harold Macmillan, *Tides of Fortune, 1945–1955*, Macmillan, London, 1969, pp. 560–2.
3   Sir Anthony Eden, *Full Circle*, Cassell, London, 1960, p. 274.
4   Macmillan, *House of Commons Debates*, 24 January 1957, c. 399.
5   Howard, *Brassey's Annual, 1959*, p. 76.
6   Vice-Admiral J. Hughes-Hallett, CB, DSO, MP, 'The central organisation for defence', *Royal United Services Institute for Defence Studies Journal*, November 1958, pp. 488–93.
7   General Eisenhower, 1 April 1952 (i.e. first anniversary of SHAPE), *Keesing's Contemporary Archives, 1952*, p. 12141.
8   Winston Churchill, *House of Commons Debates*, 28 March 1952, cc. 189–202.
9   *Statement of Defence*, Cmd 9075, 18 February 1954.
10   Field Marshal Viscount Montgomery, KG, GCB, DSO, 'The panorama of warfare in a nuclear age', *Royal United Services Institute for Defence Studies Journal*, November 1956.
11   General Gruenther, 8 June 1954, *Keesing's 1954*, p. 13640.
12   Churchill, *House of Commons Debates*, 30 July 1952, c. 1495.
13   Eden, *Full Circle*, pp. 372–3.
14   Marshal of the Royal Air Force Sir John Slessor, GCB, DSO, MC, 'British defence policy', *Foreign Affairs*, July 1957, pp. 551–63.
15   Sandys, *House of Commons Debates*, 13 February 1957, c. 1309.
16   *Report on Defence: Britain's Contribution to Peace and Security*, Cmnd 363, February 1958.
17   Churchill, *House of Commons Debates*, 1 March 1955, c. 1897.
18   Sandys, *House of Commons Debates*, 13 February, cc. 1310–11.
19   Sandys, *House of Commons Debates* 16 April 1957, c. 1761.
20   *The Times*, 5 April 1957.
21   Slessor, *Foreign Affairs*, July 1957.
22   Alastair Buchan, 'Their bomb and ours', *Encounter*, January 1957, pp. 11–18.
23   Shinwell, *House of Commons Debates*, 16 April 1957, c. 1996.
24   Strachey, *House of Commons Debates*, 17 April 1957, c. 2026.
25   Sandys, *House of Commons Debates*, 26 February 1959, c. 1418.
26   Head, *House of Commons Debates*, 27 April 1960, c. 261.
27   Lieutenant General Sir John Cowley, letter to the *Times*, 20 December 1979.

8

DENIS HEALEY
AND RATIONAL DECISION-
MAKING IN DEFENCE

PETER NAILOR

When the Labour Party under the leadership of Harold Wilson won the general election of October 1964 it had been out of office for thirteen years. It was faced, therefore, with a number of problems and difficulties over and above any immediate political issues that had to be dealt with. Only the Prime Minister himself and two of his colleagues had previously held senior office, and there was only a sprinkling among the rest of the leading members of the party in Parliament who had held any ministerial office at all. Although most of them had wide parliamentary experience, an immediate problem was how they would take to Whitehall life: how quickly they would settle in to the business of office-holding, how soon they might learn to master a brief and how they would deal with permanent officials who, at least as much as the House of Commons, judge strengths and weaknesses by strange and tribal standards.[1]

A second problem was that the machinery of government into which these new ministers had to fit was changing, at two levels. The new government added to the pace of change at the higher level by making a number of alterations in departmental structures; for example, it split the Treasury in two, and set up a new Ministry of Technology. Institution-building of this sort had already been a feature of government for some years, but it sometimes meant that experienced groups of officials were broken up and reallocated to unfamiliar conglomerations, with effects on their ability to respond to the demands made upon them by the new government.

The lower level of change was reflected in the patterns of administration within these institutions and departments. The end of the 1950s and the beginning of the 1960s had seen a rapid development of new managerial techniques and procedures, based, in part, upon a fundamental reassessment of the needs of government institutions for information and for planning data, given the changing role of government itself: but sometimes precipitated simply by the development of new equipment, which could handle information more efficiently and expeditiously.[2] In fact the age of the computer had been signalled, and the British government was taking a lead, not merely in stimulating research into computers and their accompanying software, but in employing them in its business. There was, as a consequence of these parallel developments, a new concern with forecasting, planning and trying to foresee the consequences of long-term policy decisions. It was true, of course, that the ability to look ahead was as dependent as it ever had been upon the quality of the policy assumptions that were fed into the forecasts, but there was no doubt about the improved mechanical ability of government departments to draw conclusions from sets of assumptions projected a long way into the future.

It was also the case that the new 'office machines' gave organisations a better ability to sift and arrange data about current operations, and hence to have better information and a quicker indication of what was happening on production schedules and financial commitments. All these developments gave a better hope of better management control; and British interest in them was markedly heightened by what was happening in the United States. The American government, particularly in the Department of Defense from 1958 onwards, was also using new techniques to control current projects and future plans. The new mechanisms of systematic analysis are most often associated with the name of Robert McNamara, whose administrative style depended to a marked extent upon such modes of analysis; but the movement had started before his appointment.[3]

The types of techniques that were applied in the United Kingdom and in the United States were broadly similar, but the pattern of application was rather different, and reflected both the difference in the roles of ministers in the two countries and the extensive differences in the governmental patterns of administration.[4] Functional costing, or 'output budgeting', was first advocated in the United States by the Hoover Commission in 1949, and first used as an experiment in the United Kingdom by the War Office in the 1920s; it is a system of presenting expenditure costs which not only identifies the physical objects on which money is spent but also the policy purposes which it is intended should be achieved. It also provides for costs to be identified and measured over a longish period of time: costs which include operating expenses and the associated costs that arise over and above the construction of equipment. This type of forecasting gives a better prospect of identifying bulges in future budget levels, but it requires that items to be included in any budget should be split into separate inputs, or 'programme elements' consisting of the immediate objects of expenditure.

Systems analysis, as another type of technique, was intended to assist in the making of choices between alternative methods of achieving specific policy objectives by identifying the assumptions and facts on which they rested, and tracing out the knowable consequences and costs of each alternative. In defence policy, systems analysis particularly directs attention to the total range of factors involved in weapon systems. Thus, if the army wants a new tank the main purpose of which is to destroy an adversary's tanks, systems analysts will look to see what alternative ways there are of killing tanks more efficiently or more cheaply: anti-tank missiles, artillery, or perhaps aircraft strikes, or something else which, from the army point of view alone, is not an obvious alternative.

Systems analysis and its associated techniques greatly improved the ability to make good choices between alternative ways of achieving specific policy objectives; but they did not allow departments to dispense with the exercise of judgement and military experience. Moreover none of them provided a mandatory discipline for ensuring that its results were fully reliable. Both in defining the assumptions which go into the analysis and in assessing its results, planners must exercise their skills and judgement to provide manageable data; and they have to do this without either knowing all the relevant facts or being able to provide a satisfactory intellectual proof that their judgement is correct.

Such administrative developments compounded the third problem which faced the new government. That was sheer ignorance. The British system of government gives a considerable advantage to the party in office, so far as awareness of what is going on and what the implications of what has been decided will mean. The opposition was not in much better case than ordinary members of the public to find out about the really important details, and the general implications, of government decisions. The parliamentary procedures for obtaining information by question and debate, and through the scrutiny afforded by the select committee system, were not then, and probably are not now, an adequate substitute for 'looking at the books' and reading the telegrams and minutes. It is not really so much that the actual business of government is deliberately shrouded in privacy, although that has been a persistent criticism of the British style of administration: but the business of government has become more extensive, very much more detailed, and altogether more complicated.

When Denis Healey became Secretary of State for Defence he had been the Labour Party's official spokesman on defence for about eighteen months. He had previously been the foreign affairs spokesman, succeeding Aneurin Bevan in that position in 1960. His experience in international political and military affairs went back much further, however, and in that sense he stood out among the new departmental ministers as an unusually well prepared senior colleague, with an extensive knowledge of the intellectual and policy environment of the department he was now called upon to direct.[5]

After going up to Oxford from Bradford Grammar School in 1936 and getting his degree in 1940, Healey joined the army and, like so many of his generation, found a great deal of experience concentrated in the next five years. He obtained a commission and served mainly in North Africa and Italy; by the end of the war he was a major and had been decorated and mentioned in dispatches. After unsuccessfully contesting the Pudsey and Otley constituency in 1945 he became the secretary of the international department at the Labour Party headquarters, holding the position until he was elected to Parliament for a Leeds constituency in 1952. While in the Labour Party secretariat, and for long afterwards, he was an active worker and writer on international affairs; in particular he played a significant role in supporting the study of international political and defence affairs in the United Kingdom. He was a councillor of the Royal Institute for International Affairs from 1948 to 1960 and a leading proponent in the foundation of the International Institute for Strategic Studies, set up in 1958. He kept well abreast of the welter of publications on strategic and political affairs that began to come out of America in the 1950s, and himself wrote a number of essays about the influence of nuclear weapons upon international politics and upon the Cold War. He spoke fluent French and German and, through his position in the party secretariat and on delegations to the Council of Europe and other international bodies, had a wide acquaintanceship with leading European figures in the international socialist movements. He prepared himself assiduously by reading, by discussion and by visits to foreign capitals for the responsibility which, it became increasingly clear during 1964, he might well have to assume after the general election. The opportunity arose in the same month in which the governing cabal of the Soviet Union ousted its leader, Khrushchev, and in which the Chinese Peoples' Republic exploded its first nuclear weapon.

A defence minister in a Labour government faces some special difficulties, which in 1964 were compounded by the factors arising from a long period in opposition that have already been mentioned. The Labour Party's view of the world is inevitably coloured by the ideological bias which the party embodies. On the one hand this leads to high values being put upon social well-being, internationally as well as nationally, and shades into a concern for the peaceful settlement of disputes that is sometimes manifested on the international plane in idealistic and, from some sides of the party, pacifist terms. On the other hand Labour, like social democratic parties elsewhere, has drawn sharp distinctions between the aims of socialism and the totalitarian practices and ambitions of communist (and fascist) parties. There is therefore inherently a tension between the ideals for which the party stands and the need to provide for the instruments by which states have, up till now, secured their own interests and disputed the pretensions of their rivals. The tension becomes an active issue principally when the party is in power. In practice this meant, after 1945, that the Labour Party, in office but also in opposition, found itself faced with a need to strike a balance between national security objectives which could become incompatible with each other. The requirement to rebuild, and refashion, British society and the British economy called for a heavy concentration of resources and effort that were clearly supportive of security, in general; but the emerging threat, as it was seen, of Soviet expansionism called for a collective military response by the Western powers that also involved resources and effort. In the period of the Korean war rearmament programme, from July 1950 onwards, it was arguable that the Labour government had responded too dramatically—switching resources to defence on such a scale and at such a speed that some of the domestic achievements of the immediate post-war period were threatened. Later in the 1950s Labour in opposition had heavily criticised Conservative policy over the Suez adventure, in large measure because it was the type of military response to an international dispute which the United Nations Organisation had been set up to transcend. In general, however, the broad thrust of security policies was not a matter of dispute between the main political parties: British security, in military as well as in economic terms, could no longer be conceived of solely in terms of national capabilities and, very important, the general security of Western Europe depended upon the active involvement of the United States.

In all these matters it had been the Attlee governments that had set the tone of British policies. After 1951 the Labour Party in opposition was strongly drawn to support the general line of policy but found many particular issues on which to criticise the Conservatives' performance over the years, of which Suez was one. In this respect the use of force in the Anglo-French invasion of Egypt in October 1956 was only a part of the Labour case. Force in this instance was important because it was an instrumental device: the commitment of the defence services was a subsidiary issue in parliamentary terms, although the occasion for the use of force at the end of October sharply hardened attitudes, inside as well as outside Parliament.[6]

In that matter, as in the second issue—the use of the defence services in the colonial dependencies—there was usually a delicate line to be drawn between the criticism of policy and criticism of the forces themselves. It was necessary to distinguish carefully between the basic policy and the execution of the policy in order to avoid being thought unpatriotic, or unsupportive of the soldiers whose lives were at risk; Barbara Castle, for example, was heavily criticised for commenting upon the behaviour of British troops in Cyprus. Nevertheless there was a range of opportunities in the 1950s and 1960s for the opposition to draw critical attention to the employment of the services in the 'struggles for independence' which became an increasingly salient feature of Britain's Commonwealth relationships, in South East Asia and Africa in particular. In a number of instances the army was used, it seemed, to gain time or to allow a political stalemate to become familiar. And in these circumstances it was valid enough to point up the need for flexible and acceptable political objectives to replace the services as a peace-keeping instrument of policy.

The third area was the record of the government in managing the ventures into high technology that also emerged as a constant feature of defence affairs. The pace of change accelerated markedly in this period; new weapons, new materials, new control systems and new methods of weapon delivery all contributed towards a demand for new equipment that proved extremely difficult to manage efficiently, in Britain as elsewhere. The difficulties they posed, in selection and in management, highlighted the need for better systems of control. A significant number of projects were cancelled, either because their cost rose unacceptably or because they were overtaken technically; and these experiences called into question not only the methods by which government support and management of military research and development was supervised but also the organisation of the industrial resources through which the work was carried out.[7]

But the issue which created the most dramatic difficulties for the Labour Party was the question of nuclear weapons: specifically the maintenance of a British strategic deterrent capability. The decision to go ahead with the manufacture of atomic weapons was taken by the Labour government in 1947, before the pattern of post-war relationships was determined by the 'Cold War'; the emergence of the alliance structures, and the rapid transition to thermonuclear weapons and missile-based systems of delivery, created new concerns which not only affected policy options but also created new grounds for public concern about the implications of nuclear war. Between 1959 and 1961 Labour found itself caught up in the debate about the need to control the spread of nuclear weapons, and weapon testing, which extended to demands for the country to renounce the possession of such weapons. The shape of the debate within the party was initially defined by the stance adopted by the Campaign for Nuclear Disarmament, but developed into a test of strength between the leadership and a range of parliamentary and non-parliamentary interests inside the party which urged a fundamental revision of British policy and attracted enough support in 1960 to carry resolutions embodying their views at the party conference. Gaitskell was unwilling to accept this turn of events and managed to deflect party policy away from nuclear disarmament the next year; the issue remained of considerable intrinsic importance but by the end of 1961 had come to be seen as at least as important as an issue in the relationship of the parliamentary leadership to the party conference, and to the limitations which the conference could impose upon party policy objectives.[8] Healey himself had described the intrinsic issue in an essay written in 1959:

> There is little doubt that the main aim of the British thermonuclear striking force is to provide passive deterrence for Britain in case America drops her present policy of active deterrence for NATO as a whole. Though some Englishmen [*sic*] believe that the political likelihood of Russia presenting Britain with the sort of threat to which passive deterrence would be relevant is too small to be worth preparing against, the majority, including the leaders of both the political parties, feel that the additional expenditure required to mount a passive deterrent on the basis of Britain's existing atomic resources and delivery system is small enough to be worth making. This majority might dwindle dramatically if its assumptions about the low cost of a passive deterrent prove to be mistaken.[9]

By the end of 1963 support for the CND attitude had fallen away, partly because Labour shied away from an issue which had come so close to dividing the party and partly because it appeared, in the Cuba crisis, that the policy of 'active deterrence' followed by the United States was both effective and necessary. A change of leadership in the party when Gaitskell died also helped to displace the issue. Nevertheless the concern about the dangers inherent in nuclear weapons remained, and was always likely to resurface.

The task which faced Healey, therefore, in October 1964 was to put together a set of policies which, having their roots in past policies and debates, were consonant with all the other aims of the new administration, and bore some sort of relationship to the existing state of affairs in the nation and in the party. If there was a need to examine existing programmes in the Ministry of Defence critically, there was also an opportunity to use the new methods that now lay to hand. A routine opportunity to explain what the new government intended would present itself in February 1965, when it would be necessary to produce a White Paper to accompany the defence Estimates for 1965–66; the intervening months were used to brief ministers about the existing state of affairs and to conduct interdepartmental discussions about the new government's new choices. The election campaign had committed the government 'to put our defences on a sound basis and to ensure that the nation gets value for money', but there was a lot to be done if flesh was to be put on such bones. An early determination was made to limit the scope of defence planning by pegging defence spending at £2,000 million, at 1964 prices, for 1969–70.

> I had no incentive to push further [said Healey]. It was really arbitrary. We were obsessed by the fact that there was this automatic increase in defence costs if one didn't do something. We were faced with a programme that went up from £2,000 million to £2,400 million in five years, so we decided that we would make sure that in five years time it didn't go up at all.

Towards the end of November Healey summarised his first impressions to the House of Commons:

> One thing I have already learned from my first five weeks in office . . . is that Britain is spending more on defence than any other country of her size and wealth. We are still trying to sustain three major military roles—to maintain an independent strategic nuclear striking power, to make a major contribution towards the allied defence of Western Europe, and to deploy a significant military capacity overseas, from British Guiana through the Mediterranean, Africa, and the Middle East to Hong Kong.[10]

This comment followed a major Cabinet discussion about security policy which was held at Chequers over the weekend of 21–22 November 1964. Before then presentations had been given to Healey and his departmental team of ministers, and to some of his Cabinet colleagues, on specific issues, including the planned budget for defence, and a number of the major equipment projects; all senior ministers had been provided with departmental briefs about the main items of current business, including the pressure on the pound sterling in the international money markets. In a sense the Chequers meeting was an initial stocktaking. It was also a chance to get some of the more urgent decisions out of the way.[11]

By the time the defence White Paper was published in February 1965, therefore, the shape of the new policies could be perceived; and by April 1965, when the Cabinet finally agreed to the cancellation of the TSR2 aircraft project, the decks had been cleared for the new search for effective policies to begin in earnest.

It had been a busy winter, and if the critical impetus had derived from the sense of urgency which any new government, with election pledges fresh in its mind, must always have, the style of the activity had in large part been determined by Healey himself. He quickly impressed his colleagues and the officials with whom he worked as a capable, intelligent and decisive minister. He dominated much of the debate at the November Chequers meeting, and seemed to be as much at home with detail as with broad issues of policy. He had a positive, rather combative personality, and enjoyed both having a good argument and winning it. His style suited the committee room rather more evidently than it did the House of Commons, where his touch in beating down opposition to his views was sometimes less appropriate to members' susceptibilities; and within the Ministry of Defence his inclination to use a Socratic method of discussion suited the civil servants better than it did the military, whose deference to his status sometimes led them to be more reticent and polite than was necessary or even desirable. 'He absorbed information like a sponge,' one of his personal staff once said,

> and occasionally he needed to be squeezed, to get some of the less important details out, to make room for other views and facts. He liked to make sure that he knew what had gone into the rather bland minutes that we sometimes got from the department, and he was not at all averse from hearing, from quite junior people, the full range of argument.[12]

The objectives with which he entered office were explained, in the 1965 White Paper, in this way:

> The present Government has inherited defence forces which are seriously over-stretched and in some respects dangerously under-equipped ... The present Government has therefore set in train a series of studies on defence policy; these will cover the effects on force levels and capabilities of a number of different possible courses of

action. In the light of these studies it will be possible to review our strategy, taking into account not only the economic position, but also new or reaffirmed political objectives which our strategy must be designed to implement. The purpose of these studies will try to ascertain the means by which defence expenditure during the next few years may be reduced to roughly the present figure in real terms. Meanwhile steps have already been taken to ensure that the immediate needs of our forces will be met at a cost which the nation can afford.[13]

The major steps were to alter significantly the shape and timing of the RAF re-equipment programme (cancelling three major projects and substituting for them one national programme, buying in American equipment, and setting up collaborative development programmes with European allies, principally the French). It was also decided to retain the Polaris programme, but to proceed with only four of the five submarines that had been on order. Without seriously affecting the military credibility of the submarine-based deterrent, this would defuse some of the internal opposition to the programme in the Labour Party and go part of the way towards meeting a campaign pledge to 'renegotiate the Nassau Agreement'. And it was decided to give a boost to the analytical methods by which new requirements could be evaluated, by developing existing techniques of functional costing and by setting up a new organisation to undertake operational analysis investigations and cost-effectiveness studies.

The series of defence studies that were referred to in the 1965 White Paper became known as 'The Defence Review'. In fact it was a series of studies, not all of them carried out in the same way or with the same machinery. The formal machinery that was established in Whitehall for giving a final shape to the series of issues and decisions was embodied in a structure of committees. At the top was the Defence and Overseas Policy Committee of the Cabinet (DOPC)—a body of senior ministers in which all the major interests represented in overseas and defence policy had a part, normally chaired by the Prime Minister. It dealt with a wide range of matters, but major problems were often referred to the full Cabinet. Below this ministerial committee stood the Defence and Overseas Policy (Official) Committee, with a similarly wide range of membership, composed of permanent officials and chaired by the Secretary to the Cabinet; service representation was normally limited to the Chief of the Defence Staff. Below this again the 'Defence Review Working Party' (DRWP), at a slightly less senior level, was where the submissions to the more senior committees were worked out and the sequence of papers and, if necessary, a common and agreed submission were initially arrived at.

By the time the major activity had been completed, in mid-1967, this apparatus had evolved a number of standard procedures for dealing with business. The way in which work was instigated followed two main patterns; either ministers, in DOPC, determined questions to which they required answers from departments or, working from the bottom up, the DRWP provided analyses of specific problems which were then considered by ministers, who gave their views and if necessary sent papers forward to the full Cabinet. As the extent of the work progressed a number of sub-committees of the DRWP were set up to prepare specific analyses. What was innovative in the process was that departments were not required to produce a co-ordinated and agreed statement of policy for ministers either to accept or reject. The sort of question posed by the DOPC would be in the form 'What are British interests likely to be in such and such an issue by the mid-1970s?'. And the responses to the question came, normally, in the form of analyses by departments who represented their view of British interests from the basis of their departmental expertise. These separate analyses might be submitted to ministers under cover of a summary note which briefly described the thrust of the arguments, but it was not thought desirable in a review of this importance for departments to be asked to cobble together whatever they could find that was of common significance to their separate viewpoints. They were able to present a perspective which represented only the sum of their departmental interests: and if, in some instances and on particular issues, this still created difficulties in reconciling intra-departmental causes, it still meant that—on the whole—the full range of varying departmental perspectives was the more likely to be displayed. This was particularly important to the Ministry of Defence, because it enabled differences of emphasis between them and the Foreign Office to be brought out into the open, on the extent to which British interests should be specified, and the obligation to provide military forces of some sort to meet such commitments as these interests implied. The system gave rather more play for a range of ministerial debate in the senior committee, and at this level Healey once again found himself a major and successful protagonist because of his mastery of the issues and his debating skills.

There was, however, a range of issues that were not so easily susceptible to this broad inter-departmental treatment. The Ministry of Defence itself had only been fashioned in 1964, as a result of the Mountbatten–Thorneycroft reforms that resulted in the Ministry of Defence Act of 1964. The need to put the various types of defence interests into a new federative structure had been foreseen for some time, but the moves to bring the single-service departments, and then subsequently the procurement authorities for those departments, under a single ministerial direction had been slow to develop.[14] At one level the need for a better and more cohesive management structure was based upon the increasing cost of defence; in terms of both money and skilled manpower defence had remained since the war a very big business indeed, and the loose co-ordination which had been the feature of the earlier structure was arguably outmoded in an environment in which a major weapon system might take ten years and £1,000 million to put into service. But there was also a case for the structure of defence management to reflect more accurately and sensitively the changing nature of war and the place of military force in international politics. With the advent of nuclear weapons and the emergence of deterrence as a prime objective of policy, and with the need for national security policies to be based upon an international, collective posture, it was even more clearly arguable than it had been in the past that the direction of policy must be firmly related to civilian political control and involvement. The creation of a unified Ministry of Defence went a good way to meeting this sort of point, though it still left rather in the air what the relationship between the Secretary of State for Defence and the Prime Minister, as the head of the government, was in the matter of controlling military forces in time of war.

The practical problems that emerged in 1965 meant that, in so far as the Defence Review needed to take into account departmental defence issues, the review itself took place largely within the ministry and under the supervision of the Secretary of State. The position was not so clear-cut for aerospace equipment, where the Minister of Aviation had a separate responsibility. Although the analysis of British interests in regional areas and in general matters of high-technology investment was undertaken through the collective and committee-based mechanisms of the DOPC structure, specific equipment questions were largely, though not entirely, Ministry of Defence affairs. One of the subsidiary purposes of creating 'giant' departments had in fact been to remove from the Cabinet agenda the consideration of relatively detailed issues which might be a matter of dispute between individual departments in the same area of concern. What this meant in 1966, however, was that when for example the Secretary of State eventually decided against the programme for a new class of fleet aircraft carriers, the minister for the navy no longer had any right to carry the argument through to the Cabinet; he was simply a departmental minister whose Secretary of State had ruled against him. It might be argued that this decision was hardly less significant than the cancellation of the TSR2; but the Minister of Aviation had a separate parish, and that decision therefore went to Cabinet.[15]

The results of the activities initially covered by the Defence Review were reported to Parliament in the defence White Paper of February 1966. The conclusions were broadly as follows: the determination to hold spending at £2,000 million at 1964 prices was basically sound as a reasonable target against which to plan. It could be met without reducing the nation's ability to carry out the existing range of military tasks. But this programme, 'though achieving a major cut in expenditure without any loss in military efficiency', did 'nothing to reduce the excessive cost of defence in foreign exchange'. Nor did it 'contribute to solving the second major problem which led the government to undertake the defence review—the overstretch of our military manpower'. On several occasions no units of the strategic reserve had been immediately available because of the obligations which required military commitments all over the world.

> In these conditions both recruiting and re-engagement have fallen short of the targets set; this in turn has increased the strain on our already over-stretched services. Such overstretch has the most damaging consequences in our defence policy as a whole ... Even a relatively small contraction in our present defence effort will mean that we must relinquish some of our present commitments overseas.

The White Paper went on to make points both about the need to revise NATO's strategic assumptions to fit the emerging shape of a less tense confrontation with the Soviet Union and about British military commitments outside Europe. It was in this area that the major pronouncement emerged:

> ... to maintain all our current tasks and capabilities outside Europe would impose an unacceptable strain on our overstretched forces and bear too heavily both on our domestic economy and on our reserves of foreign exchange. For all these reasons we have decided that, while Britain should retain a major military capability outside Europe, she should in future be subject to certain general limitations. First, Britain will not undertake major operations of war except in co-operation with allies. Secondly, we will not accept an obligation to provide another country with military assistance unless it is prepared to provide us with the facilities we need to make such assistance effective in time. Finally, there will be no attempt to maintain defence facilities in an independent country against its wishes.[16]

As principles of policy, these considerations seemed unexceptionable, but to planners inside the Ministry of Defence they could give no sort of guarantee that the principles would hold. The ministry might still be asked at some future time to prepare an operation that cut across any or all of them. Nevertheless the statement of intention was clear and it put extra-European interests on notice that, at some future time, Britain's willingness to involve herself in military activities would run down quite quickly. Even in the White Paper itself the declaration of principle was hedged. Discussing the Middle and Far East it went on to say:

> It is ... [there] ... that the greatest danger to peace may lie in the next decade and some of our partners in the Commonwealth may be directly threatened. We believe that it is right that Britain should

continue to maintain a military presence in this area. Its effectiveness will turn largely on the arrangements we can make with our Commonwealth partners and other allies in the coming years. As soon as conditions permit [this was a reference to the 'Confrontation' between Malaysia and Indonesia] we shall make some reductions in the forces which we keep in the area. We have important military facilities in Malaysia and Singapore as have our Australian and New Zealand partners. These we plan to retain for as long as the Governments of Malaysia and Singapore agree that we should do so on acceptable conditions. Against the day when it may no longer be possible for us to use these facilities freely, we have begun to discuss with the Government of Australia the practical possibilities of our having military facilities in that country if necessary.[17]

So far as equipment for the forces was concerned, the White Paper dealt with the re-equipment of the navy in the face of the decision not to proceed with new aircraft carriers. It then went on to the need to replace the Canberra and discussed the programme for buying a force of fifty F111 aircraft from the United States, including the offset of some of the dollar costs by American purchases of British equipment. The review also announced the decision to go ahead with new maritime reconnaissance aircraft and discussed the general implications of these decisions for the aircraft industry. Finally it commented briefly upon the new arrangements which had been announced to the House of Commons earlier in February 1966 about the reorganisation of home defence. These were basically a decision to establish a Home Defence Force and to restrict Civil Defence preparations to a new low minimum.

Domestically the Defence Review report was greeted with a good deal of interest. Parliamentary debate tended to focus upon specific issues, like the decision to abandon large aircraft carriers. This did not mean that all the commentators, inside or outside Parliament, agreed with the way in which policy was developing; but there was an acknowledgement at least of the effort the government was making to provide a credible *rationale*, even if particular decisions were strongly criticised. The representation of the results in the two-volume White Paper did not provide, in any very clear way, much of a feeling for the amount of work that had gone into the exercise. The decision not to go ahead with CVAO1 in particular was based upon an extensive series of studies, both about military function and about the relative cost-effectiveness of alternative solutions. Although there was a great deal of argument about the way in which parts of these studies had been 'fixed' by the nature of the assumptions on which they were based, nevertheless what was not in dispute was that a wide range of issues and questions had been brought out into the open simply by doing the studies.

Part II of the 1966 defence White Paper was a statement of the existing capabilities and deployments of the forces very much in the usual annual manner.[18] The explanations broke new ground in the sense only that they were more extensive and detailed than in earlier years. The meat of the Defence Review was contained in Part I.

The White Paper commented, 'We have always recognised that the Defence Review must be a continuing process and a permanent part of our policy making,' but in fact its publication represented a culmination of the process so far as the contributing departments were concerned, and there was a tendency within the Ministry of Defence to see it as a significant and finite achievement. Of course, the business of managing defence investment and deployment was recognised to be a continuous and continual process but the Defence Review itself had impinged so considerably upon the organisation that there was, as it were, a collective sigh of relief to have brought the process so far. The next step would be to get on with the development and refinement of these policies.

In practice things worked out rather differently. The domestic political environment was constrained by a number of factors, not least the smallness of the Labour majority in the House of Commons, and in the course of 1966 a general election campaign ensued. The government was returned with an enlarged majority, but an election campaign always imposes something of a hiatus upon the administrative process and 1966 was no exception. More generally, the state of the British economy began to impinge even more upon the parameters of defence planning: the rate of economic growth proved consistently unsatisfactory, and foreign exchange began to loom large as an intrinsic element affecting governmental attitudes towards NATO in general and the cost of the British Army of the Rhine in particular. The relative weakness of the pound sterling and the adverse balance of payment account were very much in the govenment's mind at this time; it was perhaps exaggerated, in the sense that Labour governments have been sensitive about their predecessors' record of having had to devalue on earlier occasions. There was no doubt that in the middle 1960s it was an issue about which senior ministers felt strongly, even to the extent of having deliberately avoided the question of devaluation for longer than now seems sensible.[19] The decisions which had been taken in 1965 to purchase equipment from overseas, over and above the programmes of purchases which the previous administration had determined upon, also began to make the defence contribution to the balance of payments very prominent.

The impetus for suggesting revised arrangements to offset some of these costs with the German government, and for a general reappraisal of NATO strategy, were accentuated during 1966 by the French government's decision to withdraw from the military organisations of the alliance. This led to hurried discussions about what could be done, both to ensure France's continuing participation in the alliance as a whole and to repair the gaps in the military dispositions due to her withdrawal.

Outside Europe the two events which affected defence planning were the ending of the Indonesian confrontation with Malaysia, which meant the removal of a considerable burden upon the defence services, and the indirect effect of the growingly contentious United States involvement in Vietnam on the the stability of South East Asia and on Anglo-American relations in general. The Labour government had identified South East Asia as an area in which Britain could still play a role in maintaining stability, and the Americans were pressing for a contribution to the effort in Vietnam. By any standard Britain's direct interest was small and her indirect interest, as the government saw it, lay more in persuading the Americans to limit their involvement than in joining them. In this attitude Britain shared common ground with many of the United States' allies and friends, but as a factor that impinged upon defence planning it had specific overtones, not least because the determination not to become involved threatened to put a strain upon other parts of her multi-faceted relationship with the United States.[20]

In sum, therefore, the Defence Review could not be regarded as anything more than a statement of general intentions, good for a limited period and perhaps not justifying the amount of work that went into it. On the other hand, by cleareng the mind and evaluating British interests in a more positive and cohesive way than had previously been done the exercise at least gave the government and the planners in the Ministry of Defence a clearer idea of where they were and where they wanted to go.

Partly as a result of the new factors the defence White Paper of February 1967 was much more in the line of a standard annual explanation of continuing defence problems.[21] The introductory section referred to the need for tight control of the defence budget, to the need to relieve overstretch in manpower and to reduce overseas expenditure. It also gave something more than a routine bob towards the importance of disarmament and arms control policy. Most of the introductory chapter, however, was concerned with the revision of NATO stategy and the redeployment of forces in the field and of resources at headquarters that followed on the review of commitments and obligations in the Defence Review, and with the changes that were possible after the end of 'confrontation' and the decision to evacuate Aden by the end of the year.

It was also possible to discern perspectives that were expected to be important for the rest of the 1960s and into the 1970s; there was a heavy emphasis on Europe, NATO and arms control. The changes in organisation in command and headquarters had a number of interesting aspects. At its most senior levels the scientific staff organisation in the Ministry of Defence was substantially reshaped, and a new body called the Programme Evaluation Group (PEG) was set up to advise the Secretary of State and his senior colleagues. The group was a small mixed military and civilian cell which effectively acted as an extension of the Secretary of State's private office. It was intended to be as it were, a prism which could be set athwart the stream of collective advice that came to the Secretary of State from the department: an independent source of evaluation which would allow him a wider scope to review the assumptions as well as the content of papers that were submitted to him. It created a number of difficulties. PEG was not intended to fulfil the same sort of heterodox function that the Foreign Office Planning Staff, for example, had within the FCO. Its time perspectives were much shorter and much more directly related to current policy studies than the Planning Staff had been set up to deal with. Although there was a formal connection with the Defence Operational Analysis Establishment (DOAE), it was by no means clear how such licensed unorthodoxy could function effectively in a large department which already had a federative structure that was by no means common in Whitehall. The advice that came to Ministers in the Defence department was not collated only through the Permanent Under Secretary; it emerged as a stream of opinion from the military staffs, the civilian financial and management staffs and the scientific staffs. In this sense the Secretary of State for Defence was already provided with a range of opinions which, potentially at least, were more diverse than many of his colleagues in the Home departments had.[22]

The other feature of note about the environment in which the defence White Paper appeared was that it was debated in the Commons at about the time the Prime Minister and Foreign Secretary were beginning consultations in Europe to pave the way for Britain's renewed application to join the European Communities. In this sense the emphasis on her interests and obligations outside Europe was seen, or could be seen, as a continuing attempt by the government to maintain a range of policies which, while the emphasis might vary, were as wide and diverse as any that their predecessors had tried to follow. The difference was going to be that they would be more restrained, and cheaper.

A substantive step towards the resolution of these problems was taken in the supplementary statement on defence policy which was published in July 1967.[23] The emphasis on Europe and NATO became much more pronounced, and what was set out in this new, and quite short, document was the basic decision to withdraw in the foreseeable future from mainland bases east of Suez and from the commitment to maintain forces outside Europe. The general pattern and timescale of withdrawal were sketched out, ministers were despatched to the Middle and Far East and to Australia to explain what the government had in mind, and proposals were put forward for cushioning friends and allies against some of the strategic and economic consequences, and for handing over the resources that would be left on site which it might be sensible to retain.

The two 1967 papers together mark a distinct stage of development in so far as they were principally concerned with a time frame beyond the end of the decade. The July paper in particular was the culmination of an exercise which had set out both to define British interests and to limit the extent to which British capabilities could be stretched to meet them. It was a careful delimitation of the resources, in terms of money and men, which the United Kingdom could afford to allocate to these various commitments, obligations and aspirations. There was thus a note of satisfaction in the conclusion to the July paper:

> We have been working continuously for almost three years on a major review of defence, revising Britain's overseas policy, formulating the role of military power to support it, and planning the forces required to carry out this role. This Statement marks the end of that process. The decisions in it have been reached after extensive consultations with our allies, to whose views we have given full weight. They spring from the best assessment we can make of Britain's interests and responsibilities as they will develop in a changing world.[24]

The Defence Review had sought to create a framework within which long-term policy objectives and shorter-term imperatives could be woven into a cohesive pattern that would result in an orderly set of efficient, and economical, activities. It was deliberately pitched at a higher level of conceptual rigour than departments usually had the time or the resources to allow; and this feature of the exercise, to which Healey himself attached importance, was instrumental in highlighting both the divergence between the sort of axiomatic assumptions on which policy is sometimes based and the conclusions to which logical analysis pointed, and also the sense of achievement which suffused parts of Whitehall when the activity was completed. That is not to say that either the logic or the achievement was universally recognised. Patrick Gordon-Walker has shown[25] how wide, diverse and persistent the range of opinions was within the Cabinet about the importance of Britain's extra-European role, and there are other, generally less coherent, accounts which supplement his version of ministerial attitudes.[26] Other parts of the national policy nexus continually intruded. The decision to re-apply for membership of the European Communities; relationships with major allies like the United

States and friends in the Commonwealth like India (which, after all, it could be claimed, was the invention of a Labour government); the impact of wars, in the Middle East no less than in Vietnam; the struggle to keep the economy prosperous and the pound strong—all represented balls that the Cabinet had to juggle with whilst it sought to erect a logical carapace within which the Ministry of Defence could go about its business. It was an inherently difficult exercise to attempt; but it was clearly a sensible thing to try to do.

All the same, the inevitable tension between a specific set of analyses and the changing circumstances to which they relate helped to constrain the utility of the review. Defence policy was to be held within whatever was possible for £2,000 million (at 1964 prices), but it was never clear (or, to be fair, it was not tested) how far this initial determinant represented a final political judgement about the priority to be accorded to defence. As things turned out, from November 1967 onwards, in the face of economic collapse at home, the replacement of this fundamental budgetary objective by a need to save on cash outlays in the short term removed a key element in the framework of the Defence Review; the withdrawal from mainland bases east of Suez was concertinaed and the equipment programme was again cut.[27] A totally new set of parameters was introduced, which related principally to the need to demonstrate a generalised political concern. If all major expenditure programmes are cut a little, the requirement to determine priorities is diminished. This was exactly the predicament which, within the field of defence and foreign policy, the Defence Review had been created to overcome; and the sense of disappointment and regret in the Ministry of Defence was therefore the more acute when some of the structures contained in the Review had to be knocked down.

The general principles, however, were not much affected; it was the pace, and the planned cohesion, of the withdrawal rather than the policy that were discarded. From the ministry's point of view much was salvaged, and there was a strong sense that if this were indeed the case it was in part because Healey had been there to fight. There is always a latent incompatibility between a senior minister's function as part of the Cabinet collectivity and his role as an advocate of the department for which he is the political manager *pro tem*; but in this case Healey's ability to provide leadership in the ministry was not much affected. This was due partly to his own robust resilience and partly to the expectation that any replacement, should he resign, would be less weighty in terms of Cabinet clout and less sympathetic to defence interests.

The definitive utility of the review was also recognised as intrinsically limited by its very nature. The style of defence policy and of foreign policy too, is essentially reactive and subject to influences over which the policy-making apparatus has limited control, even in the most powerful states. In that sense no Defence Review could ever be complete; the discussions over the need to reshape NATO strategy which began while the review was still in progress are a good example of the way in which important areas of policy developed alongside, but in some ways independently of, the issues with which it was primarily concerned. Not only was the current thrust of NATO doctrine felt to be inadequate, but the British interest in revising it was heightened by the implications of the withdrawal towards Europe which the Defence Review embodied. NATO strategy would probably have been reviewed in any event; but the timing was undoubtedly influenced by the general critique of British policy. And the need to press on with the revision remained an important task for the Ministry of Defence and for Healey himself, even after the shambles of the winter of 1967-68. It was important in itself, and it could be used, in the context of the governmmment's new stance towards European matters generally, to emphasise Britain's Europeanist credentials. Healey's skill and expertise, and the prominence they earned him among NATO Defence Ministers, were important in giving additional weight and visibility to British proposals and suggestions within NATO.

By the end of 1967 the NATO Council had got rid of the worst contradictions in its strategic practices. The doctrine of 'flexibility in response' which it then adopted differed significantly from the more ambitious strategy which had—with the same title—originally been described by Secretary McNamara in his speeches of 1961-62. For NATO the new strategy meant basing military plans on the forces that were actually available and maximising the conventional capability of those forces by deploying armies and air forces alike, so as to impose the greatest possible delay on an all-out Soviet attack short of using nuclear weapons. This would compel the Soviets to mass substantial forces if they wanted to advance at all into Western Europe, and to accept heavy casualties from the start, making a NATO nuclear response more likely if this prospect did not deter them altogether. Moreover it would give the NATO governments as long as possible to persuade the Soviet leaders to call off the fighting, and to decide exactly how and when to use nuclear weapons if the attempt to call a halt failed. It was, overall, a more realistic concept; even if it did not resolve NATO's problems it managed to make better sense of the handling of them.

One consequence of this new doctrine was the decision, at last carried out by governments, that their strike aircraft should carry conventional as well as nuclear weapons. Another was to focus the attention of Europeans and Americans alike on the crucial importance of the initial decision to introduce nuclear weapons into the fighting. It was realised that if NATO ever used nuclear weapons except in response to their use by the enemy it was likely to be at the tactical rather than the strategic level. Thus, when NATO set up a small Nuclear Planning Group in which for the first time the Americans discussed the details of their nuclear strategy with their non-nuclear allies, the initial tactical use of nuclear weapons was the first item on the agenda. By the end of 1969 the United States and the European allies were all satisfied that the new guidelines were understood and accepted. This was an important achievement; not only did it reconcile real differences of national interest at a point that was vital to NATO's deterrent strategy, but for the first time the United States was able to convince the Europeans that she was prepared to recognise their right to a share in formulating the doctrine for the use of her nuclear weapons. The achievement was equally important at the military level, for previously NATO commanders could have no reasonable assurance that the ministers who would have to authorise them to use nuclear weapons would be prepared to take the decision; and the ministers had no confidence that, if they did take it, the military would make sense of the terrifying powers released to them.

In parallel with these developments Healey was also instrumental in setting up what came to be called 'the Eurogroup'. This was originally an informal method of consultation between European members of NATO to discuss issues of common interest. It was in no sense a 'ganging up' against the North Americans; indeed, Healey saw part of its function as an opportunity it also offered for the United Kingdom to be seen to be forward in propagating a constructive and collective activity which has subsequently grown to be the sponsoring group for a number of specific and useful security initiatives.[28]

By the summer of 1970 Healey had been Secretary of State for Defence for nearly six years. This longevity in office was in itself unusual and undoubtedly contributed to his effectiveness in many important matters. He had outlasted virtually all his NATO colleagues, and derived a substantial advantage in Whitehall and Westminster too from his long tenure of the one office. Undoubtedly internal Labour Party politics played a part here; it is more usual for ministers to be changed around during the course of a government, but Healey's uneasy relationship with the Prime Minister of the day, Harold Wilson, prevented him from moving on to, say, the Foreign Office, as he would have liked to do. It could, however, be argued that, given the very recent creation of the new-style Ministry of Defence, the post of Secretary of State required a longer tenure; and Healey's reputation and skill as a 'technocrat' minister made him a natural choice for it. Later on, when he became Chancellor of the Exchequer, somewhat similar considerations continued to inhibit his selection for other Cabinet posts for which, intrinsically, his experience qualified him.

His period of office coincided with the high point of the period within which a belief in the usefulness and efficacy of new methods of evaluating and planning policy choices was both novel and fashionable. His administrative and political skills made him receptive to new methods, and his intellectual gifts enabled him to cope with the difficulties which the use of these techniques threw up. There is no doubt that they enabled complex organisations such as government departments to improve the ways in which business was done and to exert more effective control over some crucial managerial functions. But they had very limited application to the basic issues on which choices had to be made. The cost-effectiveness of one policy as against another was only one among many factors that determined what the final decision would be. Choices still had to be made, and the interplay between political or cultural dogma and personalities was still very important.[29]

Notes

1   A description of the early days of the government is given in the opening chapters of Sir Harold Wilson's 'personal record' of the administration: H. Wilson, *The Labour Government, 1964-70*, Weidenfeld & Nicolson and Michael Joseph, London, 1971. And there is an account of the Labour Party, during its period in opposition, which gives a good background, by Vernon Bogdanor (*The Labour Party in Opposition, 1951–64*) in the collection of essays: V. Bogdanor and R. Skidelsky (eds.), *The Age of Affluence 1951–64*, Macmillan Student Editions (MSE 274), London, 1970.

2   The most important single influence was the Plowden Committee on the Control of Public Expenditure, which sat from 1959 to 1961, and whose report was published in 1961 (Cmnd 1432), but there were a number of other major reviews as well. See John Garrett, *The Management of Government*, Penguin Books, Harmondsworth, 1972, and R. G. S. Brown, *The Administrative Process in Britain*, Methuen, London, 1970.

3   See, on McNamara, J. M. Roherty, *Decisions of Robert S. McNamara*, University of Miami Press, Miami, 1970: and, on systems analysis application in the United States, Guy Black, *The Application of Systems Analysis to Government Operations*, Praeger, New York, 1968; and A. C. Enthoven and K. W. Smith, *How Much is Enough?*, Harper & Row, New York, 1971.

4   See, particularly in regard to defence matters, D. Greenwood, *Budgeting for Defence*, Royal United Services Institution, London, 1972; R. Burt, *Defence Budgeting: the British and American Cases*, Adelphi Paper 112, International Institute for Strategic Studies, London, 1974–75: G. Kennedy, *The Economics of Defence*, Faber, London, 1975. Equally particularly in regard to the Treasury see H. Heclo and A. Wildavsky, *The Private Government of Public Money*, Macmillan, London, 1974; see also Brown, *The Administrative Process in Britain*, and Part 3 of B. L. R. Smith and D. C. Hague, *The Dilemma of Accountability in Modern Government*, Macmillan, London, 1971.

5   See G. Williams and B. Reed, *Denis Healey and the Policies of Power*, Sidgwick & Jackson, London, 1971 (hereinafter quoted as 'Williams and Reed'), and P. Nailor, 'The Healey era', in *The Royal United Services Institution Journal*, CXV, September 1970.

6   There is now an extensive literature about the Suez episode. Try, as a starter, the critique by R. Skidelsky, 'Lessons of Suez', in Bogdanor and Skidelsky, *The Age of Affluence*.

7   See, for example, *The Management and Control of Research and Development*, Ministry of Science, HMSO, 1961 (the 'Gibbs–Zuckerman Report'): the *Second Report* of the Select Committee on Science and Technology, 1968–69 (HC 213); and C. J. Hitch and R. N. McKean, *The Economics of Defense in the Nuclear Age*, Harvard University Press, Cambridge, Mass., 1960, especially chapter 13. See also M. E. Edmonds, 'Government contracting in industry: some observations on the Ferranti and Bristol-Siddeley contracts', in Smith and Hague, *The Dilemma of Accountability in Modern Government*.

8   See Williams and Reed, chapter 5, for a brief account of Healey's involvement.

9   D. W. Healey, 'Britain and NATO', in K. Knorr (ed.), *NATO and American Security*, Princeton University Press, Princeton, N.J., 1959.

10 The quotations are taken from Williams and Reed, pp. 167–8.

11 The accounts of what actually went on, and how it went on, at Chequers vary slightly among the memorialisations of those participants who have, up till now, committed themselves to paper. See, by way of example, Williams and Reed, pp. 168–72; Wilson, *The Labour Government, 1964–1970*: chapter 4.

12 Interview material.

13 *Statement on the Defence Estimates, 1965*, Cmnd 2592, February 1965.

14 See M. E. Howard, *The Central Organisation of Defence*, Royal United Services Institution, London, 1970.

15 See Williams and Reed, pp. 181 ff., and Wilson, *The Labour Government, 1964–1970*, chapter 7.

16 *Statement on the Defence Estimates, 1966: Part I, The Defence Review*, Cmnd 2901, February 1966.

17 *Ibid.*, section II, 24.

18 *Statement on the Defence Estimates, 1966: Part II, Defence Estimates 1966–67*, Cmnd 2902, February 1966.

19 The late Richard Crossman's comments in his Godkin lectures (R. H. S. Crossman, *Inside View*, Jonathan Cape, London, 1970, pp. 16–17) provided the first corrective to Sir Harold Wilson's rather bland account in his book *The Labour Government, 1964–1970*.

20 Besides specific equipment purchasing programmes—for Polaris missile systems, Hercules, Phantom and F111 aircraft, for example—the United States and United Kingdom shared a number of bilateral exchanges on nuclear and intelligence information that were of considerable importance in the defence field. British dependence on American support and understanding in economic and political matters, outside South East Asia, was also extensive.

21 *Statement on the Defence Estimates, 1967*, Cmnd 3203, February 1967.

22 See P. Nailor, 'Defence policy and foreign policy', in R. Boardman and A. J. R. Groom (eds.), *The Management of Britain's External Relations*, Macmillan, London, 1973. The Programme Evaluation Group was disbanded in 1968; although it was not, as a particular institutional device, a success, it paved the way to a reorganisation of the Defence Policy Staff, which was refashioned to include a division that had longer-range and less circumscribed responsibilities, besides a mixed military and civilian

composition. The need for a broader 'defence perspective' was, in this way, both recognised and seated more firmly within the normal hierarchial pattern of organisation.

23   *Supplementary Statement on Defence Policy, 1967*, Cmnd 3357, July 1967.

24   *Ibid.*, section VI, 1.

25   In his discussion of 'The decision to withdraw from East of Suez', P. Gordon Walker, *The Cabinet*, revised edition, Fontana/Collins, London, 1972, chapter 8.

26   Besides Sir Harold Wilson, the late Richard Crossman and Mrs Barbara Castle have published their memoirs, and other ministers have reminisced in public.

27   The general cuts were announced in the House of Commons on 16 January 1968; the defence cuts were summarised in section I of the defence White Paper: *Statement on the Defence Estimates, 1968*, Cmnd 3540, February 1968.

28   An account of the origins, aims and activities of the Eurogroup is given in a pamphlet, *The Eurogroup*, published by the NATO Information Service, Brussels, October 1975. See also D. C. R. Heyhoe, *The European Programme Group* (The Alliance and Europe, Part VI), Adelphi Paper 129, International Institute for Strategic Studies, London, 1976–77.

29   A useful view by Healey himself of the development of policy between 1964 and 1969 is given in a lecture to the Royal United Services Institution, and published in the Institution's *Journal* (vol. CX1V), December 1969. See also, by way of summary, P. Nailor, 'British defence policy in the 1960s', in *Perspectives upon British Defence Policy, 1945–1970*, University of Southampton (Department of Adult Education), September 1978.

APPENDIX 1

SECRETARIES OF STATE: CHRONOLOGY

Secretary at War

Feb 1845 to Jul 1846	Sidney Herbert	Conservative
Jul 1846 to Feb 1852	Fox Maule	Whig
Feb 1852	Robert Vernon Smith	Whig
Feb 1852 to Dec 1852	William Beresford	Conservative
Dec 1852 to Jan 1855	Sidney Herbert	Whig

Secretary of State for War and the Colonies

Dec 1845 to Jul 1846	William Ewart Gladstone	Conservative
Jul 1846 to Feb 1852	Earl Grey	Whig
Feb 1852 to Dec 1852	Sir John Pakington, Bt	Conservative
Dec 1852 to Jun 1854	Fifth Duke of Newcastle	Whig

Secretary of State for War

Jun 1854 to Feb 1855	Fifth Duke of Newcastle	Whig
Feb 1855 to Feb 1858	Fox Maule, Lord Panmure	Whig
Feb 1858 to Jun 1859	Lieutenant General Jonathan Peel	Conservative
Jun 1859 to Jul 1861	Sidney Herbert, Lord Herbert of Lea	Liberal
Jul 1861 to Apr 1863	Sir George Cornewall-Lewis, Bt	Liberal
Apr 1863 to Feb 1866	Earl de Grey and Ripon	Liberal
Feb 1866 to Jul 1866	Marquess of Hartington	Liberal
Jul 1866 to Mar 1867	Lieutenant General Jonathan Peel	Conservative
Mar 1867 to Dec 1868	Sir John Pakington, Bt	Conservative
Dec 1868 to Feb 1874	Edward Cardwell	Liberal
Feb 1874 to Apr 1878	Gathorne Gathorne-Hardy	Conservative
Apr 1878 to Apr 1880	Frederick Stanley	Conservative
Apr 1880 to Dec 1882	Hugh Childers	Liberal
Dec 1882 to Jun 1885	Marquess of Hartington	Liberal
Jun 1885 to Feb 1886	William Henry Smith	Conservative
Feb 1886 to Aug 1886	Henry Campbell-Bannerman	Liberal
Aug 1886 to Jan 1887	William Henry Smith	Conservative
Jan 1887 to Aug 1892	Edward Stanhope	Conservative
Aug 1892 to Jun 1895	Henry Campbell-Bannerman	Liberal
Jun 1895 to Nov 1900	Marquess of Lansdowne	Conservative
Nov 1900 to Sep 1903	William St John Brodrick	Conservative
Sep 1903 to Dec 1905	Hugh Arnold-Forster	Conservative
Dec 1905 to Jun 1912	Richard Burdon Haldane	Liberal
Jun 1912 to Mar 1914	John Edward Bernard Seely	Liberal
Mar 1914 to Aug 1914	Herbert Henry Asquith	Liberal
Aug 1914 to Jul 1916	Earl Kitchener of Khartoum	Coalition

Jul 1916 to Dec 1916	David Lloyd-George	Coalition
Dec 1916 to Apr 1918	Seventeenth Earl of Derby	Coalition
Apr 1918 to Jan 1919	Viscount Milner	Coalition
Jan 1919 to Feb 1921	Winston S. Churchill	Coalition
	(also Secretary of State for Air)	
Feb 1921 to Oct 1922	Sir Laming Worthington-Evans, Bt	Coalition
Oct 1922 to Jan 1924	Seventeenth Earl of Derby	Conservative
Jan 1924 to Nov 1924	Stephen Walsh	Labour
Nov 1924 to Jun 1929	Sir Laming Worthington-Evans, Bt	Conservative
Jun 1929 to Aug 1931	Thomas Shaw	Labour
Aug 1931 to Nov 1931	Marquess of Crewe	National
Nov 1931 to Jun 1935	Viscount Hailsham	National
Jun 1935 to Nov 1935	Viscount Halifax	National
Nov 1935 to May 1937	Alfred Duff Cooper	National
May 1937 to Jan 1940	Leslie Hore-Belisha	National
Jan 1940 to May 1940	Hon. Oliver Stanley	National
May 1940 to Dec 1940	Anthony Eden	Coalition
Dec 1940 to Feb 1942	David Margesson	Coalition
Feb 1942 to Jul 1945	Sir James Grigg	Coalition
Jul 1945 to Oct 1946	John James Lawson	Labour
Oct 1946 to Oct 1947	Frederick Bellenger	Labour
Oct 1947 to Feb 1950	Emanuel Shinwell	Labour
Feb 1950 to Oct 1951	John Strachey	Labour
Oct 1951 to Oct 1956	Brigadier Antony Head	Conservative
Oct 1956 to Jan 1958	John Hare	Conservative
Jan 1958 to Jul 1960	Christopher Soames	Conservative
Jul 1960 to Jun 1963	John Profumo	Conservative
Jun 1963 to Oct 1963	Joseph Godber	Conservative
Oct 1963 to Apr 1964	James Ramsden	Conservative

Minister for the Co-ordination of Defence

Mar 1936 to Jan 1939	Sir Thomas Inskip	National
Jan 1939 to Apr 1940	Admiral Lord Chatfield	National

Minister of Defence

May 1940 to Jul 1945	Winston S. Churchill	Coalition
Jul 1945 to Dec 1946	Clement Attlee	Labour
Dec 46 to Feb 1950	Albert Victor Alexander	Labour
Feb 1950 to Oct 1951	Emanuel Shinwell	Labour
Oct 1951 to Mar 1952	Winston S. Churchill	Conservative
Mar 1952 to Oct 1954	Earl Alexander of Tunis	Conservative
Oct 1954 to Apr 1955	Harold Macmillan	Conservative
Apl 1955 to Dec 1955	Selwyn Lloyd	Conservative
Dec 1955 to Oct 1956	Sir Walter Monckton	Conservative
Oct 1956 to Jan 1957	Brigadier Antony Head	Conservative
Jan 1957 to Oct 1959	Duncan Sandys	Conservative
Oct 1959 to Jul 1962	Harold Watkinson	Conservative
Jul 1962 to Apr 1964	Peter Thorneycroft	Conservative

Secretary of State for Defence

Apr 1964 to Oct 1964	Peter Thorneycroft	Conservative
Oct 1964 to Jun 1970	Denis Healey	Labour
Jun 1970 to Jan 1974	Lord Carrington	Conservative
Jan 1974 to Mar 1974	Ian Gilmour	Conservative
Mar 1974 to Oct 1976	Roy Mason	Labour
Oct 1976 to May 1979	Frederick Mulley	Labour
May 1979	Francis Pym	Conservative

APPENDIX 2

SECRETARIES OF STATE:
BIOGRAPHY AND BIBLIOGRAPHY[1]

Albert Victor ALEXANDER, first Earl Alexander of Hillsborough (1885–1965)

Labour MP Sheffield (Hillsborough) 1922–31, 1935–50. Parliamentary
Secretary to Board of Trade 1924; First Lord of Admiralty 1929–31, 1940–45,
1945–46; Minister without Portfolio 1946; Minister of Defence 1946–50;
Chancellor of Duchy of Lancaster 1950–51. Viscount 1950; Earl 1963.
Papers in Churchill College, Cambridge (not all available for research).

Field Marshal Sir Harold Rupert Leofric George Alexander, first Earl
ALEXANDER of Tunis (1891–1969)

C-in-C Middle East 1942–43; C-in-C Eighteenth Army Group 1943; C-in-C
Fifteenth Army Group 1943–44; Supreme Allied Commander, Mediterranean,
1944–45; Governor General of Canada 1946–52; Minister of Defence
1952–54. Viscount 1946; Earl 1952
Biography: N. Nicholson, *Alex* (1973).
Papers in PRO, WO 214/1–69 (relating mainly to 1944–45 period).

Hugh Oakley ARNOLD-FORSTER (1855–1909)

Liberal Unionist MP Belfast (West) 1892–1906; Conservative MP Croydon
1906–09. Parliamentary Secretary to Admiralty 1900–03; Secretary of State
for War 1903–05.
Biography: Mary Arnold-Forster, *The Rt Hon H. O. Arnold-Forster: a
Memoir* (1910).
Papers in British Library Add. MSS 50275–50357 (including detailed day-to-
day War Office diary).

Herbert Henry ASQUITH, first Earl of Oxford and Asquith (1852–1928)

Liberal MP Fife (East) 1886–1918; Paisley 1920–24. Secretary of State for
Home Affairs 1892–95; Chancellor of Exchequer 1905–08; Prime Minister
1908–16; Secretary of State for War 1914; Leader of Liberal Party 1908–26;
Earl of Oxford and Asquith 1925.
Biography: J. A. Spender and Cyril Asquith, *The Life of Lord Oxford and*

---

[1] The reader's attention is drawn to two valuable publications which detail the
location of various collections of private papers of politicians and public servants:
Cameron Hazlehurst and Christine Woodland, *A Guide to the Papers of British
Cabinet Ministers, 1900–1951*, Royal Historical Society, London, 1974; and
Chris Cook (ed.), *Sources in British Political History, 1900–1951*, 4 vols,
Macmillan, London, 1975–77.

Asquith (1932); R. Jenkins, *Asquith* (1964).
Autobiography: *The Genesis of War* (1923); *Fifty Years of Parliament* (1926); *Memories and Reflections* (1928).
Papers in Bodleian Library.

Clement Richard ATTLEE, first Earl Attlee (1883–1967)

Labour MP Stepney (Limehouse) 1922–50; Walthamstow (West) 1950–55. Under Secretary of State of War 1924; Chancellor of Duchy of Lancaster 1930–31; Postmaster General 1931; Lord Privy Seal 1940–42; Secretary of State for Dominion Affairs 1942–43; Lord President of the Council 1943–45; Deputy Prime Minister 1942–45; Prime Minister 1945–51; Minister of Defence 1945–46; Deputy Leader of Labour Party 1931–35; Leader of Labour Party 1935–55; Earl 1955. KG 1956;
Biography: under preparation by K. Harris.
Autobiography: *As It Happened* (1955).
Papers at University College, Oxford (forty-one boxes) and Churchill College, Cambridge (two files).

Frederick John BELLENGER (1894–1968)

Labour MP Notts (Bassetlaw) 1935–68. Financial Secretary to War Office 1941–46; Secretary of State for War 1946–47.
No papers have survived.

William BERESFORD (1798–1883)

Conservative MP Harwich 1841–47; Essex (North) 1847–65.
Secretary at War 1852.
No papers are known to have survived.

William St John Fremantle BRODRICK, first Earl of Midleton (1856–1942)

Conservative MP Surrey (West) 1880–85; South West Surrey (Guildford) 1885–1906. Financial Secretary to War Office 1886–92; Under Secretary for War 1895–98; Under Secretary for Foreign Affairs 1898–1900; Secretary of State for War 1900–03; Secretary of State for India 1903–05. Ninth Viscount Midleton 1907; Earl 1920.
Autobiography: *Records and Reactions,1856–1939* (1939).
Papers in PRO 30/67.

Sir Henry CAMPBELL-BANNERMAN (1836–1908)

Liberal MP Stirling Burghs 1868–1908. Financial Secretary to War Office 1871–74 and 1880–82; Parliamentary Secretary to Admiralty 1882–84; Chief Secretary for Ireland 1884–1885; Secretary of State for War 1886 and 1892–95; Prime Minister 1905–08; Leader of Liberal Party 1899–1908. GCB 1895.
Biography: J. A. Spender, *The Life of Rt Hon Sir H. Campbell-Bannerman* (1923); John Wilson, *CB: a Life of Sir Henry Campbell-Bannerman* (1973).
Papers in British Library, Add. MSS 41206–52 and 52512–21.

Edward CARDWELL, Viscount Cardwell (1813–1886)

Liberal Conservative MP Clitheroe 1842–47, Liverpool 1847–52; Liberal MP Oxford City 1853–74; Secretary of Treasury 1845–46; President of Board of Trade 1852; Chief Secretary for Ireland 1859–61; Chancellor of Duchy of Lancaster 1861–64; Secretary of State for the Colonies 1864–66; Secretary of State for War 1868–74. Viscount 1874.
Biography: Sir R. Biddulph, *Lord Cardwell at the War Office* (1904); A. B. Erickson, *E. T. Cardwell: Peelite* (1959).
Papers in PRO 30/48.

Peter Alexander Rupert Carrington, sixth Baron CARRINGTON (1919–)

Parliamentary Secretary to Ministry of Agriculture and Fisheries 1951–54; Parliamentary Secretary to Ministry of Defence 1954–56; High Commissioner for the United Kingdom in Australia 1956–59; First Lord of Admiralty 1959–63; Minister without Portfolio 1963–64; Leader of the Opposition in the House of Lords 1964–70; Secretary of State for Defence 1970–74; Secretary of State for Energy 1974; Chairman of Conservative Party 1972–74. Secretary of State for Foreign Affairs 1979– . Baron 1938. KCMG 1958;
No papers have been retained.

Sir Alfred Ernle Montacute CHATFIELD, first Baron Chatfield (1873–1967)

Fourth Sea Lord 1919–20; Assistant Chief of Naval Staff 1920–22; Third Sea Lord 1925–28; C-in-C Atlantic Fleet 1929–30; C-in-C Mediterranean Fleet 1930–32; First Sea Lord and Chief of Naval Staff 1933–39; Minister for Co-ordination of Defence 1939–40. KCMG 1919; GCB 1934; Baron 1937.
Biography: under preparation by Professor A. Temple Patterson.
Autobiography: *The Navy and Defence* (1942); *It Might Happen Again* (1947).
Papers in National Maritime Museum CHT1–9.

Hugh Culling Eardley CHILDERS (1827–96)

Liberal MP Pontefract 1859–85; South Edinburgh 1886–92. Secretary for Education Department, Melbourne, 1851–52; Auditor General of Melbourne 1852–53; Collector of Customs, Melbourne, 1853–56; Commissioner of Trade and Customs, Victoria, 1856–57; Agent General of Victoria 1857–58; Civil Lord of Admiralty 1864–65; Financial Secretary to Treasury 1865–67; First Lord of Admiralty 1868–71; Chancellor of Duchy of Lancaster 1872–73; Secretary of State for War 1880–82; Chancellor of Exchequer 1882–85.
Biography: E. S. E. Childers, *The Life and Correspondence of Rt. Hon. Hugh Childers, 1827–1896* (1901).
Papers in Library of the Royal Commonwealth Society, London.

Sir Winston Leonard Spencer CHURCHILL (1874–1965)

Conservative MP Oldham 1900–04; Liberal MP Oldham 1906; Manchester (North West) 1906–08, Dundee 1908–22; Conservative MP Essex (Epping) 1922–45; Essex (Woodford) 1945–64. Under Secretary for Colonies 1905–08;

President of Board of Trade 1908–10; Secretary of State for Home Affairs 1910–11; First Lord of Admiralty 1911–15 and 1939–40; Chancellor of Duchy of Lancaster 1915; Minister of Munitions 1917–19; Secretary of State for War and Air 1919–21; Secretary of State for Colonies 1921–22; Chancellor of Exchequer 1924–29; Prime Minister 1940–45 and 1951–55; Minister of Defence 1940–45 and 1951–52; Leader of Opposition 1945–51. KG 1953.

Biography: Randolph S. Churchill and Martin Gilbert, *Winston S. Churchill* (1966–75, continuing). Volume IV (1975) deals with the period 1917–1922.

Autobiography: *The World Crisis* (1923–31); *The Second World War* (1948–54).

Papers at present closed but will be available at Churchill College, Cambridge, and on microfilm in PRO 31/19.

Sir George CORNEWALL-LEWIS Bt (1806–63)

Liberal MP Herefordshire 1847–52; Radnor Boroughs 1855–63. Secretary of Board of Control 1847–48; Under Secretary at Home Department 1848–50; Financial Secretary to Treasury 1850–52; Chancellor of Exchequer 1855–58; Home Secretary 1859–61; Secretary of State for War 1861–63; Editor *Edinburgh Review* 1852–55.

Biography: Sir G. F. Lewis, *Letters of the Rt Hon Sir George Cornewall-Lewis, Bt* (1870).

Papers in National Library of Wales (as yet unlisted).

Robert Offley Ashburton-Crewe Milnes, second Baron Houghton, Marquess of CREWE (1858–1945).

Lord President of Council 1905–08 and 1915–16; Secretary of State for Colonial Affairs 1908–10; Lord Privy Seal 1908–11 and 1912–15; Secretary of State for India 1910–11 and 1911–15; President of Board of Education 1916; Ambassador to Paris 1922–28; Secretary of State for War 1931. Baron 1885; Earl 1895; KG 1908; Marquess 1921.

Biography: James Pope-Henessy, *Lord Crewe, 1858–1945: the Likeness of a Liberal* (1955).

Papers in Cambridge University Library.

Edward George Villiers Stanley, seventeenth Earl of DERBY (1865–1948)

Conservative MP South East Lancashire 1892–1906. Financial Secretary to War Office 1900–03; Postmaster General 1903–05; Under Secretary War Office 1916; Secretary of State for War 1916–18 and 1922–24; Ambassador to Paris 1918–20. Lord Stanley 1893; Earl 1908; KG 1919.

Biography: Randolph S. Churchill, *Lord Derby, King of Lancashire* (1959).

Papers in Liverpool City Libraries 920 (DER) 17 and PRO WO 137 (War Office papers 1922–24).

Sir Alfred DUFF COOPER, first Viscount Norwich (1890–1954)

Conservative MP Oldham 1924–49, Westminster (St Georges) 1931–45. Financial Secretary to War Office 1928–29 and 1931–34; Financial Secretary to Treasury 1934–35; Secretary of State for War 1935–37; First Lord of Admiralty 1937–38; Minister of Information 1940–41; Chancellor of Duchy of Lancaster 1941–43; Representative of the British Government to the French Committee for National Liberation 1943–44. GCMG 1948; Viscount 1952.
Autobiography: *Old Men Forget* (1953).
Papers (in the possession of Sir Rupert Hart-Davis) not available for research and family letters in the British Library closed until 2009.

Sir Robert Anthony EDEN, first Earl of Avon (1897–1977)

Conservative MP Warwickshire (West) 1923–57. Parliamentary Under Secretary for Foreign Affairs 1931–33; Lord Privy Seal 1933–35; Minister without Portfolio for League of Nations Affairs 1935; Secretary of State for Foreign Affairs 1935–38. 1940–45 and 1951–55; Secretary of State for Dominion Affairs 1939–40; Secretary of State for War 1940; Prime Minister 1955–57. KG 1954; Earl 1961.
Autobiography: *Full Circle, Facing the Dictators, The Reckoning* (1960–65).
Papers will eventually pass to Birmingham University Library.

Gathorne GATHORNE-HARDY, first Earl of Cranbrook (1814–1906)

Conservative MP for Leominster 1856–65; Oxford University 1865–78. Under Secretary for Home Affairs 1858–59; President of Poor Law Board 1866–67; Secretary of State for Home Affairs 1867–68; Secretary of State for War 1874–78; Secretary of State for India 1878–80; Lord President of the Council 1885 and 1886–92. Viscount 1878; Earl 1892.
Biography: A. E. Gathorne-Hardy, *Gathorne-Hardy, First Earl of Cranbrook* (1910).
Papers in Suffolk County Record Office.

Sir Ian GILMOUR, Bt (1926–   )

Conservative MP Central Norfolk 1962–74; Chesham and Amersham 1974–   . Editor *Spectator* 1954–59; Parliamentary Under Secretary for Defence (Army) 1970; Minister of State for Defence (Procurement) 1971–72; Minister of State for Defence 1972–74; Secretary of State for Defence 1974; Chairman of Conservative Research Department 1974–75; Lord Privy Seal 1979–   . Third Baronet 1977.

William Ewart GLADSTONE (1809–98)

Conservative MP Newark 1832–46; Liberal Conservative MP Oxford University 1846–65; Liberal MP South Lancashire 1865–68; Greenwich 1868–80; Midlothian 1880–85; Edinburgh 1885–95. Junior Lord of Treasury 1834; Under Secretary for War and Colonies 1835; Vice-President of Board of Trade 1841–43; President of Board of Trade 1843–45; Secretary of State for

War and Colonies 1845–46; Chancellor of Exchequer 1852–55, 1859–65, 1866 and 1873–74; Leader of House 1868; Prime Minister 1868–74, 1880–85, 1886 and 1892–94.
Biography: John Morley, *The Life of W. E. Gladstone* (1903); Philip Magnus, *Gladstone: a Biography* (1954); Eric Eyck, *Gladstone* (1938).
Papers in British Library Add. MSS 44086–835.

Joseph Bradshaw GODBER , Baron Godber (1914–1980)

Conservative MP Grantham 1951–79. Assistant Whip 1955–57; Joint Parliamentary Secretary of Ministry of Agriculture, Fisheries and Food 1957–60; Joint Under Secretary at Foreign Office 1960–61; Minister of State at Foreign Office 1961–63 and 1970–72; Secretary of State for War 1963; Minister of Labour 1963–64; Minister of Agriculture, Fisheries and Food 1972–74 Baron, 1979.
No papers were retained.

George Frederick Samuel Robinson, second Earl De GREY AND RIPON, first Marquess of Ripon (1827–1909)

Liberal MP Hull 1852–53; Huddersfield 1853–57; Yorkshire (West Riding) 1857–59. Under Secretary at War Office 1859–61 and 1861–63; Under Secretary at India Office 1861; Secretary of State for War 1863–66; Secretary of State for India 1866; Lord President of the Council 1868–73; Governor General of India 1880–84; First Lord of Admiralty 1886; Secretary of State for Colonies 1892–95; Lord Privy Seal 1905–08. Viscount Goderich 1833, second Earl de Grey and Ripon 1859, Marquess of Ripon 1871.
Biography: L. Wolf, *Life of the First Marquess of Ripon* (1921).
Papers in British Library Add. MSS 43510–644.

Sir Henry George Grey, Viscount Howick, third Earl GREY (1802–94)

Whig MP Winchelsea 1826–30; Higham Ferrers 1830–31; Northumberland 1831–32; North Northumberland 1832–41; Sunderland 1841–45. Under Secretary for Colonies 1830–33; Under Secretary for Home Affairs 1845; Secretary at War 1835–39; Secretary of State for War and Colonies 1846–52. Viscount Howick 1832; Earl Grey 1845.
Papers in Durham University Library.

Sir Percy James GRIGG (1890–1964)

National MP Cardiff (East) 1942–45. Principal Private Secretary to successive Chancellors of Exchequer 1921–30; Financial Member of Government of India 1934–39; Secretary of State for War 1942–45. KCB 1932.
Autobiography: *Prejudice and Judgement* (1948).
Papers in Churchill College, Cambridge (post-1945 papers closed).

Sir Douglas McGarel Hogg, first Viscount HAILSHAM (1872–1950)

Conservative MP St Marylebone 1922–28. Attorney General 1922–24 and 1924–28; Lord Chancellor 1928–29 and 1935–38; Secretary of State for War 1931–35; Lord President of the Council 1938. Kt 1927; Baron 1928; Viscount 1929.

Biography: R. F. V. Heuston, *Lives of the Lord Chancellors, 1885–1940* (1964).

No papers have survived.

Richard Burdon HALDANE, first Viscount Haldane of Cloan (1856–1928)

Liberal MP Haddingtonshire (Lothian East) 1885–1911. Secretary of State for War 1905–12; Lord Chancellor 1912–15 and 1924. Viscount 1911.

Biography: Sir Frederick Maurice, *Haldane* (1937–39); D. Sommer, *Haldane of Cloan* (1960); Stephen Koss, *Lord Haldane: Scapegoat for Liberalism* (1969); E. M. Spiers, *Haldane: An Army Reformer* (1980).

Autobiography: *Before the War* (1920); *Autobiography* (1929).

Papers in National Library of Scotland MS 5901–6108 (including daily letters to his mother and sister).

Edward Frederick Lindley, Baron Irwin, third Viscount and Earl of HALIFAX (1881–1959)

Conservative MP West Riding (Ripon) 1910–25. Parliamentary Under Secretary for Colonies 1921–22; President of Board of Education 1922–24 and 1932–35; Minister of Agriculture and Fisheries 1924–25; Viceroy of India 1926–31; Secretary of State for War 1935; Lord Privy Seal 1935–37; Lord President of the Council 1937–38; Foreign Secretary 1938–40; Ambassador to Washington 1941–46. Baron Irwin 1925; GCSI 1926; KG 1931; third Viscount Halifax 1934; Earl of Halifax 1944.

Biography: Earl of Birkenhead, *Halifax: the Life of Lord Halifax* (1965).

Autobiography: *Fullness of Days* (1957).

Papers in possession of the second Earl of Halifax but lists are available at the National Register of Archives and British Library. Papers as Viceroy in India Office Library.

John Hugh HARE, first Viscount Blakenham (1911–)

Conservative MP Woodbridge 1945–50; Sudbury and Woodbridge 1950–63. Minister of State for Colonial Affairs 1955–56; Secretary of State for War 1956–58; Minister of Agriculture, Fisheries and Food 1958–60; Minister of Labour 1960–63; Chancellor of Duchy of Lancaster 1963–64. Viscount, 1963.

No papers have been retained.

Spencer Compton Cavendish, Marquess of HARTINGTON, eighth Duke of Devonshire (1833–1908)

Liberal MP Lancashire (North) 1857–68; Radnor 1869–80; Lancashire (North East) 1880–85; Liberal Unionist MP North Lancashire (Rossendale) 1885–91.

Under Secretary of State for War 1863–66; Secretary of State for War 1866 and 1882–85; Postmaster General 1868–71; Chief Secretary for Ireland 1871–74; Secretary of State for India 1880–82; Lord President of the Council 1895–1903. KG 1892. Asked to form a government on three occasions—1880 and twice in 1886—but refused each time. Lord Cavendish 1834; Marquess of Hartington 1858; Duke 1891.
Biography: Bernard Holland, *The Life of Spencer Cavendish, Eighth Duke of Devonshire* (1911).
Papers in Devonshire collection, Chatsworth House, Derbyshire.

Brigadier Antony Henry HEAD, first Viscount Head (1906–   )

Conservative MP Carshalton 1945–60. Assistant Secretary to Committee of Imperial Defence 1940–1; Secretary of State for War 1951–56; Minister of Defence 1956–57; High Commissioner for Nigeria 1960–63; High Commissioner for Malaysia 1963–66.Viscount 1960.
No papers have been retained.

Denis Winston HEALEY (1917–   )

Labour MP Leeds (South East) 1952–55, Leeds (East) 1955–   . Head of Internal Department of Labour Party 1946–52; Secretary of State for Defence 1964–70; Chancellor of Exchequer 1974–79.
No papers have been retained.

Sidney HERBERT, first Baron Herbert of Lea (1810–61)

MP South Wiltshire 1832–60 (Conservative 1832; Liberal Conservative 1841; Liberal 1857). Secretary to Board of Control 1834–35; Secretary to Admiralty 1841–45; Secretary at War 1845–46 and 1852–55; Colonial Secretary 1855; Secretary of State for War 1859–61. Baron 1861
Biography: Baron Stanmore, *Sidney Herbert, Lord Herbert of Lea: a Memoir* (1906).
Papers at Wilton House, Wiltshire.

Leslie HORE-BELISHA, first Baron Hore-Belisha (1893–1957)

Liberal MP Plymouth (Devonport) 1923–31; National Liberal MP Plymouth 1931–45. Parliamentary Secretary to Board of Trade 1931–32; Financial Secretary to Treasury 1932–34; Minister of Transport 1934–37; Secretary of State for War 1937–40; Minister of National Insurance 1945. Baron 1954.
Biography: R. J. Minney, *The Private Papers of Hore-Belisha* (1960), based on an uncompleted autobiography.
Papers in the possession of Miss Hilda Sloane (not available for research).

Sir Thomas Walker Hobart INSKIP, first Viscount Caldecote (1876–1947)

Conservative MP Bristol (Central) 1918–29, Hampshire (Fareham) 1931–39. Solicitor General 1922–24, 1924–28 and 1931–32; Attorney General 1928–29 and 1932–36; Minister for Co-ordination of Defence 1936–39; Secretary of

State for Dominion Affairs 1939 and 1940; Lord Chancellor 1939–40; Lord Chief Justice 1940–46. Kt 1922; Viscount 1939.
Biography: R. F. V. Heuston, *Lives of the Lord Chancellors, 1885–1940* (1964).
Papers in Churchill College, Cambridge (consisting of copies of diary entries for 1938 and 1939–40 but not yet generally available for research).

Sir Horatio Herbert KITCHENER, first Earl Kitchener of Khartoum (1850–1916)

Commanding Officer, Khartoum Expedition, 1898; Chief of Staff, South Africa, 1899–1900; C-in-C South Africa 1900–02; C-in-C India 1902–09; Agent and Consul General in Egypt 1911–14; Secretary of State for War 1914–16. KCMG 1894; Baron 1898; Viscount 1902; Earl 1914; KG 1915;
Biography: Sir George Arthur, *Life of Lord Kitchener* (1920); Sir Philip Magnus, *Kitchener: Portrait of an Imperialist* (1958); G. A. Cassar, *Kitchener* (1977).
Papers in PRO 30/57 and WO 159 (papers of his private secretary, Sir Herbert Creedy); India Office Library (papers of military secretary, William Birdwood) and British Library Add. MSS 52276–8 (papers of his ADC, Major Marker).

Henry Charles Keith Petty-Fitzmaurice, fifth Marquess of LANSDOWNE (1845–1927)

Under Secretary at War Office 1872–74; Under Secretary for India 1880; Governor General of Canada 1885–88; Viceroy of India 1888–94; Secretary of State for War 1895–1900; Secretary of State for Foreign Affairs 1900–05; Minister without Portfolio 1915–16. Viscount Clanmaurice 1845; Earl of Kerry 1863; Marquess 1866. GCMG 1884; KG 1895;
Biography: Lord Newton, *Lord Lansdowne: a Biography* (1929).
Papers in the possession of eighth Marquess, Bowood Park, Calne, Wilts. (not available while new biography being completed).
Papers as Governor General in Public Archives of Canada and as Viceroy in India Office Library.

John James LAWSON, first Baron Lawson (1881–1965)

Labour MP Durham (Chester le Street) 1919–49. Financial Secretary to War office 1924; Parliamentary Secretary to Ministry of Labour 1929–31; Secretary of State for War 1945–46. Baron 1950.
Autobiography: *A Man's Life* (1932).
Papers in possession of his daughter but none relating to period at War Office.

John Selwyn Brooke LLOYD, Baron Selwyn-Lloyd (1904–78)

Conservative MP Wirral 1945–76. Minister of State for Foreign Affairs 1951–54; Minister of Supply 1954–55; Minister of Defence 1955; Secretary of State for Foreign Affairs 1955–60; Chancellor of the Exchequer 1960–62; Lord Privy Seal and Leader of Commons 1963–64; Speaker of Commons 1971–76. Baron 1976.

Autobiography: *Mr Speaker, Sir* (1976), *Suez, 1956: A Personal Account* (1978)
Papers were retained but are not as yet available for research

David LLOYD-GEORGE, first Earl Lloyd-George of Dwyfor (1863–1945)

Liberal MP Carnarvon Boroughs 1890–1945. President of Board of Trade 1905–08; Chancellor of Exchequer 1908–15; Minister of Munitions 1915–16; Secretary of State for War 1916; Prime Minister 1916–22. Earl 1945.
Biography: Malcolm Thomson, *David Lloyd-George* (1948); J. Griggs, *The Young Lloyd-George* (1973); Kenneth Morgan, *Lloyd-George: Family Letters, 1885–1936* (1973).
Autobiography: *War Memoirs* (1935–36).
Papers in Beaverbrook Library (including ten boxes relating to War Office period) and family letters in National Library of Wales MSS 20403–93.

Maurice Harold MACMILLAN (1894–   )

Conservative MP Stockton on Tees 1924–29, 1931–45; Bromley 1945–64. Parliamentary Secretary to Ministry of Supply 1940–42; Parliamentary Under Secretary for Colonies 1942–43; Minister Resident in North West Africa 1942–45; Secretary of State for Air 1945; Minister of Housing and Local Government 1951–54; Minister of Defence 1954–55; Secretary of State for Foreign Affairs 1955; Chancellor of Exchequer 1955–57; Prime Minister 1957–63.
Autobiography: *Winds of Change* (1966), *The Blast of War* (1967), *Tides of Fortune* (1969), *Riding the Storm* (1971), *Painting the Way* (1972), *The End of the Day* (1973), of which the third volume covers the period as Minister of Defence.
Papers will not be available until after death.

Henry David Reginald MARGESSON, first Viscount Margesson (1890–1965)

Conservative MP West Ham (Upton) 1922–23; Warwickshire (Rugby) 1924–42. Government Chief Whip and Parliamentary Secretary to Treasury 1931–40; Secretary of State for War 1940–42. Viscount 1942.
Papers in Churchill College, Cambridge (but not generally available).

Roy MASON (1924–   )

Labour MP Barnsley 1953–   . Minister of State (Shipping) at Board of Trade 1964–67; Minister of State for Defence (Equipment) 1967–68; Postmaster General 1968; Minister of Power 1968–69; President of Board of Trade 1969–70; Secretary of State for Defence 1974–76; Secretary of State for Northern Ireland 1976–79.
No papers have been retained.

Sir Alfred Milner, first Viscount MILNER (1854–1925)

High Commissioner for South Africa 1897–1905; Member of the War Cabinet 1916–18; Secretary of State for War 1918–19; Secretary of State for Colonies 1919–21. KCB 1895; Baron 1901; Viscount 1902. KG 1921;
Biography: Cecil Headlam, *The Milner Papers* (1931–33); A. M. Gollin, *Proconsul in Politics* (1964).
Papers in Bodleian Library and PRO 30/30.

Sir Walter Turner MONCKTON, first Viscount Monckton of Brenchley (1891–1965)

Conservative MP Bristol (West) 1951–57. Director General of Press and Censorship Bureau 1939–40; Minister of Information 1940–41; Solicitor General 1945; Minister of Labour and National Service 1951–55; Minister of Defence 1955–56; Paymaster General 1956–57. Viscount 1957.
Papers in Bodleian Library,

Frederick William MULLEY (1918–   )

Labour MP Sheffield Park 1950–   . Minister of Air 1965–67; Joint Minister of State at Foreign and Commonwealth Office 1967–69; Minister for Disarmament 1967–69; Minister of Transport 1969–70; Minister for Transport (Department of Environment) 1974–75; Secretary of State for Education 1975–76; Secretary of State for Defence 1976–79.
No papers have been systematically retained.

Henry Pelham Fiennes Pelham Clinton, fifth Duke of NEWCASTLE (1811–64)

Whig MP South Nottinghamshire 1832–46; Falkirk Burghs 1846–51. Lord of Treasury 1834–35; Chief Secretary to Lord Lieutenant of Ireland 1846; Secretary of State for War and Colonies 1852–54; Secretary of State for War 1854–55; Secretary of State for Colonies 1859–64. Duke 1851. KG 1860
Papers in Nottingham University Library.

Sir John Somerset PAKINGTON, Bt, first Baron Hampton (1799–1880)

Conservative MP Droitwich 1837–74. Member of Inquiry into the State of the Army before Sebastopol 1855; Secretary of State for War and Colonies 1852; First Lord of Admiralty 1858–59 and 1866–67; Secretary of State for War 1867–68; First Civil Service Commissioner 1875. Bt 1846; GCB 1859; Baron 1874.
Papers in Worcestershire County Record Office.

Fox Maule, second Baron PANMURE, eleventh Earl of Dalhousie (1801–1874)

Liberal MP Perthshire 1835–37; Elgin Burghs 1838–41; Perth 1841–52. Under Secretary of State for War and Colonies 1835–41; Vice-President of Board of Trade 1841; Secretary at War 1846–52; Secretary of State for War 1855–58. Baron 1852; Earl 1860.

Biography: Sir G. B. Scott-Douglas and Sir G. D. Ramsay, *The Panmure Papers* (1908).
Papers in Scottish Record Office.

General Jonathan PEEL (1799–1879)

Tory MP Norwich 1826–31; Huntingdon 1831–68. Army officer 1815–63. Major General 1854; Lieutenant General 1859. Surveyor General of Ordnance 1841–46; Secretary of State for War 1858–59 and 1866–67. Racing enthusiast who won Derby in 1844.
No papers are known to have survived.

John Denis PROFUMO (1915–   )

Conservative MP Kettering 1940–45; Stratford on Avon 1950–63. Joint Parliamentary Secretary to Ministry of Transport and Civil Aviation 1952–57; Parliamentary Under Secretary for Colonies 1957–58; Parliamentary Under Secretary for Foreign Affairs 1958–59; Minister of State for Foreign Affairs 1959–60; Secretary of State for War 1960–63.
Papers have been retained but are not available for research.

Francis Leslie PYM (1922–   )

Conservative MP Cambridgeshire 1961–   . Assistant Government Whip 1962–64; Opposition Whip 1964–67; Deputy Chief Opposition Whip 1967–70; Parliamentary Secretary to Treasury and Government Chief Whip 1970–73; Secretary of State for Northern Ireland 1973–74; Secretary of State for Defence 1979–   .

James Edward RAMSDEN (1923–   )

Conservative MP Harrogate 1954–74. Parliamentary Private Secretary for Home Affairs 1959–60; Under Secretary and Financial Secretary to War Office 1960–63; Secretary of State for War 1963–64; Minister of State (Army) 1964.
Papers retained are limited to engagement books.

Duncan Edwin SANDYS, Baron Duncan Sandys (1908–   )

Conservative MP Lambeth (Norwood) 1935–45; Wandsworth (Streatham) 1950–74. Financial Secretary to War Office 1941–43; Parliamentary Secretary to Ministry of Supply 1942–44; Minister of Works 1944–45; Minister of Supply 1951–54; Minister of Housing and Local Government 1954–57; Minister of Defence 1957–59; Minister of Aviation 1959–60; Secretary of State for Commonwealth Relations 1960–64; Secretary of State for Colonies 1962–64. Baron 1974.
Papers in Churchill College, Cambridge, but are not as yet available for research.

John Edward Bernard SEELY, first Baron Mottistone (1868–1947)

Conservative MP Isle of Wight 1900–04; Liberal MP Isle of Wight 1904–06 and 1923–24; Liverpool (Abercromby) 1906–10; Derbyshire (Ilkeston) 1910–22. Under Secretary for Colonies 1908–11; Under Secretary for War Office 1911–12; Secretary of State for War 1912–14; Parliamentary Under Secretary for Ministry of Munitions 1918–19; Under Secretary of State for Air 1919. Baron 1933.
Autobiography: *Adventure* (1930); *Fear and be Slain: Adventure by Land, Sea and Air* (1931).
Papers in Nuffield College, Oxford (including six boxes of War Office papers and two boxes of CID papers).

Thomas SHAW (1872–1938)

Labour MP Preston 1918–31. Minister of Labour 1924; Secretary of State for War 1929–31.
No papers have survived.

Emanuel SHINWELL, Baron Shinwell (1884–   )

Labour MP Linlithgowshire 1922–24 and 1928–31; Durham (Seaham) 1935–50; Durham (Easington) 1950–70. Financial Secretary to War Office 1929–30; Parliamentary Secretary to Department of Mines at Board of Trade 1924 and 1930–31; Minister of Fuel and Power 1945–47; Secretary of State for War 1947–50; Minister of Defence 1950–51. Baron 1970.
Autobiography: *Conflict without Malice* (1955); *I've lived through it all* (1973).
Papers will eventually be made available to a suitable library.

Robert Vernon SMITH, Baron Lyveden (1800–73)

Whig MP Tralee 1829–31; Northampton 1831–59. Junior Lord of Treasury 1830–34; Joint Secretary to Board of Control for India 1835–39; Under Secretary for War and Colonies 1839–41; Secretary at War 1852; President of Board of Control 1855–58. Baron 1859; GCB 1872.
No papers are known to have survived.

William Henry SMITH (1825–91)

Conservative MP Westminster 1868–85; Westminster (Strand) 1885–91. Secretary to Treasury 1874–77; First Lord of Admiralty 1877–80; Secretary of State for War 1885–86 and 1886–87; Leader of House and First Lord of Treasury 1887–91; Warden of Cinque Ports 1891.
Biography: Sir H. E. Maxwell, *The Life and Times of Rt Hon W. H. Smith* (1893); Viscount Chilston, *W. H. Smith* (1965).
Papers as Secretary of State for War in PRO WO 110.

Sir Arthur Christopher John SOAMES, Baron Soames (1920–   )

Conservative MP Bedford 1950–66. Parliamentary Under Secretary for Air 1955–57; Parliamentary and Financial Secretary to Admiralty 1957–58; Secretary of State for War 1958–60; Minister of Agriculture, Fisheries and Food 1960–64; Ambassador to France 1968–72; Vice-President of Commission of European Communities 1973–76; Lord President of the Council and Leader of the Lords 1979; Governor of Rhodesia 1979–80. Kt 1972. Baron 1978.
No papers have been retained.

Edward STANHOPE (1840–93)

Conservative MP Mid-Lincolnshire 1974–85. Horncastle 1885–93. Parliamentary Secretary to Board of Trade 1875–78; Under Secretary for India 1878–80; Vice-President of the Council 1885–86; President of Board of Trade 1886; Secretary of State for Colonies 1886–87; Secretary of State for War 1887–92.
Biography: Aubrey Newman, *The Stanhopes of Chevening* (1965).
Papers in Kent Record Office.

Sir Frederick Arthur STANLEY, sixteenth Earl of Derby (1841–1908)

Conservative MP Preston 1865–68; North Lancashire 1868–85; Blackpool 1885–86. Civil Lord of Admiralty 1868; Financial Secretary to War Office 1874–77; Financial Secretary to Treasury 1877–78; Secretary of State for War 1878–80; Secretary of State for Colonies 1885–86; President of Board of Trade 1886–88; Governor General of Canada 1888–93; President of British Empire League 1904. Baron 1886; Earl 1893; KG 1897; GCVO 1905.
Papers at Knowsley, Lancashire.

The Hon. Oliver Frederick George STANLEY (1896–1950)

Conservative MP Westmorland 1924–45; Bristol (West) 1945–50. Parliamentary Under Secretary of State for Home Affairs 1931–33; Minister of Transport 1933–34; Minister of Labour 1934–35; President of Board of Education 1935–37; President of Board of Trade 1937–40; Secretary of State for War 1940; Secretary of State for Colonial Affairs 1942–45.
No papers have survived.

Evelyn John St Loe STRACHEY (1901–63)

Labour MP Birmingham (Aston) 1929–31; Dundee 1945–50; Dundee (West) 1950–63. Under Secretary for Air 1945–46; Minister of Food 1946–50; Secretary of State for War 1950–51.
Biography: Hugh Thomas, *John Strachey* (1973).
Papers in the possession of his widow but are not available for research.

George Edward Peter THORNEYCROFT, Baron Thorneycroft (1909–)

Conservative MP Stafford 1938–45; Monmouth 1945–66. Parliamentary Secretary to Ministry of War Transport 1945; President of Board of Trade 1951–57; Chancellor of Exchequer 1957–58; Minister of Aviation 1960–62; Minister of Defence 1962–64; Secretary of State for Defence 1964; Chairman of Conservative Party 1975– . Baron 1967.
No papers have been retained.

Stephen WALSH (1859–1929)

Labour MP South West Lancashire 1906–29. Parliamentary Secretary to Ministry of National Service 1917; Parliamentary Secretary to Local Government Board 1917–19; Secretary of State for War 1924.
No papers have survived.

Harold Arthur WATKINSON, first Viscount Watkinson (1910–)

Conservative MP Woking 1950–64. Parliamentary Secretary to Ministry of Labour and National Service 1952–55; Minister of Transport and Civil Aviation 1955–57; Minister of Defence 1957–62. Viscount 1964.
No papers have been retained.

Sir Laming WORTHINGTON-EVANS, Bt (1868–1931)

Conservative MP Colchester 1910–29; Westminster (St George's) 1929–31. Parliamentary Secretary to Ministry of Munitions 1916–18; Minister of Blockade 1918–19; Minister of Pensions 1919–20; Minister without Portfolio 1920–21; Secretary of State for War 1921–22 and 1924–29; Postmaster General 1923–24. Bt 1916. GBE 1922.
Papers in Bodleian Library.

INDEX